REAL CITY

Paris

REAL CITY

Paris

www.realcity.dk.com

Previously published as the popular eGuide series

LONDON, NEW YORK,
MELBOURNE, MUNICH AND DELHI
www.dk.com

Produced by Departure Lounge LLP

Contributors
Maryanne Blacker, Rosa Jackson, Katherine Spenley, Julie Street, Richard Woodruff

Photographer
Britta Jaschinski

Reproduced in Singapore by Colourscan
Printed and bound in China by Hung Hing Offset Printing Company Limited

First American Edition, 2007
07 08 09 10 9 8 7 6 5 4 3 2 1

Published in the United States by
DK Publishing, Inc.,
375 Hudson Street, New York, New York 10014

ISSN: 1933-4567
ISBN: 978-0-75662-688-4

The information in this Real City guide is checked annually

This guide is supported by a dedicated website which provides the very latest information for visitors to Paris; please see page 7 for the web address and password. Some information, however, is liable to change, and the publishers cannot accept responsibility for any consequences arising from the use of this book, nor for any material on third party websites, and cannot guarantee that any website address in this book will be a suitable source of travel information.
We value the views and suggestions of our readers very highly. Please write to:
Publisher, DK Eyewitness Travel Guides,
Dorling Kindersley, 80 Strand, London WC2R 0RL.

Contents

The Guide

Real City Paris

Stay ahead of the crowd with **Real City Paris**, and find the best places to eat, shop, drink and chill out at a glance.

The guide is divided into four main sections:

Introducing Paris – essential background information on the city, including an overview by one of the authors, the top tourist attractions, festivals and seasonal events, and useful travel and practical information.

Listings – eight themed chapters packed with incisive reviews of the best the city has to offer, in every price band and chosen by local experts.

Street Finder – map references in the listings lead you to this section, where you can plan your route and find your way around.

Indexes – the By Area and By Type indexes offer shortcuts to what you are looking for, whether it is a bar in the 6th arrondissement or an Italian restaurant.

The Website

www.realcity.dk.com

By purchasing this book you have been granted free access to up-to-the-minute online content about Paris for at least 12 months. Click onto **www.realcity.dk.com** for updates, and sign up for a free weekly email with the latest information on what to see and do in Paris.

On the website you can:

- **Find the latest news** about Paris, including exhibitions, restaurant openings and music events

- Check what other readers have to say and **add your own comments** and reviews

- **Plan your visit** with a customizable calendar

- See at a glance **what's in and what's not**

- Look up listings by name, by type and by area, and check the **latest reviews**

- **Link directly** to all the websites in the book, and many more

How to register

> Click on the Paris icon on the home page of the website to register or log in.

> Enter the city code given on this page, and follow the instructions given.

> The city code will be valid for a minimum of 12 months from the date you purchased this guide.

city code: **paris61094**

introducing paris

How to spend your time in Paris? Whatever your interests – dining in fine restaurants or local bistros, exploring cultural attractions, checking out the social scene or shopping in designer boutiques – Paris will deliver. Our contributors have selected the best of what the city has to offer and we open with a lowdown that sets the scene for this perennially exciting city.

INTRODUCING PARIS

Despite the tired old clichés, Paris is a complex city that continues to surprise and entrance. Like many people who choose to live here, I came for a short trip – and almost a decade later I still can't imagine why I'd want to be anywhere else. It's almost impossible to be indifferent to Paris. A city that's clever, beautiful, demanding and hedonistic – what is there not to love? Here are a few of the reasons why this city sparkles for me.

Katherine Spenley

Left Bank/Right Bank

A grasp of the great Left Bank/Right Bank divide is crucial to understanding Paris. Traditionally, the Left Bank (south of the Seine) is home to the intelligentsia, students and creative types, and the Right Bank is where everyone else lives. In reality, this ceased to be the case long ago. Some cite the demise of St-Germain's jazz scene as the beginning of the end; others bemoan the day Armani took over Le Drugstore, an emblematic neighbourhood meeting place. The more practical point simply to escalating property prices. One thing's for sure: while many best-selling authors and art dealers still live on the Left, the struggling artists and musicians are long gone. Of course, La Sorbonne's students still swarm the cafés nearby, but today's thinkers now tend to live in the historically working-class 10th, 11th, 19th or 20th *arrondissements* on the Right Bank.

Being Beautiful

Like a supermodel on the bus, Paris's beauty is impossible to ignore. There are, of course, less pretty parts to the city, but gorgeous monuments are everywhere and the city's beauty is one of its defining characteristics. Unsurprisingly, this kind of backdrop to everyday life has an impact on the mundane. Bad day at work? The Eiffel Tower. Heartbreak issues? Opéra. Existential crisis? Palais Royal. The end result? Parisians understand the power of beauty. The city has a history of ambitious urban planning from Haussmann's avenues to Mitterand's Louvre pyramids *(see p106)* and now Chirac's Musée du Quai Branly *(see p106)* and Mayor Delanë's regeneration of Les Halles (Map 10 G4). The architects of the most recent projects hope to never hear the phrase *pas très beau*. Declaring that something "isn't very beautiful" is the most damning of Parisian insults...

Getting Away With It

...which puts their reputation for rudeness into perspective. In Paris, people aren't necessarily rude, but they are always demanding. Like a petulant princess, Paris regularly has foot-stamping outbursts; but actually, they are one of her best qualities. One just needs to look at

a city primer

recent French revolutions and protests to realise that taking to the streets is effective here. A Parisian's first demonstration is like their first date: a rite of passage that opens their eyes to what might happen if they play their cards right. Take, for example, the maximum 35-hour working week. Anywhere else, this concept would seem unreasonable, but here, somehow, they get away with it. The threat of the tantrum that would otherwise ensue seems enough to maintain the status quo. The city's collective diva-ish demands can seem more than a little difficult at times, but these outbursts do seem to work, and in the end Parisians get what they want: namely a fabulous city and an enviable lifestyle. No-one talks about a work-life balance here; the whole idea would seem absurd to a Parisian, and *la qualité de la vie* or "quality of life" is what is most important.

La Vie en Rose

It's therefore not surprising that the romantic side of things is taken very seriously. Just as the city really is as beautiful as the clichés suggest, it also really is incredibly romantic and seductive. The men *do* stop you in the street to tell you you're pretty, the women *do* wear complex lingerie on a daily basis, and if you visit this city in love, it *does* seem as if it has been designed especially for you. It's the perfect place to be with your perfect person. Paradoxically, Parisians believe that the good things in life are equally valid when sampled alone. It's not just accepted, it's expected that sometimes you'll want to walk in the Jardin des Tuileries (Map 9 C4), go to the theatre or eat oysters *tout seule*. The key is always to be in pursuit of pleasure. Use your brain, indulge your eyes, feast your senses, never accept anything that's not good enough, revel in emotion of all kinds and you should enjoy an authentic Parisian experience.

✅ The Good Value Mark

Cities can be expensive, but if you know where to go you can always discover excellent-value places. We've picked out the best of these in the Restaurants, Shopping, and Hotels chapters and indicated them with the pink Good Value mark.

INTRODUCING PARIS

Paris's top attractions are the sights and museums that make up every first- and second-time visitor's must-see list. The "big three" museums (the Musée d'Orsay, the Musée du Louvre and the Centre Pompidou) in particular boast extraordinarily rich collections; the cathedral of Notre Dame and the Eiffel Tower are city icons; and taking a stroll in the Jardin du Luxembourg or along the Champs-Elysées is a quintessential Parisian experience.

Eiffel Tower
`8 E5`

Champ de Mars, 7ème • 01 44 11 23 23 • Ⓜ Champs de Mars Tour Eiffel
≫ www.tour-eiffel.fr Open 9:30am–midnight daily

Built for the 1889 World Fair and to mark the centenary of the French Revolution, the 324 m (1,063 ft) Tour Eiffel was intended to be a temporary structure. Today it draws six million visitors annually. If you walk up to either of the first two levels, queues for the lifts are shorter. **Adm**

Jardin du Luxembourg
`16 E4`

Entrances on rue Auguste Comte & rue Guynemer, 6ème
01 42 34 23 89 • Ⓜ Odéon Open 7:30am–9pm (winter 8:15am–4:30pm)

The quintessential Parisian "garden" is a well-kept expanse of orchards, chestnut trees and classical statues. Bourgeois locals read, stroll, and play tennis or chess, and excellent free photo exhibitions along the park's perimeter railings are regularly held.

Musée du Louvre
`10 E5`

Rue de Rivoli, 1er • 01 40 20 50 50 • Ⓜ Palais Royal Musée du Louvre
≫ www.louvre.fr Open 9am–6pm Thu & Sat–Mon, 9am–9:45pm Wed & Fri

A former royal palace, the Louvre has major galleries dedicated to the Etruscans, Egyptians, Greeks, and European and Islamic art. It houses some 35,000 works, though crowds still flock to the most famed masterpieces such as the *Mona Lisa* and *Venus de Milo*. I M Pei's striking main entrance cleverly juxtaposes the new with the old. **Adm**

top attractions

Musée d'Orsay
`9 C5`

1 rue de Bellechasse, 7ème • 01 40 49 48 14 • RER Musée d'Orsay
>> www.musee-orsay.fr Open 9:30am–6pm daily (to 9:45pm Thu)

A former railway station is the spectacular setting for this sizable collection of Western art that includes painting, furniture, sculpture, architecture and photography. The upper level is justifiably famed for its exquisite Impressionist and Post-Impressionist masterpieces. **Adm**

Centre Pompidou
`11 A5`

Place Georges Pompidou, 4ème • 01 44 78 12 33 • Ⓜ Rambuteau
>> www.centrepompidou.fr Open 11am–9pm daily (to 11pm Thu)

This dynamic cultural centre boasts the largest modern art collection in Europe and is also famous for its exoskeletal architecture, which highlights the building's structural workings using colour-coded pipes. The temporary exhibitions are unfailingly excellent. **Adm**

Notre Dame
`16 H2`

Place du Parvis Notre Dame, 1er • 01 42 34 56 10 • Ⓜ St-Michel
>> www.cathedraledeparis.com Open 7:45am–6:45pm daily

This masterpiece of Gothic church architecture dominates the Ile de la Cité. With the years of grime recently removed from its stonework, the detailed biblical sculptures on the façade and the ornate flying buttresses at the rear are even more impressive. Climb up the tower for a close inspection of its famous gargoyles. **Adm**

>> *From April to November, the Batobus river shuttle links sights such as the Eiffel Tower and the Louvre*

INTRODUCING PARIS

Arc de Triomphe

Place Charles de Gaulle, 8ème • 01 55 37 73 77
Ⓜ Charles de Gaulle Etoile Open 10am–11pm daily

Completed in 1836, this arch features four relief panels depicting
Napoleon's triumphs. Beneath it is the tomb of the Unknown Soldier,
where an eternal flame commemorates the dead of the two world
wars. There are excellent views from the top of the arch. **Adm**

Champs-Elysées
8 G2

Ⓜ Charles de Gaulle Etoile, Franklin D Roosevelt, Champs-Elysées Clemenceau

France's most famous avenue has certainly changed since Marie de
Medici first created a path through the surrounding fields (*champs*)
in 1616. Today, this street's exclusive boutiques, hotels, chain stores
and fast-food eateries pay the most expensive retail rents in Europe. It's
all about strolling, window-shopping and, above all, people-watching.

Cimetière du Père-Lachaise
12 H4

Blvd de Ménilmontant, 20ème • 01 55 25 82 10 • Ⓜ Père-Lachaise
➤➤ www.pere-lachaise.com Open 8am–6pm Mon–Fri, 8:30am–6pm Sat,
9am–6pm Sun (winter to 5:30pm Mon–Sat)

A resting place for thousands of famous dead, the city's biggest
cemetery also draws museum-weary tourists to its tranquil setting.
The often ostentatious tombs house an impressive roll call that
includes Proust, Chopin, Balzac, Oscar Wilde and Jim Morrison.

14
➤➤ www.realcity.dk.com

top attractions

Sainte-Chapelle

16 G1

4 boulevard du Palais, 1er • 01 53 73 78 51 • Ⓜ St Michel
Open 9:30am–6:30pm daily (winter 10am–5pm)

Consecrated in 1248, this royal chapel was designed to hold Louis IX's collection of holy relics. The lower level features a star-painted ceiling, but it's the upper level's wrap-around, stained-glass windows depicting Old Testament scenes that steal the show. **Adm**

Sacré Cœur

4 G2

35 rue du Chevalier de la Barre, 18ème • 01 53 41 89 00 • Ⓜ Abbesses
➤➤ www.sacre-coeur-montmartre.com Open 9am–6:45pm (winter 10am–5:45pm)

Perched atop the city's highest point, this huge white-domed basilica was built using funds generated by public subscription and completed in 1919. Inside, the golden mosaics are the main draw, but most people come for the grand vistas from the terrace and top of the dome. **Adm**

Château de Versailles

01 30 83 76 20 • RER Versailles-Rive Gauche
➤➤ www.chateauversailles.fr Open 9am–6:30pm Tue–Sun (winter to 5:30pm)

In his usual spirit of self-glorification, Louis XIV transformed his father's hunting lodge into France's most sumptuous château in the late 17th century. The vast gardens were landscaped by André Le Nôtre, while painter Charles Le Brun embellished the interiors, where highlights include the Hall of Mirrors. Arrive early to avoid the busloads. **Adm**

INTRODUCING PARIS

Springtime in Paris is traditionally the city's most magical and romantic season. Lily-of-the-valley is sold on street corners on May Day to celebrate the return of warmer weather. The annual Fête de la Musique kicks off summer on 21 June, followed by outdoor music festivals and dance and theatre performances as well as the Bastille Day balls on the 13 or 14 July, where you can dance the night away crying "Liberté, Egalité, Fraternité".

Foire du Trône

Pelouse de Reuilly, 12ème, Ⓜ Liberté/Porte Dorée www.foiredutrone.com Open 11:45–11 daily (to 1am Fri & Sat)

This colossal fun fair began in AD 957, when merchants first met up with farmers to trade grain and wine. Today at this site to the east of the city, instead of wheat sacks and wine barrels there are 350 attractions, including a giant Ferris wheel, gravity-defying rides and carousels, and clouds of candy floss. **End Mar–end May**

Portes Ouvertes

Ateliers d'Artistes de Belleville (AAB), 32 rue de la Mare, 20ème, 01 46 36 44 09, www.ateliers-artistes-belleville.org

There's more to the Paris art scene than majestic museums and pricey private galleries, as the annual Belleville Artists Open Studios confirms. For four days, more than 250 artists in this multi-ethnic *quartier* (Map 12 F2) open their doors to the public. Pick up a map from the AAB and set about discovering the neighbourhood's cornucopia of painters, photographers and jewellers, along with the bistros, funky cafés and shops. **Mid-May**

Summer Music Festivals

Festival de St-Denis, 01 48 13 06 07, www.festival-saint-denis.fr; Paris Jazz Festival & Festival Classique au Vert, Esplanade du Château de Vincennes, 12ème, Ⓜ Chateau de Vincennes; Fête de la Musique, www.fetedelamusique.culture.fr

Throughout the summer, Paris is alive with the sound of all kinds of music. St-Denis Gothic basilica *(see p114)* is the glorious backdrop to a month-long classical- and world-music festival starting in June. At the same time, as part of the **Paris Jazz Festival** (Jun–Jul), both big-name and experimental jazz artists strike up in the Bois de Vincennes in a series of open-air afternoon concerts. Noise-pollution laws are in abeyance at the **Fête de la Musique**'s all-day and all-night extravaganza on 21 June. The summer solstice is fêted by appreciative crowds as international and world-music acts, serious professionals, one-man bands and musical wannabes play their kind of music in varied locations all over the city. The **Festival Classique au Vert** (Aug– Sep) rounds off the summer with classical music wafting over the lawns of the Bois de Vincennes. **Jun–Sep**

spring and summer

La Marche des Fiertés LGBT (Gay Pride)
www.marche-inter-lgbt.org

This vivacious and flamboyant celebration of gay, lesbian, bi- and transsexual culture draws 650,000 performers and onlookers. A week of exhibitions, events and parties climaxes in the parade, which kicks off at 2pm and dances its way to place de la Bastille (Map 17 D2). **End Jun**

Le Quatorze Juillet (Bastille Day)

France's national holiday recalls the storming of the Bastille in 1789 and the beginning of the Republic. By 10am, hordes pack the Champs-Elysées for a glimpse of French military might and the president reviewing the troops. Later that night, thousands gather under the Eiffel Tower to watch the fireworks display at Trocadéro, as others head off for more partying at the *bals des pompiers* (firemen's balls) held in stations all over the city. Some of these kick off the previous night, when Parisians can also dance their hearts out on place de la Bastille. **13–14 Jul**

Paris Plage

The Seine becomes the seaside for a month as palm trees, deck chairs, and vast amounts of sand appear along the Right Bank (from the Louvre to Pont de Sully) and the Left Bank at Port de la Gare (Map 22 F2) . **Mid Jul–mid Aug**

Le Tour de France
See the action at www.letour.fr

The world's best road cyclists descend on Paris each year for the final stage of the Tour de France. Riders loop past place de la Bastille before completing nine laps around the Champs-Elysées, place de la Concorde and rue de Rivoli, including a final sprint up the Champs-Elysées to the finish line. **End Jul**

La Fête des Tuileries
Jardin des Tuileries, 1er
Open 11am–midnight daily (to 1am Fri & Sat)

After the spring Foire du Trône, a similar array of rides and attractions springs up around the rue de Rivoli boundary of the Jardin des Tuileries (Map 9 D4). **Aug–Sep**

17

INTRODUCING PARIS

While to others September may just mark the end of the summer holidays, for Parisians it's a time when they can enjoy cultural happenings and openings. Take Jazz à la Villette's musical adventures or La Nuit Blanche, when clubs, museums, and swimming pools stay open all night. Perhaps the best nocturnal celebration is on New Year's Eve, which sees the Champs-Elysées packed with happy revellers who congregate to ring out the old and ring in the new.

Les Journées du Patrimoine
www.journeesdupatrimoine.culture.fr

As part of a Europe-wide initiative, normally inaccessible public and private buildings in Paris open their doors to the public and allow a fascinating free glimpse of hidden architectural treasures. It's a rare opportunity to explore some of the most unusual historic sights in the city on one weekend. **Mid-Sep**

Jazz à la Villette
www.cite-musique.fr, Ⓜ Porte de Pantin

La Villette's annual week-long jazz fest spills out into the Cité de la Musique (see p129), local bars and the park (for free open-air concerts). There's a penchant for innovative and experimental music, with appearances by big international names as well as local favourites. **Sep**

Festival d'Automne
01 53 45 17 00, www.festival-automne.com

Parisians are jolted out of their summer slumber with the arrival of this forward-looking, city-wide arts festival, showcasing new talent from around the world. It's all about music, opera, theatre and dance not previously shown in France; the kind of productions that make you sit up and pay attention. **Sep–Dec**

La Nuit Blanche
Check out all the activities at www.paris.fr

The brainchild of Mayor Delanoë, "Sleepless Night" is designed to keep Parisians up all night with a hefty dose of culture. And it's all free, from nocturnal swimming sessions and a 3am art crawl through the Centre Pompidou, to techno concerts. A must for the culturally curious, night owls and insomniacs. **Early Oct**

Le Fiac
www.fiacparis.com

This international contemporary arts fair attracts leading modern art galleries from around the world. They gather under the impressive shadow of the Grand Palais or set up in the Cour Carrée of the Louvre to show off their wares. **End Oct**

autumn and winter

Photography Shows
Paris Photo, Carousel du Louvre (Map 10 E5), www.parisphoto.fr
Le Mois de la Photo, venues across the city

Now into its 11th year, the ticketed **Paris Photo** show exhibits all aspects of photography, from the early masters to contemporary work, with a different focus each year. Every two years photography fans find themselves spoilt for choice as the show coincides with the more erudite citywide celebration of the art of photography called **Le Mois de la Photo**. Watch out for free exhibitions in galleries and all the major museums, as well as some interesting fringe events. **Nov**

Paris sur Glace
Place de l'Hôtel de Ville, 4ème (Map 17 A1); place Raoul Dautry, 15ème (Map 19 B1) Both open noon–8pm Mon–Fri, 9am–8pm Sat & Sun

It might not be a frozen lake in the Alps, but in the depths of winter, an open-air Paris ice rink can be equally enchanting. Two rinks are open to the public free of charge – the one in front of the grandiose Hôtel de Ville is the largest and perhaps the prettiest, ringed with fir trees and twinkling lights when night falls. Skates are available for hire. **Early Dec–early Mar**

Le Réveillon (New Year's Eve)
While some Parisians prefer to spend their Réveillon (or Fête de St-Sylvestre) sitting around the table supping oysters and reminiscing, more spirited folk take to the streets. Crowds throng the Champs-Elysées, bars around Bastille teem and the Quartier Latin is alive with people throwing their arms around each other and screeching "Bonne année!". **31 Dec**

Présences
Maison de la Radio France (Map 13 2A)

The most adventurous annual festival of contemporary classical music in the city sees world-class ensembles perform an impressive range of avant-garde music, including new commissions and world premieres programmed around a major 21st-century composer. All events are free. **Feb**

INTRODUCING PARIS

Paris's public transport network (RATP) comprises the Métro, the RER (suburban train service), buses and trams, and is both efficient and reasonably priced. Taxis and the Batobus (water bus) service provide alternatives, but visitors often find that it is easier, quicker and more rewarding to explore the heart of Paris on foot. The following information covers the key aspects of getting around Paris; for further details, see www.eparis.co.uk.

Arrival

Paris has two airports: Roissy Charles de Gaulle is the largest and handles international flights; Orly serves national and European destinations.

Roissy Charles de Gaulle

The most popular public-transport link is RER B (via the Roissyrail bus), with a journey time of around 30 minutes into central Paris. Alternatively, Roissybus will drop you at Opéra, taking 50 minutes. Both services run approximately 6am–11:30pm. Air France also runs two bus services: to Porte Maillot and Etoile (5:45am–11pm) and to Gare de Lyon and Montparnasse (7am–9:30pm). For details of times and ticket prices, check the **ADP** website. **Bus de Nuit** bus services run through the night. For hassle-free transfers, you can book a shuttle bus (try **Paris Airports Service** or **Airport Connection**) direct to your hotel. The price depends on the number of passengers (usually about 16–25€ per person) but is cheaper than taking a taxi (around 50€). Limousine transfers are offered by companies such as **Airport Limousine Service** (around 100€).

Orly

To get into town by train, there are three options: catch the Orlyval shuttle train that connects with RER B, the Orlyrail bus for RER C, or the Jetbus to get on to the Métro. Alternatively, you can travel direct to Denfert-Rochereau on the Orlybus service, which takes around 30 minutes. Air France coaches take around 30 minutes to reach Montparnasse and Invalides. Check the **ADP** website for details. Taxi, shuttle bus and limousine services are also available from Orly – check the websites of **PariShuttle**, **Airport Connection** and **Airport Limousine Service** for more details.

By Train

Paris has six long-distance train stations, each serving a different region. All train stations are centrally located and have Métro stations, bus stops and taxi ranks nearby. High-speed services between the UK, Germany and Benelux are provided by **Eurostar** and **Thalys**; within France, the railway network is run by **SNCF**.

Getting Around

Central Paris is compact and easy to tackle on foot, but the excellent public transport system is a pleasure to use.

Public Transport

Paris's Métro system is one of the best in the world, and still improving – most recently with the addition of hi-tech driverless trains on the new line 14. The Métro runs from 5:30am to 1am, and is the quickest and most reliable way of getting across town. Short hops (especially those involving transfers) are not recommended, however, as they often take longer – and involve more legwork – than simply walking from A to B.

Buses are faster than the Métro over short distances, with the added bonus of being able to see where you're going, but it is at night-time that the bus network really comes into its own: Noctambuses (see the **RATP** website) are the only form of public transport in operation between 1 and 5am. These are very user-friendly and a must for night owls who don't want to take taxis – they operate outwards from the centre, leaving Châtelet hourly on the half hour and leaving their end stops hourly on the hour to travel back into town. Travel passes are valid, but single tickets (see below) are not. Fares start at 2.30€.

Single tickets, valid on all public transport, cost 1.40€ each, or 10.70€ for a carnet (book) of ten. A Métro trip uses one ticket – including transfers, as long as you don't leave the Métro system. (Inattentive travellers beware: it is not always possible to change direction without exiting the station.) Bus and tram journeys within central Paris also use one ticket each, but transfers are not permitted.

The Carte Mobilis (5.40€ for zones 1 and 2) allows you to travel on all bus, Métro, RER and tram lines all day. The Carte Orange (be sure to get the photo

ID card or risk a fine) offers the same deal on a weekly (Mon–Sun only; 15.70€) or monthly (calendar month only; 51.50€) basis. The tourist option is the Paris Visite ticket – available for 1, 2, 3 or 5 days. As well as unlimited travel, this offers discounts on tours and some shops (such as Les Galeries Lafayette), but at 8.35€ for the 1-day version, you really do have to use the discounts to get your money's worth.

Tickets (but not passes) must be validated at the start of your journey – either in station turnstiles (Métro and RER) or as you board buses and trams. When travelling by bus, you should also show your ticket to the driver.

Taxis

The best way to get a taxi is to queue at one of the city's many taxi ranks. This is often quicker and cheaper than calling for a cab, and easier than hailing one on the street (they never stop near a rank). You'll find taxi ranks at railway stations and at bigger Métro stops, for a full list and more tips on Parisian taxis, see **www.paris-taxi.net**.

Driving

There is really little benefit to driving in Paris: the city is well known for its aggressive drivers and if you must take to the road, you will need nerves of steel and an up-to-date map of the city's labyrinthine one-way systems. Drivers from outside the EU should also carry an international licence. The city speed limit is 50 km/h (31 mph) – though many drivers ignore this – and parking spaces are as sparse as they are expensive.

Bicycles & Roller Blades

Bicycle hire is possible (try **Paris à Velo c'est Sympa**) and cycle maps are available from major Métro stations. Hiring roller blades is also an option *(see p18)*, but the streets of Paris are not the place for novices. Take care – drivers have scant respect for any other road users' rights or safety.

Tours

There are plenty of guided walks, bus tours and river cruises to choose from – full listings can be found on the tourist-office website *(see p231)* and at **http://paris.city-discovery.com**. For a low-key boat trip, take to the canal *(see p106)*. Some of the less obvious tour options are detailed below.

Fat Tire Bike Tours offers day- and night-time bicycle tours around Paris. Tours take 4 hours or more but are not strenuous, and children are catered for with tandems and child seats.

If you prefer posing to pedalling, join a **City Segway Tour**. These offer a unique opportunity to experience Paris by electric scooter – and you do get to practise before you hit the streets.

For stunning aerial views, take a helicopter tour with **Helifrance Paris**, or see the city the romantic way from a hot-air balloon (try one of the trips run by **France Montgolfiers**).

The flexible option is **AlloVisit**'s tour – this can be taken at your leisure, guided only by your mobile phone. Or, if you're feeling self-indulgent, you can order a tailor-made itinerary from **Edible Paris**: anything goes, as long as it is something to do with food.

Directory

ADP (Aéroports de Paris)
01 48 62 22 80 (CDG)
01 49 75 15 15 (Orly)
www.adp.fr

Airport Connection
01 43 65 55 55
www.airport-connection.com

Airport Limousine Service
01 40 71 84 62

AlloVisit
04 95 04 95 32 or 08 92 68 33 14
www.voxinzebox.com

Bus de Nuit
08 10 02 02 02

City Segway Tours
01 56 58 10 54
www.citysegwaytours.com

Edible Paris
www.edible-paris.com

Eurostar
08 92 35 35 39
www.eurostar.fr

Fat Tire Bike Tours
01 56 58 10 54
www.fattirebiketoursparis.com

France Montgolfiers
08 10 60 01 53

Helifrance Paris
01 45 54 95 11

Paris Airports Service
01 55 98 10 80
www.parisairportservice.com

Paris à Velo c'est Sympa
01 48 87 60 01
www.parisvelosympa.com

PariShuttle
01 53 39 18 18
www.parishuttle.com

RATP
01 92 68 77 14 • www.ratp.fr

SNCF
36 35 • www.sncf.com

Thalys
35 36 or 08 92 35 35 36
www.thalys.com

Paris is not a difficult city for most visitors, although people with special needs can find it tricky to access information and get around. The city's Office du Tourisme has an excellent website packed with useful information and suggestions, and several welcome centres dotted around the city, which increase significantly in number over the summer months. The following is some essential practical information; for further tips and information, check www.eparis.dk.com.

Disabled Travellers

Unfortunately, much of Paris's public-transport network is inaccessible to wheelchair- (and pram-) users, though wheelchair-friendly buses are gradually replacing the old stock. On the Métro, only line 14 has stair-free access at all stations. Station staff rarely go out of their way to help, but leaflets about disabled facilities are available at main stations, and there is a **Compagnons du Voyage** service which provides helpers to accompany disabled people on public transport (25€ per hour). Guide dogs can ride on public transport, but owners must pay 50% of the fare for them.

Taxi drivers are bound by law to assist disabled passengers and accept guide dogs, but not all cabs are equipped to carry wheelchairs.

The French **Tourisme & Handicaps** association has a useful list of disability-friendly accommodation, restaurants, cultural sites and leisure facilities, which is also posted on the **Office du Tourisme de Paris** website. There are separate criteria for those catering to physical, mental, hearing and visual disabilities.

There are several organizations that specialize in guided tours of the city for disabled people – check with the tourist office for information.

Emergencies and Health

French pharmacists are highly trained and therefore authorized to sell some medicines that are not available over the counter at home. As they can also usually direct you to the nearest doctor, they are always a good first port of call for minor ailments. After hours, a note on the door will direct you to the nearest late-opening pharmacy; alternatively, try **Pharmacy les Champs** – one of the few that stay open all night. Paris's hospitals all have A&E departments, but if your French isn't up to scratch, you may prefer to try the **American Hospital in Paris** or the **Hertford British Hospital**. Both are private, so check beforehand that your insurance will cover the cost. Check www.magicparis.com for a list of English-speaking doctors.

Gay and Lesbian Travellers

The legal age of sexual consent is 16 and Parisians are generally very tolerant of same-sex relationships. The most openly gay areas, with lots of gay bars and clubs, are in the 1st–4th arrondissements. The **Lesbian & Gay Centre Paris** is on hand for support.

Left Luggage

Paris's six main stations all have left-luggage facilities. The airports do not.

Listings/What's On

Pariscope and *Officiel des Spectacles* are well-known, comprehensive listings magazines. The tourist office also publishes a free monthly guide called *Where: Paris*, available from information kiosks across town. The website www.novaplanet.com gives a more underground perspective on what the city has to offer.

Money

If you need to exchange cash, banks usually offer a better rate of exchange than the *bureaux de change* that are clustered around the tourist hotspots and along the Champs-Elysées, even once you have taken commission into account. Withdrawing cash from an ATM is a much simpler – and usually cheaper – way of getting your euros. Your bank will usually offer a competitive exchange rate, but may charge more commission for small transactions, so it is best to withdraw larger rather than smaller amounts. Check with your bank before you leave home.

Opening Hours

Most **restaurants** close between lunch and dinner, while **cafés** typically stay open from the morning until the end of the afternoon, when restaurants re-open. **Brasseries** often remain open until very late. **Bars** (and bar-like cafés) tend to open from mid-afternoon until the early hours. Some late bars stay open until around 6am.

Shops and **restaurants** are generally closed on Sundays – though some shops (typically tobacconists and general stores) open briefly on Sunday morning. The exceptions to this rule are generally found in the Marais and along the Champs-Elysées. Late-night shopping is on Thursdays until 9pm.

Most **museums** and many **shops** are closed on Mondays. Small shops may also close for lunch, as do many local bank and post office branches. Parks tend to open from dawn to dusk daily.

Public holidays are 1 Jan, 1 May, 8 May, 14 Jul, 15 Aug, 1 Nov, 11 Nov, 25 Dec, Easter Monday, Ascension and Whit Monday. Paris closes down on these days, and anywhere that does open will usually keep Sunday hours. The city also practically shuts down in August for the summer break; during this month, it is always best to phone ahead to check that your restaurant, bar or boutique of choice is open.

Phones and Communications

Many public telephone boxes are falling into disrepair and, given the rise in use of mobile phones, they are often left unrepaired. If they do work, you will most likely need to use a phonecard (available from Métro stations and *tabacs*). Some cafés and bars have public phones.

Non-residents cannot buy a French SIM card, though if you know a resident, they can buy one on your behalf. Phone-hire companies advertise at airports, but they rarely offer significant savings over a roaming contract.

Internet cafés are springing up all over the city – especially along the Champs-Elysées. Small local places offer good deals but little availability, and have a habit of closing down at short notice. Visit **www.pidf.com** for an up-to-date list of internet cafés, or try **Café Psycho** or **Paris-Cy** if you have trouble getting online elsewhere.

Stamps are sold by many *tabacs*, some hotels and most postcard vendors. Post boxes are yellow and are marked "La Poste".

Security

Everyone must carry ID (passport or EU identity card) at all times. Police may – and in the case of ethnic minorities, frequently do – ask to see it. Certain areas in the north of Paris – La Goutte d'Or *(see p164)* in particular – are best avoided after dark.

Tipping

In restaurants, cafés and bars, service is usually included, but most Parisians will round up their drinks bill to the nearest euro, and leave a couple of euros for good service in a restaurant or café. Where service is not included, you should leave around 15%. Taxi drivers and hairdressers expect a similar percentage, and in hotels you should tip porters a couple of euros per item, and other hotel staff the same amount per day.

Tourist Information

The main **Office du Tourisme de Paris** is located at 25 rue des Pyramides, 1er. 0892 683 000 (Map 10 E3) and is one of seven permanent welcome centres. In addition, there are numerous seasonal welcome centres that are open from June through August. Check the website *(see directory)* for details.

Directory

Ambulance (SAMU)
15

American Hospital in Paris
63 blvd Victor Hugo, Neuilly-sur-Seine
Ⓜ Pont de Levallois-Bécon
01 46 41 25 25
www.american-hospital.org

Café Psycho
13 rue de Médicis, 6ème
01 43 25 21 81

Compagnons du Voyage
01 53 11 11 12
www.compagnons.com

Dentist (SOS Dentaire)
01 43 37 51 00

Directory Assistance
12

Doctor on Call (SOS Médécin)
08 20 33 24 24

English-Language Help (SOS Help)
01 46 21 46 46

Fire Brigade (Pompiers)
18

Hertford British Hospital
3 rue Barbès, Levallois-Perret
Ⓜ Anatole France • 01 46 39 22 22
www.british-hospital.org

Lesbian & Gay Centre Paris
3 rue Keller, 11ème
01 43 57 21 47 • www.cglparis.org

Office du Tourisme de Paris
www.parisinfo.com

Paris-Cy
8 rue de Jouy, 4ème
01 42 71 37 37 • www.paris-cy.com

Pharmacy les Champs
84 ave des Champs-Elysées, 8ème
01 45 62 02 41

Police
17

Tourisme & Handicaps
01 44 11 10 41
tourisme.handicaps@club-internet.fr

Yellow Pages (Pages Jaunes)
www.pagesjaunes.fr

restaurants

Restaurants alone are reason enough to come to Paris, whether you're seeking a slice of history, a dash of panache or a pinch of perfection. What sets French chefs apart is their mastery of technique, which has filtered down to a young generation of bistro chefs whose creative cuisine highlights seasonal ingredients. The current trend is for "tapas" – elegant food served in tiny portions.

RESTAURANTS

After a few years of angst, Parisian chefs have shed their worries about where they stand on the world's gastronomic stage. These days, the key word is fun – whether that means serving gourmet hot dogs as part of a "fooding" event *(see p30)*, turning out market-inspired cooking in the tiny kitchen of a 20-seat bistro, or opening a tapas-style annexe to an *haute-cuisine* temple. In my ten years as a Paris food writer, restaurants have never felt so inspired.

Rosa Jackson

Food with Great Views

Despite a lack of tall buildings, this beautifully preserved city still offers breathtaking views. Even after 400 years, it's hard to beat the one from **La Tour d'Argent** *(see p37)*. Over the river **La Maison Blanche** *(see p44)* offers a similarly dramatic panorama. And diners at **Au Bon Acceuil** *(see p42)* can feast their eyes on that Paris icon, Le Tour Eiffel.

Designer Dining

Design no longer plays second fiddle to food in the capital. Superchef Alain Senderens has gone for a space-age look at **Senderens** *(see p45)*, while at Baccarat's **Le Cristal Room** *(see p44)*, designer Philippe Starck has left his mark. Most recently, Pierre Gagnaire got in on the act too, with the marine-themed fish-scale wall at **Gaya Rive Gauche** *(see p42)*.

Eating Alfresco

There can be no greater pleasure than claiming an outdoor table in Paris, whether it's wobbling on a narrow pavement or elegantly set in a hotel courtyard. Be sure to nab an outside table at **Le Square Trousseau** *(see p56)*, savour the garden setting of the **Restaurant du Palais-Royal** *(see p28)*, or enjoy the bucolic square at **Kastoori** *(see p48)*.

choice eats

Romantic Rendezvous

You don't have to try very hard to muster up romance in Paris. Snuggle up in red surroundings at the candlelit **Chez Toinette** *(see p51)*, sink into Moroccan splendour at **Le Souk** *(see p55)*, or pull out all the stops with a luxurious dinner at **L'Ambroisie** *(see p33)*. If your stomach's a-flutter, stick to simple yet sensual fare in a vintage brasserie instead.

Neo-Bistros

The city has a huge number of bistros with market-inspired menus and compact kitchens manned by just one or two cooks. At **Le Timbre** *(see p39)*, you can watch British native Chris Wright toil in his tiny kitchen, while Yves Camdeborde at **Le Comptoir du Relais St-Germain** *(see p38)* continues to reinvent the bistro genre with his five-course set menu.

Small Plates

Emulating their Spanish rivals, Parisian chefs have embraced the tapas tradition. Joël Robuchon's **Atelier** *(see p41)* encourages high-class nibbling, while at **Le Salon d'Hélène** *(see p39)*, the chef draws on her Basque roots to present an inventive tasting menu. **Bellota-Bellota** *(see p40)* provides a more authentic Spanish tapas experience.

Au Pied de Cochon *former market eatery* `10 G4`
6 rue Coquillière, 1er • 01 40 13 77 00
>> www.pieddecochon.com Open 24/7

The signature dish of humble grilled pig's trotter with Béarnaise sauce is one to try at this jolly 24-hour brasserie in the heart of Les Halles, the city's former central food market. It's great for a meal of onion soup and briny oysters, too, and gets lively after 2am, when theatre folk and clubbers tend to drop by. **Expensive**

L'Ardoise *seasonal menus* `9 C3`
28 rue du Mont Thabor, 1er • 01 42 96 28 18
Open lunch & dinner Tue–Sat, dinner only Sun

Pierre Jay's bistro is one of the few in Paris to open on Sundays, but that's only one reason to visit. Local office workers and Parisians in the know congregate here for the great-value food, ranging from pig's trotters to pan-fried scallops with oyster mushrooms. Desserts are not their strong point though. **Moderate**

Restaurant du Palais Royal *real class* `10 F3`
110 galerie Valois, 1er • 01 40 20 00 27
Open lunch & dinner Mon–Sat

In summer, a table on the terrace here is hotly sought-after, so book ahead. In winter the jewel-toned dining room is a treat, and the Mediterranean-inspired food is consistently delicious. (The chef claims to make the best risotto in Paris.) For dessert, try *millefeuilles* filled with fruit and crème Chantilly. **Moderate**

L'Espadon *luxury lunching* `9 D2`
Hôtel Ritz, 15 place Vendôme, 1er • 01 43 16 30 80
>> www.ritzparis.com Open lunch & dinner daily

L'Espadon delivers everything you'd expect of the Ritz: sumptuous surroundings, smooth (and surprisingly unsnooty) service and simply fabulous food. The lunch menu (75€) is a bargain, entitling diners to a lavish four-course feast, including a stunning cheese trolley and coffee with *mignardises* (tiny cakes). **Expensive**

Chez Vong *flavourful Oriental* `10 H4`

10 rue de la Grande Truanderie, 1er • 01 40 26 09 36
» www.chez-vong.com Open lunch & dinner Mon–Sat

Those who despair of ever finding great Chinese food in Paris are relieved to discover this discreet Les Halles restaurant. Among the plants and chinoiserie, discriminating diners savour authentic steamed fish, Peking duck and prawns in lotus leaf. Not cheap, but the freshness and flavour justify the price. **Moderate**

La Tour de Montlhéry *late-night joint* `10 G4`

5 rue des Prouvaires, 1er • 01 42 36 21 82
Open lunch & dinner Mon–Fri

Hearty food (mutton chops, stuffed cabbage) and a noisy, smoke-filled atmosphere are the order of the day at this round-the-clock haunt in Les Halles. Closely packed tables mean that there is often cross-table chat; luckily, the flowing wine helps make conversation a breeze. **Moderate**

Café Moderne *creative cuisine* `10 G2`

40 rue Notre-Dame-des-Victoires, 2ème • 01 53 40 84 10
Open lunch & dinner Mon–Fri, dinner only Sat

Achieving a balance between hip and inviting isn't easy, but Café Moderne proves that it can be done – and well. The cosy red banquettes accommodate a cosmopolitan bunch who contentedly polish off dishes such as thyme-flavoured lamb in filo pastry, and squid filled with Parmesan. **Moderate**

Le Meurice *heavenly hotel dining* `9 D3`

Hotel Meurice, 228 rue de Rivoli, 1er • 01 44 58 10 10
» www.meuricehotel.com Open lunch & dinner Mon–Fri

The cloud-painted ceiling, gilt galore and cushy chairs put you in just the right relaxed frame of mind to appreciate the subtle tastes of Yannick Alleno's understated creations. Try a lightly smoked salmon chunk wrapped in paper-thin crisp potato, John Dory dotted with cumin or the most delicate lemon meringue tart. **Expensive**

Aux Lyonnais *revitalized bistro* `10 F2`

32 rue St-Marc, 2ème • 01 42 96 65 04
Open lunch & dinner Tue–Fri, dinner Sat

French super-chef Alain Ducasse has rejuvenated an 1890s restaurant into a classic bistro complete with burnished red façade, zinc bar, tiles and majestic mirrors. This is updated regional food at its finest – *sabodet* (pork sausage), eggs poached in red wine, and irresistible Saint-Marcellin cheese. **Moderate**

» *Cheap: under 13€ for a main course; moderate: 13–20€; expensive: over 20€*

Chez Georges *quintessential bistro* `10 G3`
1 rue du Mail, 2ème • 01 42 60 07 11
Open lunch & dinner Mon–Sat

On this quiet corner, the glorious old Paris bistro of film and fiction is alive and well and full to the rafters every night. Its success rides on the winning combination of a worn but grand interior, maternal waitresses and good, honest food such as duck with ceps and plump profiteroles doused in chocolate. **Moderate**

Le Petit Dakar *African chic* `11 C5`
6 rue Elzévir, 3ème • 01 44 59 34 74
Open lunch & dinner daily

Thanks to its link with the shop opposite selling African art and *objets*, Le Petit Dakar would look right at home on the pages of *Marie Claire Maison*. Its menu is limited to just a few reliably tasty Senegalese classics such as *thieb'oudjen* (fish stew) or *maffé* (meat in peanut sauce). **Cheap**

Rue Ste-Anne *noodle central* `10 E2`
Demand from Japanese ex-pats has created many great noodle shops in the *10ème*, particularly on rue Ste-Anne. Higuma (at No. 32bis), with an army of dextrous wok-handlers in the open kitchen, is a favourite. Try a giant bowl of ramen topped with grilled pork, rice with tempura, or *yakisoba* (stir-fried noodles). Nearby, Laï Laï Ken (at No. 7) is equally popular with a young clientele who comes for more of the same. **Cheap**

Le Fooding
Journalist Alexandre Cammas invented the concept of "Le Fooding" in 1999 and it has been gaining ground ever since. The word mixes "food" and "feeling" and aims to modernize and democratize the fusty image of French gastronomy. The creation of big "eat-in" events with famous chefs in the kitchen are designed to open the minds of the young to exciting tastes in an atmosphere more akin to a pop concert than a grand restaurant. Entry fees for events vary and details of future fixtures can be found at *www.lefooding.com*. Adventurous fusion cookery that typifies Le Fooding's ethos is much to the fore in restaurants such as **Market** *(see p44)*, **Le Salon d'Hélène** *(see p39)* and **Senderens** *(see p45)*.

Anahï *South American hideaway* 11 B3
49 rue Volta, 3ème • 01 48 87 88 24
Open dinner only daily

Sisters Carminia and Pilat brought a little bit of Latin
America to this old Parisian deli almost 20 years ago.
Since then, they've converted a stylish crowd, including
the occasional celeb, to the joys of Argentinian beef,
Mexican stews and assorted South American titbits.
The snug atmosphere is appealing, too. **Moderate**

Les Enfants Rouges *winning wine bar* 11 C4
9 rue de Beauce, 3ème • 01 48 87 80 61
Open lunch & dinner Thu & Fri, lunch only Tue, Wed & Sat

Run by the couple behind the legendary Montmartre
bistro Le Moulin à Vins – now Café Burq *(see p50)* –
this intimate wine bar guarantees a serious selection
of wines from both well-known and up-and-coming
producers. Also on the menu is simple but robust
French grub and a festive atmosphere. **Moderate**

L'Ambassade d'Auvergne *hearty fare* 11 A4
22 rue du Grenier St-Lazare, 3ème • 01 42 72 31 22
>> www.ambassade-auvergne.com Open lunch & dinner daily

This two-storey tavern with heavy oak beams and
dangling hams has a well-earned reputation for
serving up Auvergne on a plate. That means sturdy
farmhouse food that's perfect for an icy winter's
evening (if slightly less appealing in the height of
summer). Pork and cabbage are menu staples, from
cabbage soup with Roquefort cheese to braised pork
with cabbage and white beans. Also on offer is the
famed regional Salers beef, as well as lamb and fish
dishes. The highlight, however, has to be the *aligot*,
a creamy potato and Tomme cheese mixture,
delivered to the table in a large copper dish, that is
then teased into long ribbons by deft waiters and
served as a side dish. Admittedly, you've got to be in
the mood for an intense cholesterol hit. There's also
a great selection of regional cheeses, and *eau de vie*
(fruit-based brandy) to round things off. **Moderate**

Les Petits Marseillais *southern comfort* `11 B5`

72 rue Vieille du Temple, 3ème • 01 42 78 91 59
Open lunch & dinner daily

A trendy crowd frequents this lively bistro run by two friends from Marseille – they're the nice guys behind the bar. Food has a southern bent: pasta with baby squid and saffron, duck with polenta and Parmesan. As quarters are close, getting into a conversation with your neighbours is also on the menu. **Moderate**

R'Aliment *trendy organic bites* `11 C4`

57 rue Charlot, 3ème • 01 48 04 88 28
Open lunch & dinner Tue–Sat

Plenty of colour in the decor makes this funky organic eatery popular with a young, design-conscious set. Soups, quiches and daily-changing hot dishes – such as vegetable gratin with squash seeds, and fried grouper with roasted potatoes – are prepared directly behind the bar, within view of the customers and filling the room with wholesome smells. It's a good idea to bring a book or a friend as service can be slow. **Moderate**

Le Potager du Marais *vegetarian food* `11 A5`

22 rue Rambuteau, 3ème • 01 42 74 24 66
Open lunch & dinner daily

It may be vegetarian and organic, but that doesn't mean it's all tofu and sprouts. Instead, tuck into tasty dishes such as meat-free pasta carbonara with chanterelles, minestrone and chunky tarts. No incense and batik throws either, just a galley-style room with pared-back decor and an emphasis on healthy eating. **Cheap**

Le Pamphlet *quick-change menu* `11 C4`

38 rue Debelleyme, 3ème • 01 42 72 39 24
Open lunch & dinner Tue–Fri, dinner only Sat & Mon

The menu at this Pyrenees bistro takes its lead from seasonally available produce and changes several times a week; one day, rack of Pyrenean lamb, the next, glazed suckling pig. Owner-chef Alain Carrère – an aficionado of butter and cream – can be gruff, but generally a friendly atmosphere reigns. **Moderate**

L'As du Fallafel *Middle-Eastern mecca*

17 B1

34 rue des Rosiers, 4ème • 01 48 87 63 60
Open all day Sun–Fri

One of many falafel joints on the bustling rue des Rosiers, but undoubtedly the best. The "special", with crunchy chickpea balls cooked to order, fried aubergine, shredded cabbage, hummus and spicy sauces will convert non-believers. This is the epitome of fast food, so don't expect to linger. **Cheap**

L'Ambroisie *classy cuisine*

17 C1

9 place des Vosges, 4ème • 01 42 78 51 45
Open lunch & dinner Tue–Sat

Bernard Pacaud's food is sedate and sophisticated, just like the interior of this 17th-century townhouse with high ceilings and gilt flourishes. High-end dining means polished cooking, artistic presentation and deluxe ingredients (lobster, foie gras, truffles). Service is efficient but sometimes frosty. **Expensive**

Brasseries

When you want a vintage setting, straightforward food, professional waiters and great atmosphere, nothing can beat a Parisian brasserie. Many of the city's most historic examples belong to the Flo group, whose owner Jean-Paul Bucher founded the empire in 1968 with the purchase of **Brasserie Flo**, which resembles a hunting lodge but still has the feel of an Alsatian tavern.

Nearby, another Flo flagship, **Julien**, brings a dash of class to this gritty part of town, near the Gare de l'Est, with its glitzy Art-Nouveau interior. Perhaps the most beloved Flo brasseries, however, are the Art-Deco **La Coupole** – no longer a bona fide literary haunt, but still a great venue – and the more intimate **Le Balzar**, whose purchase by the group sparked an outcry among its intellectual habitués. The typical brasserie fare of *choucroute*

(shredded, fermented cabbage, also known as *sauerkraut*), enormous seafood platters, steaks and sole meunière is generally good enough in Flo brasseries to prevent the regulars from grumbling, and the desserts, such as giant ice-cream sundaes and parfaits, can be spectacular.

Among the independent brasseries, the **Brasserie de l'Isle St-Louis** is a favourite for its tavern-like interior and view of Notre Dame's elegant rear. Near the Gare St-Lazare, **Garnier** is known for its outstanding seafood and rather glamorous setting, while the down-to-earth **Le Grand Colbert**, next to the Palais Royal, may have the oldest interior – part of the dining room dates from the 17th century. Whatever the brasserie, try not to be tempted by the more complex dishes – the kitchens can get overwhelmed at peak times, resulting in slapdash preparations. For contact details, *see pp224–5*.

Restaurants

La Canaille *eccentric eating*
4 rue Crillon, 4ème • 01 42 78 09 71
>> www.lacanaille.fr
Open lunch & dinner Mon–Fri, dinner only Sat

In this quirkily laid-back literary café, don't be surprised if the waiter hands you his note pad and asks you to write down your food order. The French cuisine with a twist – salmon in a crunchy peanut sauce, for example – is reliably good. **Cheap**

17 C3

L'Enoteca *Italian know-how*
25 rue Charles V, 4ème • 01 42 78 91 44
Open lunch & dinner daily

17 C2

This welcoming wine bar is *the* place to try both Italian wine (there are some 30,000 bottles in the cellar) and choice Italian food. Dishes such as swordfish *carpaccio* with pesto, risotto with asparagus, and *bunet* (chocolate flan), together with unpretentious service and decor, mean reservations are advisable. **Moderate**

Robert et Louise *rustic bliss*
64 rue Vieille du Temple, 4ème • 01 42 78 55 89
Open lunch & dinner Tue–Sat

11 B5

More like a country kitchen than a Paris restaurant, this is the kind of place where you get to watch your steak being chopped off an enormous side of beef and thrown on to the wood-fire griddle to sizzle. The atmosphere might be smoky and the staff can be rude, but the food is good and filling. **Moderate**

Le Vieux Bistro *timeless attraction*
14 rue du Cloître Notre Dame, 4ème • 01 43 54 18 95
Open lunch & dinner daily

16 H2

Despite its touristy address, The Old Bistro retains an authentic feel, including a dining room that looks as if it hasn't changed in decades, and a cache of regulars who never tire of dishes such as Lyonnais sausage with potatoes, *boeuf bourguignon* and *tarte tatin*. Portions are generous; the service likewise. **Moderate**

✓ *Good value*   >> www.realcity.dk.com

Mon Vieil Ami *modest inventiveness*   `17 A2`
69 rue St-Louis-en-l'Ile, 4ème • 01 40 46 01 35
Open lunch & dinner Wed–Sun

Distinguished French chef Antoine Westerman's take on Alsatian cuisine bears no hint of pedestrian pork and cabbage. Instead, it's all about innovative food combinations to match the unmistakably modern interior of his one Paris bistro. Westerman's culinary mastery lurks behind a demure, easily missed façade; in fact, compared to many eateries on the tiny Ile St-Louis, Mon Vieil Ami seems very low-key indeed. All the action is inside and on the plate: generous servings of chicken with caramelized *sauerkraut* and potato purée, and roast cod with carrots, raisins and dates. It's lighter and more varied than traditional Alsatian fare, but that's because a Michelin three-star chef devised the menu. Westerman might not be flinging the pans out back, but he's there in spirit, and that means that the bistro is fast becoming an old friend to many. **Moderate**

L'Osteria *risotto central*   `17 C1`
10 rue de Sévigné, 4ème • 01 42 71 37 08
Open lunch & dinner Tue–Fri, dinner only Mon

Toni Vianello is the risotto maestro; he's even written a cookbook on the subject, and his risottos are simply sensational – especially the one with pheasant and black truffles. This is some of the finest Italian food around and, as a result, tables are jam-packed, often with designers and political gurus. **Moderate**

Anahuacalli *a trip down Mexico way*   `16 H3`
30 rue des Bernardins, 5ème • 01 43 26 10 20
Open dinner daily & lunch Sun

Cooking from south of the border doesn't come much better than this; forget runny guacamole and dry taco shells, this is *mole poblano* (turkey cooked with chocolate) territory. It's serious regional Mexican food with very good margaritas served up by charming staff, albeit in a rather subdued atmosphere. **Moderate**

Restaurants

Fogon St-Julien *Spanish class* `16 H2`
10 rue St-Julien-le-Pauvre, 5ème • 01 43 54 31 33
Open lunch & dinner Sat & Sun, dinner only Tue–Fri

Owner-chef Alberto Herraiz dishes up some of the best Spanish food in Paris in this sunny dining room on one of the city's oldest streets. His quest for quality ingredients is evident in his elegant tapas and superb paella Valenciana: saffron-stained rice topped with plump chicken, rabbit, snails and vegetables. **Moderate**

Le Cosi *rugged cuisine* `16 G4`
9 rue Cujas, 5ème • 01 43 29 20 20
Open lunch & dinner Mon–Sat

Corsica has its own mountain cuisine featuring unusual cheeses, outstanding charcuterie and long-simmered stews, and the red walls of this bistro create a suitably warm setting for this hot-blooded food. Expect a sophisticated spin on rustic ingredients, with pulses, *brocciu* (a ricotta-like cheese) and *cabri* (kid) featuring large on the menu. If you've room for dessert, do try the delicious *fiadone* cheesecake. **Moderate**

Les Délices d'Aphrodite *Greek odyssey* `20 H1`
4 rue de Candolle, 5ème • 01 43 31 40 39
>> www.mavrommatis.fr Open lunch & dinner Mon–Sat

With a dining room done out in cool Mediterranean blue, a ceiling of trellised ivy, and good-quality Greek food, from *dolmades* to spit-roasted lamb, this is the perfect antidote to a grey day in Paris. The service is typically Greek too – it can be slow but it comes with a smile, so relax. **Moderate**

Le Reminet *sugar and spice* `16 H3`
3 rue des Grands-Degrés, 5ème • 01 44 07 04 24
Open lunch & dinner Thu–Mon ✓

This romantic little bistro just gets better and better, thanks to chef Hugues Gournay's passion for food. His interest in spices results in dishes such as lamb chops with a cumin-and-red-pepper crust. Desserts are outstanding and service couldn't be more helpful. A 13€ lunch menu is available (Mon, Thu and Fri). **Moderate**

36 ✓ *Good value* For the very latest on Paris go to >> **www.realcity.dk.com**

La Tour d'Argent   *fine food with a view*   `17 A3`
15–17 quai de la Tournelle, 5ème • 01 43 54 23 31
>> www.tourdargent.com   Closed Mon & Tue lunch

Views don't get much more Parisian than this, and
the cuisine doesn't get more ageless: the restaurant
has been serving the same pressed-duck recipe
since 1890. It's kid-glove treatment all the way, but
you don't have to blow the budget. The lunch menu
is great value and the view's the same. **Expensive**

Restaurant Marty   *Art Deco dining*   `21 A2`
20 avenue des Gobelins, 5ème • 01 43 31 39 51
>> www.marty-restaurant.com   Open lunch & dinner daily

The Marty stands out among Parisian brasseries on
two counts: it is independent, and chef Thierry Colas
has an *haute cuisine* pedigree. As a result, the food
goes beyond brasserie classics. Try salmon sautéed
with grapes and served with a celeriac purée, or veal
with herb butter and violet mustard. **Moderate**

Le Pré Verre   *a modern twist on the classic*   `16 G3`
8 rue Thénard, 5ème • 01 43 54 59 47
Open lunch & dinner Tue–Sat

The Delacourcelle brothers do French classics with a
nod to the modern. Chef Philippe is a fan of herbs
and spices, and it shows in his pairing of rabbit with
cumin, adding ginger to shallot sauce, showering
squid with sesame vinaigrette or popping parsley in
the strawberry dessert. The cuisine is slightly fusion,
but with an emphasis on good, sustaining food
(such as mashed potato with foie gras). Perched on
a corner in the scholarly Quartier Latin, this *bistrot à
vins* is very much a neighbourhood favourite,
attracting cooing couples, conversing academics,
serious suits and curious visitors. It's casual and
friendly, with a wooden floor and walls dotted with
vintage jazz LPs. *Très* cool – especially in summer,
when the doors are flung back and the tables spill
on to the street. The wine list is worthy, and the
lunch menu is a bargain. **Moderate**

Restaurants

Abazu *Japanese cool* `16 F2`
3 rue André-Mazet, 6ème • 01 46 33 72 05
Open lunch & dinner Tue–Sat, dinner only Sun

Teppanaki restaurants are rare in Paris, so it's surprising to find this Zen oasis in the heart of bustling St-Germain. On the main floor you can watch the sharp-knifed chefs at work, grilling fresh, raw ingredients before the customers' eyes, while the downstairs room feels calmer thanks to a small fountain. **Moderate**

Allard *old timer* `16 F2`
41 rue St-André-des-Arts, 6ème • 01 43 26 48 23
Open lunch & dinner Mon–Sat

Allard doesn't seem to have changed much since the 1940s, and that's just the way its regulars like it. Against a backdrop of weathered wallpaper, visitors mix with the neighbourhood's bourgeois, who flock here for hearty dishes such as Bresse chicken with mushrooms and the *canard aux olives*. **Moderate**

Le Comptoir du Relais St-Germain `16 F2`
9 carrefour de l'Odéon, 6ème • 01 43 29 12 05
Open lunch & dinner daily

Chef Yves Camdeborde made his gastronomic name at the ground-breaking Régalade. He now runs this highly popular, tiny restaurant in a boutique hotel. A relaxed lunchtime brasserie menu makes way for a formal dinner menu, where the chef displays his talent with just six carefully chosen dishes. **Expensive**

L'Epi Dupin *creative cooking* `15 C3`
11 rue Dupin, 6ème • 01 42 22 64 56
Open lunch & dinner Tue–Fri, dinner only Mon

Chef François Pasteau's bistro is full day and night thanks to a mix of imaginative cooking (mackerel in a hazelnut-and-fennel crust and pigeon with braised onions), fast, friendly service and a cosy old dining room. Blackboard specials reflect the best produce the seasons have to offer. **Moderate**

Yen *a slice of Tokyo* `16 E2`
22 rue St-Benoît, 6ème • 01 45 44 11 18
Open lunch & dinner Mon–Sat

If you have a yen for noodles, this is the place to satisfy your craving. The neighbourhood couldn't be more Parisian, but once in the wood dining room you could easily be in Tokyo. At lunchtime, try a bento box; at dinner, the speciality is *soba* – buckwheat noodles served with a delicious dipping sauce. **Moderate**

Le Timbre *a modern touch*   `15 D5`
3 rue Ste-Beuve, 6ème • 01 45 49 10 40
Open lunch & dinner Tue–Sat, dinner only Mon

Garret-like Le Timbre serves refined French food (roast pigeon with mango and ginger chutney, Jerusalem artichoke purée with truffle oil) with a dash of the British, thanks to its Mancunian owner. Cleverly arranged around the long counter, the dining room encourages conviviality. **Moderate**

La Ferrandaise *classic helpings*   `16 F3`
8 rue de Vaugirard, 6ème • 01 43 26 36 36
Open lunch & dinner Tue–Fri, dinner only Sat

La Ferrandaise is named after a race of mountain cattle and chef Nicolas Duquenoy's cooking features enlightened classic dishes with predictably fine meat. Try cream of Jerusalem artichokes with foie gras, suckling lamb in a herb crust and tempting *crêpes au chocolat* to finish. **Moderate**

Le Salon d'Hélène *southwest-side story*   `15 D3`
4 rue d'Assas, 6ème • 01 42 22 00 11
Open lunch & dinner Tue–Sat

French chefs in general don't tend to stray too far from formality – but there are exceptions, and Hélène Darroze is one of them. In an effort to make her south-western cooking more accessible, she opened Le Salon d'Hélène, a more reasonably priced, more casual eatery on the floor below her Michelin two-star restaurant. Rather than a three-course-plus-cheese meal, Darroze took to tapas – she hails from France's Basque country, and the Spanish influence is evident in her cooking. Graze on a range of beautifully presented small dishes (oyster with foie gras "ice cream", langoustine tempura, duck liver with dried fruit) from the comfort of a plush pink sofa, bar-style high chairs with raised tables or a banquette loaded with cushions. Darroze comes from a family of chefs and also spent time in Alain Ducasse's restaurant in Monte Carlo, so diners are in capable, and creative, hands. **Expensive**

Restaurants

L'Ami Jean *Basque is best* 8 G5
27 rue Malar, 7ème • 01 47 05 86 89
Open lunch & dinner Tue–Sat

Some of the best bistro chefs in Paris come from the French Basque region, and Stéphane Jégo, who owns this tavern-like bistro, is one of them. Jégo cooks up specialities such as *axoa* (veal stew) alongside more modern inventions like marinated scallops with shaved ewe's-milk cheese. **Moderate**

Bellota-Bellota *simple Spanish pleasures* 8 G5
18 rue Jean-Nicot, 7ème • 01 53 59 96 96
Open lunch & dinner Mon–Sat

This breezy, tiled bar-cum-grocery is devoted to Spain's finest ham: ruby-red meat from black-footed Iberian pigs that graze on acorns *(bellotas)*. And it's the acorns that give the ham its wonderful flavour. Excellent manchego cheese, anchovies, olives and tuna are also on offer. Perfect for lunch or a late supper. **Moderate**

L'Arpège *art appreciation* 15 A1
84 rue de Varenne, 7ème • 01 45 51 47 33
Open lunch & dinner Mon–Fri

Chef Alain Passard caters for the serious food connoisseur. His food is close to art, which seems appropriate given that the Musée Rodin *(see p107)* is just opposite. The wine list is almost as long as *War and Peace*, the decor is discreetly modern and the prices are rather steep. In recent times, Passard has shunned red meat, preferring instead to serve fish, shellfish, poultry and – his overriding passion of late – vegetables. In L'Arpège's kitchen at least, *légumes* have finally been granted their rightful place alongside fish and meat as diet staples. Passard prides himself on retaining the unique colours and flavours of his ingredients; consequently, his food looks as if it has escaped the pages of a glossy art mag. Tender lobster braised in Jura wine and his signature dessert, a candied 12-flavour tomato filled with dried and fresh fruit, nuts and spices, are beautiful to look at and even better to eat. **Expensive**

L'Atelier de Joël Robuchon *hot spot* `15 D1`
5 rue de Montalembert, 7ème • 01 42 22 56 56
➤➤ www.robuchon.com Open lunch & dinner daily

He might not be a household name outside France, but in Paris Joël Robuchon stands for French cuisine at its most refined. Gastronomes were devastated when he announced his retirement from the restaurant world at the age of 51, and his comeback was the subject of rumours for years. Now in his early 60s, Robuchon has not only opened what is probably the most modern restaurant in Paris, but also runs a sister restaurant, La Table de Joël Robuchon, in the 16th as well as a twin establishment in Tokyo. What is all the fuss about? Well, his potato purée for one, made from the flavourful *ratte* variety and with nearly as much butter as potato. At L'Atelier, diners sit around two bars in the compact, red-and-black lacquered dining room (there are no individual chairs and tables), while cooks toil in the open kitchen, slightly removed from the communal counters. You can order a little – from a selection of about 20 small plates inspired by Asia, Spain and offerings from the best Parisian chefs – or a lot, as it is also possible to have a blow-out three-course meal of full-sized offerings without feeling rushed. Some of the most outstanding dishes are *spaghetti à notre façon* (an Alsatian take on carbonara), turbot with the famous potato purée and, among the smaller plates, clams stuffed with garlic and a crisp mackerel tart with Parmesan cheese. Desserts, such as the chartreuse soufflé, are served in small portions to allow for grazing. Telephone reservations are possible only for 11:30am and 6:30pm; otherwise, be prepared to queue alongside Left Bank lawyers and publishers who are willing to swallow their pride for extraordinarily good food. **Expensive**

➤➤ *In France, bread is broken at the table, and can just be put on the tablecloth if there's no side plate*

Restaurants

Au Bon Accueil *a success story*
`8 F5`
14 rue de Monttessuy, 7ème • 01 47 05 46 11
Open lunch & dinner Mon–Fri

Lying in the shadow of the Eiffel Tower, this bistro is teeming most days and nights (often with out-of-towners in the tourist season). Owner Jacques Lacipière has refurbished it to give it a trendier edge and better lighting, but the seasonal menu remains good quality and the service is always agreeable. **Moderate**

Gaya Rive Gauche *stellar seafood*
`15 C1`
44 rue du Bac, 7ème • 01 45 44 73 73
Open lunch & dinner Mon–Fri, dinner only Sat

With celebrity three-Michelin-star chef Pierre Gagnaire at the helm, this fish restaurant attracts smart Left-Bank intellectuals. The young team under his management produce sophisticated seafood dishes such as the signature starter of pressed crab with cauliflower and wilted sorrel. **Expensive**

Café Constant *simply delicious*
`8 F5`
139 rue St-Dominique, 7ème • 01 47 53 73 34
Open lunch & dinner Tue–Sat

As head chef at the luxury hotel Le Crillon *(see p183)*, Christian Constant trained many of the best bistro chefs in Paris today, including Christian Etchebest of Le Troquet *(see p59)*. Constant is gradually colonizing the rue St-Dominique with this eponymous café; his classic restaurant, Le Violon d'Ingres; and most recently, La Table de la Fontaine, an affordable fish house. But Café Constant is the locals' favourite, and it's here that the chef can express his casual side (he is often seen having lunch here, which shows how comfortable he is with this simpler style of cooking). The menu is something of a nostalgia trip –*oeufs mimosa*, pumpkin soup with Gruyère, veal Cordon Bleu, profiteroles and *île flottante*, all prepared just as they should be. Like the food, the setting doesn't put on airs – white walls, old tile floors and red banquettes – and the staff are exceptionally friendly. **Moderate**

Best Places to Buy Food to Go
Long limited to a sandwich or a quiche, takeaway food in Paris is growing more varied. For salads, hot dishes and perhaps a slice of pâté, stop by any neighbourhood *charcutier/traiteur*, where you will be charged according to the weight of your order. The gourmet counters at Le Bon Marché's **Grande Epicerie** offer more exotic options, as do those at **Galeries Lafayette**. British-style sandwiches are sold at **Cojean**, while top chef Alain Ducasse and baker Eric Kayser provide high-class sandwiches at **Be**. Perhaps the best meal to go, though, is the falafel sandwich at **L'As du Fallafel** *(see p33)*, the pick of Lenny Kravitz and other discriminating chickpea fans. For 5€, it's heaven on a plate. For other contact details, *see p225.*

Flora *provincial elegance* `8 F2`
36 avenue George V, 8ème • 01 40 70 10 49
Open lunch & dinner Mon–Sat

This stylish restaurant's menu is influenced by southern France (chef Flora Mikula was born in Provence), but also dips into even sunnier lands, such as Turkey, Morocco and India. Mikula has a sure touch with produce and lots of finesse, as dishes such as lobster with wild mushrooms in coral vinaigrette attest. **Moderate**

Le Bistrot Napolitain *perfect pizza* `8 H1`
18 avenue Franklin D Roosevelt, 8ème • 01 45 62 08 37
Open lunch & dinner Mon–Fri

Down-to-earth bistros are thin on the ground in these parts, which explains the popularity of this Italian *trattoria*. It's hard to resist the crisp-crusted classic pizzas, such as Margherita, but the *carpaccio*, fish and pasta are equally tempting. Perfect for a quick bite after the cinema, but book ahead. **Moderate**

Garnier *a fishy business* `3 C5`
111 rue St-Lazare, 8ème • 01 43 87 50 40
Open lunch & dinner daily

Sup on freshly shucked oysters at the bijou oyster bar just inside the door, or take an impeccably laid table near the window and watch the commuters from nearby Gare St-Lazare grind by. The setting is elegant, waiters are considerate and the seafood is a cut well above that of most Paris brasseries. **Expensive**

L'Angle du Faubourg *cornering success* `2 G5`
195 rue du Faubourg St-Honoré, 8ème • 01 40 74 20 20
» www.taillevent.com Open lunch & dinner Mon–Fri

Boosted by the success of his Michelin three-star restaurant, Taillevent, owner Jean-Claude Vrinat opened this more cost-conscious bistro. Contemporary in look, it combines both the classical and the modern in the kitchen, serving attractive dishes such as braised veal cheeks to an upmarket clientele. **Moderate**

Restaurants

Maison Blanche · *a drop of the Med* · 8 G3

15 avenue Montaigne, 8ème • 01 47 23 55 99
›› www.maison-blanche.fr
Open lunch & dinner Mon–Fri, dinner only Sat & Sun

The Pourcel twins just love the Mediterranean and it shows in their inventive menu. A plate of roast pigeon fillets with pan-fried peaches and *cacao* accompanied by a penthouse view of Paris might not come cheap, but extravagance has its rewards. **Expensive**

Market · *exemplary innovations* · 9 A2

15 avenue Matignon, 8ème • 01 56 43 40 90
›› www.jean-georges.com   Open breakfast, lunch & dinner daily

Jean-Georges Vongerichten, the whizz kid behind New York's Mercer Kitchen and Vong, has returned to his French roots with this fashionable spot. Celebrities and local suits can't get enough of his clever food, such as raw-tuna spring roll or "burnt" foie gras with a dried fruit compote. **Expensive**

Le Cristal Room · *glass act* · 8 E2

La Maison Baccarat, 11 place des Etats-Unis, 16ème
01 40 22 11 10 Open breakfast, lunch & dinner Mon–Sat

A giant chandelier immersed in an aquarium gives a clue as to who was in charge of decorating the new Baccarat museum and boutique: the daring and witty Philippe Starck. Formerly a private residence, this mansion is now, literally, a crystal palace, with glass and mirrors creating dizzying optical effects. The in-store restaurant, a showcase for Baccarat's crystal and porcelain, has become a huge hit thanks to its ironic-but-chic decor and simple, yet deliciously prepared, food. What can you expect to eat? Most of the modish folk who come here probably don't care all that much, but dishes such as a frothy soup of *potimarron* (a type of pumpkin that tastes like chestnut) and the very good club sandwich show that the kitchen is far from careless. If you have any money left over, you can pick up a jewel or accessory as a souvenir. Be sure to book ahead. **Expensive**

Senderens *less haute cuisine* `9 C2`

9 place de la Madeleine, 8ème • 01 42 65 22 90
>> www.lucascarton.com
Open lunch & dinner Tue–Fri; dinner only Sat & Mon

At the age of 65, iconic French chef Alain Senderens decided he no longer wanted to be part of the Michelin star system and so "gave back" his three stars and changed the concept of his original restaurant, Lucas Carton. It is now far less formal and stuffy. Meals are roughly two-thirds cheaper, too. Dishes still bear his cerebral approach to cuisine how-ever, with creative fusions combining pigeon, crab meat and tea or roasted cod with chorizo cream sauce. And each dish is still accompanied by a (now-optional) wine that harmonizes perfectly with it. Senderens bought this spot in 1985, perhaps because he worked here as a young *saucier* for the renowned chef Soustelle. Today, the apprentice is very much the acclaimed master, even if in Michelin's eyes his restaurant is now only worth two stars. **Expensive**

Savy *regional traditions* `8 G3`

23 rue Bayard, 8ème • 01 47 23 46 98
Open lunch & dinner Mon–Fri

An old-fashioned bistro, both in decor and disposition, that provides welcome relief from the 24-carat designer shops and salons of nearby avenue Montaigne. Comfort food, from coddled eggs to rib steak with bone marrow and matchstick potatoes, is served up in comfortable surroundings. **Moderate**

A Toutes Vapeurs *all steamed up* `3 C5`

7 rue de l'Isly, 8ème • 01 44 90 95 75
Open until 11pm Mon–Sat

Waistline-watchers and the health conscious love the little *paniers* (baskets) of vegetable, fish and meat combinations at this self-service eating house – all cooked while you wait. Choose a pre-prepared basket, a flavoured oil and, presto, it's in and out of the chrome "dry" steamer in minutes. **Cheap**

>> *A three-course* prix-fixe *menu, though often limited in choice, is much cheaper than eating à la carte*

L'Astrance *top tables*

7 C5

4 rue Beethoven, 16ème • 01 40 50 84 40
Open lunch & dinner Mon–Fri

This six-year-old, 25-seat dining room near Trocadéro is arguably the most exciting restaurant to have opened in Paris this century (though Joël Robuchon's Atelier *(see p41)* is a close rival). Pascal Barbot and Christophe Rohat (who runs the dining room) worked with Alain Passard at L'Arpège *(see p40)* before branching out on their own with a style that reflects Barbot's time as a chef in Sydney. Asian spices turn up in all sorts of unexpected places, but never shock the palate. Minimalist names on the menu create an element of suspense, but first come surprise nibbles: soup made with nearly burnt bread (much more intriguing than it sounds) or an avocado and crab *millefeuille* flavoured with almond oil and a tiny Granny Smith julienne. Then comes "The Pea", a frothy green cream topped with crisp, golden-brown shavings of baked Tomme d'Auvergne cheese and a fresh pea pod lined with plump, tender peas. "The Mackerel" shows what Barbot can do with a humble fish: boneless fillets come coated in spiced crumbs, on a bed of Asian-style spinach with sesame. More *amuse-gueules*, such as herb-infused sorbets and an eggshell filled with eggy cream, pave the way for inventive desserts combining fruits and spices. The sober – but not off-puttingly so – grey dining room, its walls decorated with gilt-framed mirrors, puts the spotlight on the food. So cherished are reservations here (you must book exactly one month ahead) that foodies congratulate each other on their success in securing a table. **Expensive**

La Grande Armée *modern classic* `7 E1`
3 avenue de la Grande Armée, 16ème • 01 45 00 24 77
Open breakfast, lunch & dinner daily

Jointly owned by the Costes brothers and designer Jacques Garcia, this contemporary take on the classic brasserie is more bordello red and leopard skin than beer and brass. Count on dependable food (duck shepherd's pie), a stylish crowd and a surprisingly cosy atmosphere. Great for breakfast, too. **Moderate**

La Butte Chaillot *contemporary cuisine* `7 D3`
110bis avenue Kléber, 16ème • 01 47 27 88 88
>> www.buttechaillot.com
Open lunch & dinner Sun–Fri, dinner only Sat

Part of chef Guy Savoy's restaurant empire, La Butte Chaillot is sleek and modern – even if its decor is a little too brown for some tastes. However, the modern cuisine is spot on, particularly the sea bass with crisp vegetables and an orange reduction. **Moderate**

Le Petit Rétro *trad French* `7 C2`
5 rue Mesnil, 16ème • 01 44 05 06 05
>> www.petitretro.fr
Open lunch & dinner Mon–Fri, dinner only Sat

In keeping with its authentic Belle Epoque decor, Le Petit Rétro is a bastion of traditional French cooking. Melt-in-your mouth duck liver pâté and creamy veal stew never go out of fashion, which is precisely why this not-so-little bistro is always brimful. **Moderate**

L'Entrédejeu *packed-out bistro* `1 D2`
83 rue Laugier, 17ème • 01 40 54 97 24
Open lunch & dinner Tue–Sat

Does Paris need another bistro? Of course it does, when it's as good as this one. The space is cramped and smoky, but locals crowd in nonetheless for the daily-changing menu, which might include spot-on dishes such as veal *en cocotte* with new potatoes or rack of lamb with a salsify *jus*. **Moderate**

>> *A pichet (carafe) of house wine is usually good value and very drinkable*

Restaurants

La Braisière `2 H2`
54 rue Cardinet, 17ème • 01 47 63 40 37
Open lunch & dinner Mon–Fri, dinner only Sat

Newly promoted to Michelin-star status, chef Jacques Faussat is proud of his Southwest origins and some of his dishes are inspired by the cooking of the Gers. Others – like the signature starter of blue lobster with mangos – are rather more exotic. Popular with well-heeled local residents. **Expensive**

Le Bistrot d'à Côte Flaubert *a treat* `2 F3`
10 rue Gustave Flaubert, 17ème • 01 42 67 05 81
» www.michelrostang.fr Open lunch & dinner daily

It's no surprise that *haute cuisine* chef Michel Rostang's first bistro turned out to be more sophisticated than many of its genre. The period interior, and walls of kaleidoscopic majolica ceramics and old Michelin guides, provide a convivial setting in which to sample consistently good bistro cooking. **Moderate**

Casa Olympe *fixed-menu finesse* `4 F5`
48 rue St-Georges, 9ème • 01 42 85 26 01
Open lunch & dinner Mon–Fri

Dominique Versini, aka Olympe, is a diva of the Paris restaurant scene. The compact, ochre-painted dining room showcases her fine cooking, which draws on her Corsican roots. The three-course, 38€ menu offers simple dishes, like potato salad with truffle shavings, that highlight the quality of the ingredients. **Moderate**

Kastoori *Indian idyll* `4 F4`
4 place Gustave Toudouze, 9ème • 01 44 53 06 10
Open lunch & dinner daily

There aren't many Indian restaurants in Paris where you can enjoy a fairly authentic meal in warm, tasteful surroundings, or on a quiet pavement terrace. Hence the popularity of Kastoori, with its carefully spiced – if not chilli-potent – food. The 8€ lunch menu is one of the city's best bargains. **Cheap**

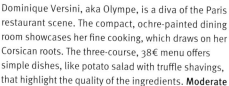

48   ✓ *Good value*

For the very latest on Paris go to » www.realcity.dk.com

Rose Bakery *daytime distraction*
46 rue des Martyrs, 9ème • 01 42 82 12 80
Open during the day Tue–Sun

This café is dedicated to typically British products (from baked beans to sausages), many of them organic. Quiches, soups and snack-sized pizzas satisfy the lunch crowd, but the big draw is the childhood-fantasy cakes, from tangy lemon tarts to sticky toffee pudding. The decor is as simple as the food. **Cheap**

Velly *down-to-earth bistro*
52 rue Lamartine, 9ème • 01 48 78 60 05
Open lunch & dinner Mon–Fri

Just off the old-fashioned rue des Martyrs, Velly is the kind of bistro everyone hopes to find in Paris. In a no-frills setting, the real star is the food, prepared with seasonal ingredients and attention to presentation. Regulars love the *oeuf cocotte* with foie gras, and meaty mains like *onglet de veau* with salsify fritters. **Moderate**

Chez Dom *funky West African*
34 rue Sambre et Meuse, 10ème • 01 42 01 59 80
Open dinner only Mon–Sat

Typical of the *quartier*, Chez Dom serves authentic Senegalese food. Flower-printed tablecloths set the cheerful tone, and a glass of potent *ti ponch* arrives even before you've asked for it. Boldly spiced meat and fish stews will have you licking the plate, but try to save room for the "sexy chocolate" dessert. **Moderate**

Martel *trendy French-Algerian*
3 rue Martel, 10ème • 01 47 70 67 56
Open lunch & dinner Mon–Fri, dinner only Sat

The latest haunt of couscous-loving fashionistas is this bistro in the interesting and up-and-coming 10th. Among the most popular dishes are the "lovers' arti-choke" a spiky treat to be shared, and lamb tagine with almonds, prunes and apricots, but it's hard for the food to compete with the glamorous crowd. **Moderate**

Restaurants

Café Burq *fashionable French* `4 E2`

6 rue Burq, 18ème • 01 42 52 81 27
Open dinner only Tue–Sat

Formerly a sepia-toned wine bar, the Moulin à Vins, this bistro has been reborn as a slick hang-out for Montmartre's young artists, film-makers and media folk. The mostly classic French food is decent enough, but what people really come for is the joyous, if smoky, atmosphere. **Moderate**

Terminus Nord *classy destination* `5 A4`

23 rue de Dunkerque, 10ème • 01 42 85 05 15
>> www.terminusnord.com Open lunch & dinner daily

Despite its position opposite the busy northern railway station, the august Terminus Nord is no tourist trap, just one of the city's most handsome brasseries. Refuel post-journey on onion soup and fresh seafood served by white-suited waiters under the gaze of huge frescoes and turn-of-the-20th-century posters. **Moderate**

Chez Michel *from Brittany with love* `5 A4`

10 rue de Belzunce, 10ème • 01 44 53 06 20
Open lunch & dinner Tue–Fri, dinner only Mon

There's no mistaking Thierry Breton's roots: the menu is piled high with hearty seasonal offerings from his native Brittany. And to quash any doubt, he also sports the Breton flag on his chef's whites. While the area isn't very chic, the restaurant, with its red velvet banquettes and farmhouse-style seating in the basement, is nicely perched behind the imposing St-Vincent-de-Paul church, and the food is very smart indeed. The blackboard specials echo the seasons and carry an additional cost but they're worth it – game-lovers are well catered for in the cooler months with pigeon, wild boar and venison. At other times, try plump, fresh scallops with velvety celeriac purée. Breton's Paris-Brest, choux pastry filled with hazelnut butter cream, is pure dessert happiness. The service can be excruciatingly slow, but the staff are affable, and if there's any tension it melts when the food appears. **Moderate**

✓ *Good value*   >> www.realcity.dk.com

Chez Toinette *neighbourhood bistro* `4 E2`
20 rue Germain-Pilon, 18ème • 01 42 54 44 36
Open lunch & dinner Tue–Sat, dinner only Mon

You don't expect to find a discreet, candle-lit jewel like this one around the corner from bawdy Pigalle, so it's all the more surprising to discover that Chez Toinette also has seriously good food. You'll often find Provençal dishes on the menu, such as *daube de boeuf*; game is a speciality in winter. **Moderate**

Le Poulbot Gourmet *trad French food* `4 F1`
39 rue Lamarck, 18ème • 01 46 06 86 00
Open lunch & dinner Mon–Sat

It's a little out of the way, but this Montmartre restaurant has a loyal following thanks to the sincerity of its owner and of its cooking. The small dining room is the perfect place to savour dishes such as pastry-enveloped poached egg and veal kidney with morel mushrooms. **Moderate**

Lao Siam *Southeast Asian offerings* `12 G1`
49 rue de Belleville, 19ème • 01 40 40 09 68
Open lunch & dinner daily

Neither service nor decor are particularly charming, but Lao Siam is almost always packed thanks to the lip-smacking flavours of its Thai and Laotian dishes. Squid salad is a good bet to start, followed by coconut-milk curry and a giant, juicy mango. The separate non-smoking dining room is less busy. **Cheap**

La Cave Gourmande *hidden talent*
10 rue du Général-Brunet, 19ème • 01 40 40 03 30 • Ⓜ Botzaris
Open lunch & dinner Mon–Fri

This sedate neighbourhood near the Butte Chaumont park is not where you'd expect to find an up-and-coming US chef, but Paris has a few such secret eating destinations. Mark Singer puts a modern spin on traditional French dishes, so you might find escargots, but not bathed in the usual garlic butter. **Moderate**

Restaurants

La Famille *globe-trotting hit* 4 F2

41 rue des Trois-Frères, 18ème • 01 42 52 11 12
Open dinner only Tue–Sat, dinner 1st Sun of each month,
brunch 2nd–4th Sun of each month

Few Paris chefs have come to grips with fusion food, which is why La Famille, in newly fashionable Montmartre, has become such a hit. Young Basque chef Inaki Aizpitarte has had his passport stamped around the world, particularly in Latin America and Morocco, and also worked with the inventive Gilles Choukroun at Le Café des Délices before opening this restaurant with his cousin (he's the one in charge of the bar and the hip music). The short, constantly changing menu combines French (and especially Basque) ingredients with more tropical flavours,

resulting in dishes such as pan-fried foie gras with miso sauce, gambas pan-fried with passion fruit, and chocolate custard with Espelette chilli pepper. Not everything works all the time but any culinary near-misses are easily compensated for by the fact that dinner here is guaranteed fun. This is especially true of the first Sunday of each month, when the entire menu is served in tapas-like portions so that you can really do Aizpitarte's creative endeavours justice and graze your way through every dish. A help-yourself all-day brunch of French pastries and egg dishes is served on the other Sundays, making customers feel that they are really part of the family. Since the spare space is rather limited and word has already been out for a while, it's essential to book. **Moderate**

La Mascotte *old Montmartre* `4 E2`
52 rue des Abbesses, 18ème • 01 46 06 28 15
» www.la-mascotte-montmartre.com Open lunch & dinner daily

This is a neighbourhood institution, the last original *bistrot* on the rue des Abbesses, where the ambiance is the major draw. Stick to the simpler à la carte dishes or plump for the good-value 29€ menu, which might include chicken with potato purée and an almond cake with Berthillon ice cream. **Moderate**

Café Noir *eccentric surprise*
15 rue St-Blaise, 20ème • 01 40 09 75 80 • Ⓜ Porte de Bagnolet
Open lunch & dinner Mon–Fri, dinner only Sat & Sun

A thriving bar scene has put this *quartier* on the map, but if it's a good meal you're seeking here, this quirky bistro is the place to go. Located on a pedestrianized street, the restaurant's terrace tables are irresistible in summer; inside you can admire the coffee pot and hat collections while tucking into unusual dishes such as tandoori prawns with chicken livers. **Moderate**

Benisti *North African pit-stop* `12 F1`
108 boulevard de Belleville, 20ème • no phone
Open lunch & dinner Tue–Sun

Jewish, Arab and Chinese communities comfortably co-exist in Belleville, as a walk down the main boulevard will testify. One of the most popular places to stop and refuel is this Tunisian snack and pastry shop, where you can order a gargantuan grilled-meat sandwich or sip mint tea with a plate of sticky pastries. **Cheap**

Astier *fashionably shabby chic* `12 E3`
44 rue Jean-Pierre Timbaud, 11ème • 01 43 57 16 35
Open lunch & dinner Mon–Fri

Resolutely old-fashioned, Astier is as much loved for its worn decor and overrun tables as for its great-value four-course menu. That doesn't imply second-rate food: the cooking is classy and finely balanced between traditional dishes and seasonal specials. The wine list is long and worthy. **Moderate**

Restaurants

Dong Huong *Vietnamese canteen* `12 F1`
14 rue Louis-Bonnet, 11ème • 01 43 57 18 88
Open lunch & dinner Wed–Mon

When you can't face another multi-course meal, a bowl of Vietnamese noodles can be just the thing to revive your appetite. Dong Huong stands out for the quality of its *pho* (noodle soups) and grilled meats and for its large non-smoking room – a rarity in Paris. The crunchy imperial rolls are also exceptionally good. **Cheap**

L'Homme Bleu *North African local* `12 E3`
55bis rue Jean-Pierre Timbaud, 11ème • 01 48 07 05 63
Open dinner only Mon–Sat

The queue out the door attests to L'Homme Bleu's popularity (they don't take reservations, so show up early). The main floor is more atmospheric thanks to its open kitchen, but those lucky enough to get a table anywhere won't complain. Delicious couscous and fragrant tagines are the stars. **Moderate**

Crêperie Bretonne Fleurie *pancakes* `18 F2`
67 rue de Charonne, 11ème • 01 43 55 62 29
Open lunch & dinner daily

Two steps from the booming Bastille bar scene, this crêperie shows the *quartier*'s flip-side, with real Breton specialities. Proof of its authenticity is the crêpe filled with *andouille* (tripe sausage), but you can also stick to the more conventional ham, cheese and egg variations, washed down with cider. **Cheap**

Jacques Mélac *no-frills wine bar*
42 rue Léon-Frot, 11ème • 01 43 70 59 27 • Ⓜ Charonne
Open lunch & dinner Tue–Sat

There's nothing complicated about moustachioed Jacques' wine bar: cheese is hacked off a giant hunk, charcuterie is sliced before your eyes and the non-smoking room is reached through the tiny kitchen, where the day's specials such as *porc aligot* (sausage and cheesy potato mash) are prepared. **Moderate**

Le Petit Keller *retro home cooking*   `18 F1`
13bis rue Keller, 11ème • 01 47 00 12 97
Open lunch & dinner Tue–Sat

This little 1950s-vintage restaurant is popular for its great-value set menu – 11€ at lunch and 16€ in the evening. The food is more like decent home cooking than ambitious restaurant fare, which is fine with the locals who can't be bothered to whip up salmon with sorrel sauce, duck *magret* or apple crumble. **Moderate**

Le Souk *spice-scented haven*   `18 F2`
1 rue Keller, 11ème • 01 49 29 05 08
Open lunch & dinner Sat & Sun, dinner only Tue–Fri

Though it's run by chatty Algerians, Le Souk's food is totally Moroccan, with sweet and fragrant tagines and *pastillas* (poultry wrapped in crisp pastry, sprinkled with sugar) featuring alongside couscous. Tables are so sought after that there are two fixed dinner sittings, for which bookings are essential. **Moderate**

Le Bistrot Paul Bert *seasonal food*
18 rue Paul-Bert, 11ème • 01 43 72 24 01 • Ⓜ Faidherbe-Chaligny
Open lunch & dinner Mon–Sat

This place seems to have it all: an atmospheric setting, genuinely friendly service, a hip, festive crowd, intriguing (organic) wines and, best of all, great food that follows the seasons to the extent that the black-board menu changes every day. It's a little out of the way, but you're unlikely to regret the effort. **Moderate**

Le Train Bleu *vintage dining*   `18 E5`
Gare de Lyon place Louis-Armand, 12ème • 01 43 43 09 06
≫ www.le-train-bleu.com Open breakfast, lunch & dinner daily

With its stockpile of cherubs, gilt and big oak benches, Le Train Bleu is a glamorously vintage experience amid the hubbub of the Gare de Lyon train station. As you'd expect from a Belle Epoque dame, the food is a lofty take on French classics (lobster salad, veal chops) and there's a bar, too, for a quiet drink. **Moderate**

Restaurants

Le Trou Gascon *regional refinement*
40 rue Taine, 12ème • 01 43 44 34 26 • Ⓜ Daumesnil
Open lunch & dinner Mon–Fri

Devotees of serious, French southwestern cooking
hunt out this contemporary restaurant overseen by
Michelin two-star chef Alain Dutournier. Dishes such
as the surprisingly light *cassoulet* and the gutsy
regional Madiran wine make the trek to this outpost
more than worthwhile. **Expensive**

Le Square Trousseau *outstanding bistro* `18 F3`
1 rue Antoine-Vollon, 12ème • 01 43 43 06 00
Open lunch & dinner Tue–Sat

Thanks to its setting next to a leafy square, its beautifully weathered 1900s interior and the charismatic
and friendly staff, Le Square Trousseau oozes charm.
Wines from small producers complement modern
bistro fare, such as green asparagus with melon and
lamb shank in a syrupy sauce. **Moderate**

Sardegna a Tavola *authentic Italian* `18 F3`
1 rue de Cotte, 12ème • 01 44 75 03 28
Open lunch & dinner Tue–Sat, dinner only Mon

It's rare to find an authentic Italian restaurant in Paris,
let alone a Sardinian one that gives you a flavour of
this rocky, sun-baked isle. No compromises here:
both ingredients and dishes are genuine, from the
robust Sardinian wines to the pasta dishes, often
flavoured with almonds, mint or orange. **Moderate**

L'Avant Goût *top-quality bistro fare* `21 A4`
26 rue Bobillot, 13ème • 01 53 80 24 00
Open lunch & dinner Tue–Fri

Just a taste of Christophe Beaufront's creative fare and
it becomes patently clear why landing a table in here
without a reservation is impossible. The *pot-au-feu de
cochon* (pork simmered with fennel, carrot and spices),
accompanied by ginger chips, onion in cider, gherkins
and horseradish purée, is exceptional. **Moderate**

Les Cailloux *casual yet classy*

`20 H5`

58 rue des Cinq-Diamants, 13ème • 01 45 80 15 08
Open lunch & dinner Tue–Sat

The owners of Les Cailloux are on to a winning formula with this Italian wine bar-restaurant located in the villagey Butte-aux-Cailles *(see p165)*. Some 40 wines are available, half of them Italian and a few by the glass, and the food (linguine with crab, roasted pepper with mozzarella) is simple but satisfying. **Moderate**

Tricotin *Oriental roundup*

15 ave de Choisy, 13ème • 01 45 84 74 44
Ⓜ Porte de Choisy Open lunch & dinner daily

It won't win any prizes for decor or location, but Tricotin wins out with its steaming display of Chinese, Cambodian, Thai and Vietnamese dishes. It's frantic, canteen-style eating, but the food is fresh and very affordable: *pho*, the Vietnamese meal-in-a-bowl soup, is the bargain deal. **Cheap**

Natacha *family values*

`19 E1`

17bis rue Campagne-Première, 14ème • 01 43 20 79 27
Open lunch & dinner Tue–Fri, lunch only Sat

Long a fashion haunt, Natacha is a family affair, with young chef Alain Cirelli running the kitchen while his mother is front of house. And following a home-cooking tradition, many dishes are served in their casseroles: a roasted pheasant nestles in a copper pot and *hachis parmentier* (shepherd's pie) comes in a cast-iron dish. Desserts are similarly comforting. **Moderate**

Au Petit Marguery *timeless bistro*

`20 H2`

9 boulevard de Port-Royal, 13ème • 01 43 31 58 59
Open lunch & dinner Tue–Sat

This bistro is famous for its game, and in winter it serves up the classic dish *lièvre à la royale*, a complex creation involving hare, foie gras, wine and blood. Service can be grumpy, but the clientele of local gourmands tucking into pâtés and partridge creates an atmosphere of pure enjoyment nonetheless. **Moderate**

Restaurants

L'Assiette *market leader*
19 C3

181 rue du Château, 14ème • 01 43 22 64 86
Open lunch & dinner Wed–Sun, dinner only Tue

Unquestionably elitist, L'Assiette attracts bourgeois diners who find it amusing to pay through the nose for bistro cooking in a bare-wood setting. The fact remains, however, that chef Lulu draws on the finest ingredients and her food is delicious. The puddings are the kind *maman* might make. **Expensive**

Le Père Claude *excellent grill*

14 F3

51 avenue de la Motte-Piquet, 15ème • 01 47 34 03 05
Open lunch & dinner daily

Meat-lovers are well catered for in Paris but nowhere more so than at this caramel-coloured local with its glassed-in grill bar. The protein-strong mixed grill comes with steak, black pudding, lamb and chicken, and golden gratinéed potatoes. A perennial favourite with omnivorous French politicians. **Moderate**

L'Os à Moëlle & La Cave de l'Os à Moëlle *local heroes*

3 rue Vasco de Gama, 15ème • 01 45 57 27 27;
181 rue Lourmel, 15ème • 01 45 57 28 28 • Ⓜ Lourmel
Open lunch & dinner Tue–Sat

Chef Thierry Faucher produces food that is consistently satisfying and reasonably priced. Lunch (32€) and dinner (38€) are a fixed blackboard affair, and might include velvety cauliflower soup ladled over roasted thyme and crispy croutons, foie gras coated in gingerbread crumbs, or roast pigeon with chestnuts. The four-course lunch menu offers several choices, while the indulgent six-course dinner menu is set.

In contrast, the casual and cheaper La Cave de l'Os à Moëlle, opposite, features three communal tables and a 20€-buffet (you can have seconds and thirds) of robust fare. Terrines, bowls of olives and sea snails, a tureen of steaming soup and one main-course choice, such as pheasant with lentils, plus cheese, desserts and good-value wine are all included. **Moderate**

Le Troquet *upscale Basque* `14 G5`
21 rue François-Bonvin, 15ème • 01 45 66 89 00
Open lunch & dinner Tue–Sat

While this bistro in a nondescript street appears intensely old-fashioned, looks can be deceiving. Christian Etchebest's menu, while brief, is strictly seasonal and contemporary, often displaying the chef's Basque bias (fish wrapped in Bayonne ham with liberal sprinklings of Espelette pepper). **Moderate**

Chez Fung *Malay peninsula* `14 F4`
32 rue de Frémicourt, 15ème • 01 45 67 36 99
Open lunch & dinner Mon–Sat

Chez Fung offers a welcome taste of Malaysia's little-known (certainly in Paris) cuisine. The *prix-fixe* menus are great value; light, tasty starters such as omelette with ginger-peanut sauce are followed by steamed spiced fish and curries or grilled meats flavoured with lemongrass and coconut. **Moderate**

Le Suffren *neighbourhood favourite* `14 F3`
84 avenue de Suffren, 15ème • 01 45 66 97 86
Open breakfast, lunch & dinner daily

The timber and maritime theme may have given way to fashionable shades of black and orange and clubby fabric chairs, but the menu at this adored neighbourhood brasserie escaped unscathed. You'll find all the classics, from seafood platters and steaks to *choucroute*. **Moderate**

Salons de Thé
Coffee might be the brew of choice when it comes to dunking a croissant, but tea has caught on in Paris in a big way. The deservedly famous **Ladurée**, dating back to 1862, is excellent for lemon tea and multi-flavoured macaroons – they sell one of these every 25 seconds! Fuel up on a cup of strong Darjeeling and a fruit-crammed crumble at **A Priori Thé** in the glitzy Galerie Vivienne, or calm down after a serious Left Bank shopping spree with a pot of Celestial Empire at **La Maison de la Chine**. Stop by **Angelina** for mud-thick hot chocolate and gooey cakes in elegant surroundings, or, take a seat under a shady fig tree on the serene terrace of the **Grande Mosquée**'s Café Maure and sup on mint tea and honey-drizzled baklava. For contact details, *see p226.*

shopping

The capital of style, Paris has all the retail opportunities that a shopaholic might crave. The city's 20 *arrondissements* house a dazzling and diverse array, from tiny glamourpuss boutiques on serpentine streets to venerable department stores on sweeping boulevards. Trawl for luxury labels, pore over silky lingerie, search out one-off handbags or stock up on deliciously French homewares.

SHOPPING

While the Paris retail scene is constantly evolving, the major shopping areas tend to remain the same. This means couture and luxury labels in the 8th *arrondissement*, shoe shops along rue de Grenelle, and unique boutiques in the Marais and St-Germain in particular. In summer, nothing beats browsing the one-off boutiques along Canal St-Martin or trawling the elegant arcades of the historic Palais-Royal, carrier bags swinging from each arm.

Julie Street

Gourmet Goodies

Paris is a movable feast: its vibrant, roving markets are bursting with mouthwatering produce, and there are specialist food stores all over town. Try **La Maison du Chocolat** *(see p79)* for divine cocoa treats and **A L'Olivier** *(see p78)* for flavoured olive oils. The hip store **Food** *(see p71)* offers exquisite larder-fillers and cookbooks.

Parisian Accessories

The locals' innate sense of style seems to revolve around knowing how to complement minimal outfits with the perfect accessories. **Christian Louboutin** *(see p64)* and **Pierre Hardy** *(see p65)* are popular for their extravagant footwear, while **Karine Dupont**'s *(see p79)* snappy bags and **Jamin Puech's** *(see p82)* limited-edition totes are also *de rigeur*.

Vintage Finds

Long one of the world's fashion capitals, Paris is a treasure trove of vintage clothes. *Les puces (see pp164–5)* are fun, but more expensive and less well-stocked than in the past. Head instead to specialist stores such as **Yukiko** *(see p75)* for vintage fashion, **Nuits de Satin** *(see p93)* for lingerie, or **Catherine Arigoni** *(see p86)* for couture collectibles.

choice shops

Designer Fashion

If you're a logos-and-labels kind of shopper, head for the couture heartland of the Golden Triangle *(see p90)*. Other essential stops include the modern-vintage designs at **E2** *(see p91)*, the upmarket fashion chez **Zadig & Voltaire (de luxe)** *(see p88)*, and – with the hottest selection of cutting-edge unisex fashion in town – **L'Eclaireur** *(see p67)*.

Parisian Panache

Long-time resident, Australian **Martin Grant** *(see p76)* is an eternal favourite with the city's fashion crowd. The ultra-wearable, cross-generational clothes by **Vanessa Bruno** *(see p81)*, "bourgeois bohemian" designs of **Isabel Marant** *(see p94)* and savvy, colour coordinated racks at **AB33's** *(see p73)* are also worth seeking out.

Mode for Men

Urban dandies are spoiled for choice in Paris, with temptations such as avant-garde shirts from **Martin Margiela** *(see p66)*, razor-sharp trousers from **Helmut Lang** *(see p65)* and the all-male department store, **Madelios** *(see p65)*, which stocks everything from Dior to Lacoste. **Loft Design by** *(see p82)* is a haven of stylish basics for the modern man about town.

Shopping

Fifi Chachnil *ultra-feminine frills* `9 D3`
231 rue St-Honoré, 1er • 01 42 61 21 83
>> www.fifichachnil.com Open 11–7 Mon–Sat

Nobody does girly lingerie like Delphine Véron.
Think baby-doll dresses in soft candy colours,
G-strings with feathery pom-poms at the hips, lush
red bras with cute little bows – all guaranteed to
summon up the *femme fatale* in every woman. Just
browsing in this sugary pink boudoir is fun.

Christian Louboutin *fabulous footwear* `10 F4`
19 rue Jean-Jacques Rousseau, 1er • 01 42 36 05 31
Open 10:30–7 Mon–Sat

Louboutin's extravagant red-soled shoes are extremely
glamorous. Displayed in a white wall set with red
alcoves, the styles veer from fantasy (bejewelled
velvet) to resolutely feminine (leather and spidery
lace). Shoes, claims Louboutin, are like faces: some
are extraordinary front-on, others are better in profile.

by Terry *couture cosmetics* `10 F4`
21 passage Véro-Dodat, 1er • 01 44 76 00 76
>> www.byterry.com Open 10:30–7 Mon–Sat

Terry de Gunzburg, a former make-up artist and
creative director of YSL's cosmetics line for 15 years,
knows a thing or two about beauty and luxury; for
instance, that women can't get enough of it. So, she
launched "by Terry", a line of made-to-order *haute
couleur* cosmetics. Simply book a consultation with
Terry, self-described *couturier pour le visage*, to
discover what she can do to make you radiant.

The make-up, which boasts some of the most costly
pigments around, is mixed up by a team of chemists
and colourists in the lab upstairs and packaged into
silver containers, which can be personalized with
initials or a message. Each order will comprise a year's
supply of a unique product, albeit at a handsome price.
There's also a range of ready-to-wear cosmetics (a few
doors away at No. 36), but it's more interesting – and
much more Parisian – to go for the bespoke service.

Helmut Lang *master of minimalism* `10 E4`
219 rue St-Honoré, 1er • 01 58 62 53 20
» www.helmutlang.com Open 11–7 Tue–Sat

Lang's gallery-cum-boutique features a concrete stair-case flanked by two imposing, black monolithic boxes, black vinyl ottomans and art by names such as Louise Bourgeois. These clean lines are also evident in the men's and women's clothes: razor-sharp pants and jackets, figure-hugging dresses and skinny T-shirts.

Madelios *male domain* `9 C2`
23 boulevard de la Madeleine, 1er • 01 53 45 00 00
» www.madelios.com Open 10–7 Mon–Sat

A one-stop shop for men's fashion, with two floors of stylish, if faintly conservative, clothing. This means sharp suits by Dior, Paul Smith and Givenchy; stylish casuals by the likes of Lacoste and Diesel; plus a large range of accessories and shoes. Also found in-store are expert tailors and a men's beauty salon.

Pierre Hardy *his-and-hers heels* `10 F4`
156 galerie de Valois, 1er • 01 42 60 59 75
» www.pierrehardy.com Open 11–7 Mon–Sat

Former Hermès accessories designer Pierre Hardy has had a big hit with his sophisticated, own-brand range of shoes. His elegant boutique is located within the up-market arcades enclosing the Palais Royal gardens *(see p168)*: lit by a wall of coloured neon tubes, it has something of a gallery feel to it, an impression reinforced by the fact that the shoes are presented on one long black shelf running round the walls.

Hardy's women's collection revolves around vertiginous heels, daring foot "décolletés" and open-toed stilettos in nude pink and coral that fasten with lingerie straps. But fans of flatter styles are also well served with kitten heels, sexy gladiator sandals and cute ballerina shoes in candy colours. The designer's capsule men's collection includes stylish cowboy boots, kangaroo-skin lace-ups and white leather desert boots. Unusually for Paris, service is with a smile.

Shopping

L'Artisan Parfumeur *evocative scents* `10 F5`
2 rue Amiral de Coligny, 1er • 01 44 88 27 50
>> www.artisanparfumeur.com Open 10:30–7 Mon–Sat ✓

This boutique rekindles memories with its cleverly scented candles and perfumes. Premier Figuier (First Figs) is Provence on a hot summer's day, Je Me Souviens (I Remember) conjures up childhood cuddles, while Pour des Prunes (Plum Pudding) is reminiscent of a pie baking in the oven. Delicious.

Salons du Palais Royal *regal perfumes* `10 F3`
25 rue de Valois, 1er • 01 49 27 09 09
>> www.salons-shiseido.com Open 10–7 Mon–Sat

Every year Serge Lutens, Shiseido's creative director, comes up with new fragrances that are added to the range and sold exclusively in this lavish shop. Bestsellers include Rahat Loukoum, with its bittersweet almond, honey and vanilla scent, and Amber Sultan, aromatic amber spiced with evergreen rock rose.

Martin Margiela *bold fashion statements* `10 F3`
23bis & 25bis rue de Montpensier, 1er
01 40 15 06 44 (menswear), 01 40 15 07 55 (womenswear)
Open 11–7 Mon–Sat

The Belgian fashion maverick's first Paris boutique is a startling all-white space. Margiela's avant-garde mens- and womenswear tends to be on the conceptual side, but everything – apart from the weird split-toed shoes – is actually very wearable.

Maria Luisa *always in fashion* `9 C3`
2 rue Cambon, 1er • 01 47 03 96 15
Open 10:30–7 Mon–Sat

Maria Luisa has impeccable taste and a discerning eye. Her boutiques are favoured by the fashion elite who come by each season for the latest by Gaultier, Olivier Theyskens, Ann Demeulemeester and Jean-Paul Knott, to name but a few. Whether you crave cutting-edge or classic, new or established, this is prime territory.

L'Eclaireur *directional fashion* `10 G3`
10 rue Hérold, 1er • 01 40 41 09 89
>> www.leclaireur.com   Open 11–7 Mon–Sat

It might be Paris's hippest multi-brand boutique, but with no shop window it's certainly not the city's most obvious. You'll have to press the buzzer to get in to the dimly lit cavernous space, where, despite the store's ultra-trendy reputation, the welcome is warm and the staff are genuinely enthusiastic about helping customers put an outfit together.

The store's focus is on innovative, international fashion, showcasing superbly tailored men's collections by Austrian designer Carol Christian Poell and avant-garde mens- and womenswear by Japanese label Undercover. Other highlights include tactile deconstructed sweaters in vintage cashmere by LA-based designer Koi, a great selection of Linda Farrow vintage sunglasses and a more classic collection of menswear designed by actor John Malkovich that is exclusive to L'Eclaireur in France.

Ventilo *effortless chic* `9 C2`
13–15 boulevard de la Madeleine, 1er • 01 42 60 46 40
Open 10:30–7 Mon–Sat

An upmarket concept store, Ventilo sells a small but sophisticated range of women's fashion and home accessories. The look is chic with a Moroccan/Indian twist; think gorgeous fabrics, floaty *djellebas* and lots of beading and embroidery. The in-store café serves a selection of Japanese teas and world food.

Odette & Zoe *handbags galore* `10 F3`
4 rue des Petits Champs, 2ème • 01 42 61 48 75
Open 11–7 Mon–Sat

This pink boutique is packed with bags of every imaginable style, shape and colour. The focus is on fun and originality rather than famous designer labels: quirky finds include suitcases printed with Marilyn Monroe's face, practical foldaway bags by Bensimon and purses made from vintage saris.

Flavie Furst *real gems* `10 E3`
16 rue de la Soudière, 1er • 01 42 60 06 01
Open 11:30–7 Mon–Sat

Flavie Furst makes glorious jewellery, her husband Ronald makes gorgeous bags – and that means that their tiny boutique is one big temptation. Flavie, who designed accessories for Lanvin before turning to full-time jewellery-making, loves the colour and emotive qualities of precious stones, and is careful not to overpower them with extravagant designs. She creates pieces that are original, expressive and, above all, easy to wear: an effortlessly pretty pale-blue teardrop sapphire set off-centre on a silver band, a single plump Tahitian pearl draped on a delicate gold chain.

No less eye-catching are her partner's handbags, which run from totes to baguettes, all with matching make-up bags inside. The bags are made in a multitude of colours and textures, including stripes and rowdy floral prints, tweed and cowhide; few who enter can leave without buying at least one.

Lavinia *wine emporium* `9 D2`
3–5 boulevard de la Madeleine, 1er • 01 42 97 20 20
Open 10–8 Mon–Fri, 9–8 Sat

If your wine-appreciation skills need some polishing, Lavinia is the place to go. With a selection of over 6,000 bottles (including 3,000 French wines, 2,000 foreign wines and 1,000 spirits), 500 books, a staff of 15 sommeliers, dozens of glasses and decanters as well as various other wine-related paraphernalia, it's Europe's largest wine shop. The slick three-level store is maintained like a traditional wine cellar, with a temperature of 19°C (68°F), though a special section for rare wines is kept at 14°C (58°F). Prices range from a few euros a bottle through to several thousand-plus.

The glossy 80-seat, in-store restaurant serves lunch only (shark steak and chardonnay are a winning combination), though the bar is open till 8pm. In either, you can sample any wine in the store and there's no extra mark-up in price. Lavinia also holds regular tastings and runs wine courses.

For the very latest on Paris go to >> www.realcity.dk.com

Killiwatch *hip hand-me-downs*

10 G3

64 rue Tiquetonne, 2ème • 01 42 21 17 37
Open 2–7 Mon, 11–7:30 Tue–Sat

This store buys pre-worn clothing, cleans it up a treat
and puts it back out on the rails. Not just any old rags,
though – this is stylish stuff: from fur-trimmed coats to
leather minis and swirly 70s shirts. There's also club-
wear from their in-house label, non-vintage jeans and
streetwear, plus magazines and the latest club flyers.

Barbara Bui *clean-cut style*

10 H4

23 rue Etienne Marcel, 2ème • 01 40 26 43 65
» www.barbarabui.com Open 10:30–7:30 Mon–Sat

Barbara Bui's designs can be described as clothes
for style-conscious rebels: refined, with an offbeat femi-
ninity. Born and raised in Paris in a Franco-Vietnamese
family, Bui's designs subtly reflect both cultures.
Her exquisitely finished and flattering trousers are
wardrobe must-haves; ditto, her leather jackets.

Robert Le Héros *arty decor*

11 C4

13 rue de Saintonge, 3ème • 01 44 59 33 22
» www.robertleheros.com Open 1–7 Tue–Sat

This leading textile design agency that was set up by four art-school
friends now has its own boutique. Step past the jaunty red façade
and you'll find a veritable art and design laboratory with a
seasonally changing decor. The foursome's eye-catching graphic
designs in gorgeous colourways are reproduced on everything
from cushions, curtains and wallpaper to handbags and diaries.

Erik & Lydie *jewels galore*

10 H3

7 passage du Grand Cerf, 2ème • 01 40 26 52 59
Open 2–7 Tue–Sat

Seriously pretty jewellery is what Erik & Lydie do best;
contemporary and gently artistic with a slight
Victorian bent. Spidery necklaces draped with flower-
shaped stones recall the delicate garlands favoured by
a previous generation, while the slim metal chokers
wouldn't be out of place in the coolest of clubs.

Goumanyat & Son Royaume *spices* `11 C3`

3 rue Charles-François Dupuis, 3ème • 01 44 78 96 74
»» www.goumanyat.com Open 2–7 Tue–Fri, 11–7 Sat

A whiff of faraway lands emanates from this elegant little shop-cum-olfactory-museum run by Jean Marie Thiercelin, a sixth-generation spice merchant. His family started out dealing in saffron in 1809; today their business encompasses 180 spices, including pink peppercorns from Pondicherry, vanilla beans from Madagascar, black peppercorns from Kerala and sea salt and oils from around the world.

This is where Michelin-starred chefs, such as Alain Ducasse and Joel Robuchon, come to stock up on rare condiments. Poke your nose into the jars on *le bar à sniffer* to discover the vibrant aromas of star anise, cloves and nutmeg; get a lesson on spices from the gracious Monsieur Thiercelin himself; or browse the store for gifts of saffron-flavoured chocolate, caviar, fine linen aprons, plant-based bath and skincare products, kitchen utensils and heady spice mixes.

Nodus *crisp shirts and ties* `17 B1`

22 rue Vieille du Temple, 4ème • 01 42 77 07 96
»» www.nodus.fr Open 10:15–7:30 Tue–Sat, 2–7:30 Sun & Mon

Nodus pays homage to smart men, with a range of 400 shirts and over 300 different ties. This cosy branch in the Marais displays its styles in neat, colour-coded rows that cover every inch of wall and much of the floor space in between. Trendy cufflinks and tie-pins complete the experience.

The Northern Marais

This used to be a rather shabby, down-at-heel neighbourhood ignored by the crowds thronging rue des Francs-Bourgeois to the south. But thanks to the arrival of ultra-cool hotels such as **Murano Urban Resort** and the **Hôtel du Petit Moulin** *(for both see p179)* – not to mention a flurry of young designers' showrooms during Fashion Week – the area gained a hip fringe atmosphere and was quickly dubbed the "Parisian Notting Hill". Hot addresses on rue Charlot include **Martin Grant**'s chic boutique *(see p76)*, cutting-edge multi-brand store **AB33** *(see p73)*, foodie emporium **Food** *(see p71)* and textile designer **Dominique Picquier**'s eye-catching store (at No. 10). Rue de Poitou is another buzzing strip with several art galleries and quirky stores.

Shoe Bizz *fashion for feet* `11 A5`
48 rue Beaubourg, 3ème • 01 48 87 12 73
Open 10:30–7:30 Mon–Sat

Shoe Bizz zeroes in on the hottest footwear trends, reproduces the styles and sells them for a lot less than you'd pay elsewhere. Don't expect flawless finishes or sturdy quality, though. These shoes aren't meant to last forever, just as long as the style is *en vogue* – but that's more than enough.

Food *gourmet's hang-out* `11 C4`
58 rue Charlot, 3ème • 01 42 72 68 97
Open 11–1 & 2–7 Tue–Fri, 2–7 Sat

Much of the rue Charlot buzz was started by the opening of this intriguing bookstore-cum-gallery. With its wall-to-wall bookshelves, it's a foodie's paradise, where browsers linger over a range of mouthwatering cookbooks in French, English and Japanese. Food also stocks larder goodies and designer tableware.

Antik Batik *ethnic fusion* `17 C1`
18 rue de Turenne, 4ème • 01 44 78 02 00
>> www.antikbatik.fr Open 10:30–7:30 Mon–Sat, noon–8 Sun

Antik Batik sells globally inspired somethings that follow the season's trends; from flowery headscarves and crocheted bikinis for summer, to hand-knitted hats, pullovers and bags for winter. Labels such as Ordinary People, Laura Urbinati and Uniform can also be found on the shelves.

Chic on the Cheap

Dépôt-ventes are where canny Parisians shop for cut-price designer clothes. Try **Annexe des Créateurs** (40–70 per cent off previous seasons' Versace, Vivienne Westwood, Dolce & Gabbana and more), **Réciproque** (six stores in one street selling womenswear, menswear and the biggest range of second-hand Chanel in Paris) and **Dépôt-Vente de Buci** (two neighbouring stores selling everything from YSL to Yamamoto). Many stores have their own permanent sales shops, the best of which are **Et Vous**, **Cacharel** and **Kookaï**. At the cheap end of the scale, **Guerrisol** has more of a whiffy jumble-sale flavour. But this is where designers such as Gaultier trawl for inspiration, and there are real bargains to be had. For further details, *see pp227–8*.

Shopping

Abou d'Abi Bazar *affordable fashion* `17 C1`
10 rue des Francs Bourgeois, 3ème • 01 42 77 96 98
Open 2–7:15 Mon, 10:30–7 Tue–Sat, 2–7 Sun

Savvy shoppers pop in here regularly to pick up the season's must-have pieces. These include reasonably priced jeans, dresses and accessories from designers such as Vanessa Bruno, Stella Forest and Isabel Marant. Mixing and matching is a breeze, too, as the clothes on display are organized by colour.

La Chaise Longue *Marais institution* `17 C1`
20 rue des Francs Bourgeois, 3ème • 01 48 04 36 37
Open 11–7 Mon–Sat, 2–7 Sun

This tiny, two-storey home-decor boutique has become synonymous with design inventiveness and cheerful kitsch. Specializing in cheap and quirky accessories for bathrooms and kitchens – such as cocktail shakers, retro fans and miniature kitten-shaped frying-pans – LCL is the perfect hunting ground for novelty presents.

Galerie Simone *designers' creative lab* `11 C4`
124 rue Vieille du Temple, 3ème • 01 42 74 21 28
Open noon–7 Mon–Sat, 1–6 Sun

The city's coolest boutique for fashion, furniture, jewellery and accessories, Galerie Simone showcases one-offs and limited editions by some of the edgiest new designers in Paris. Check out Michel Morellini's draped leather dresses, conceptual silver jewellery by Georges Tsak and origami-inspired handbags by Sanja.

French Chain Stores

Several international high-street stores are actually of French origin: the young of body and heart make a beeline for branches of **Morgan**, **Etam** and **Kookaï** (which now has a capsule up-market collection, Creative Lab). Basic, fashion-conscious footwear can be snapped up at **André** (which also regularly invites guest designers),

while **Princesse Tam Tam** is good for bikinis and underwear (though bra sizes often stop at a B-cup). On the beauty front, **Sephora** is hard to beat, but **Yves Rocher** is also worth checking out for all-natural bath and beauty products. **Monoprix** supermarkets are great one-stop shops for (slightly older) fashion, bags, beauty products and home accessories. For further details, *see pp227–8.*

AB33 *affordable fashion*
33 rue Charlot, 3ème • 01 42 71 02 82
Open 11–8 Tue–Sun (to 9 on Thu)

Located in the heart of the retail hub that has emerged in the northern Marais, AB33 has an appealing take both on women's fashion and the shopping experience. Dynamic young owner Agathe Buchotte (the AB of the store's name) revamped an old grocer's shop with the help of her architect father, giving the space a lived-in feel with rugs, a magazine-strewn coffee table and a scattering of velvet poufs.

You won't find snooty Parisian vendors here, though; Agathe is an upbeat Marseillaise with a laid-back attitude who extends a friendly welcome to all and encourages browsing and extended trying-on sessions. She takes a highly personal approach to her buying, putting collections together as if they were her own wardrobe. And while Agathe is keenly aware of what's out there on fashion's cutting-edge, she manages to mix the season's hottest catwalk looks with clothes that are fun, easy and wearable. These are all arranged on accessible, colour coordinated rails, offering an extensive selection of mainstream lines such as Vanessa Bruno, Isabel Marant, Cabane de Zucca and celebrity jeans of choice Notify, showcased alongside delicate Italian lingerie by Kristina Ti and designer knits by rising Belgian star Christian Wijnants.

AB33 accessories, which include original jewellery creations by Marine de Diesbach and luxury leather bags by up-and-coming Danish designer Malm Strecker, have an edgier look. Agathe also produces her own line of customized suede and leather shoulder bags; clients can choose their own colours and fabric combinations (giving them a stylish one-off creation for under 300€). Allow five days for production.

Shopping

Comptoir des Cotonniers *basic needs* `11 B5`
33 rue des Francs Bourgeois, 4ème • 01 42 76 95 33
»» www.meresetfilles.com
Open 10–7:30 Mon–Sat, 1–7 Sun

French women who like stylish clothes but don't like
paying high prices for them stock up on well-designed
wardrobe basics here. The look is modern, casual
and urban: easy-to-wear jackets in wool and flannel
for winter, crisp shirts and cool dresses for summer.

Azzedine Alaïa *a well-kept secret* `17 A1`
7 rue de Moussy, 4ème • 01 42 72 19 19
Open 11–7 Mon–Sat

No tempting shop window here; just a discreet buzzer
to gain admittance to this cool address. The Tunisian
maestro's flattering cuts and curve-conscious women's
clothing are showcased in a cavernous space decorated by US artist Julian Schnabel. Don't miss the permanent sale area of old stock and samples out back.

A-poc *instant ready-to-wear* `11 B5`
47 rue des Francs Bourgeois, 4ème • 01 44 54 07 05
Open 11–7 Mon–Sat

A-poc, which stands for "A Piece of Cloth", is the brainchild of Japanese designer Issey Miyake, and it works
like this: simply cut a piece of cloth from a bolt of his
revolutionary woven-knit, non-run fabric and *voilà*, a
new top, dress or wrap. Staff in the gallery-style
space will advise how best to wear your new "poc".

Brontibay *bags of style* `17 C1`
6 rue de Sévigné, 4ème • 01 42 76 90 80
Open 11–8 Mon–Sat, 1:30–7:30 Sun

The name might be inspired by two Australian coastal
havens (Bronte Beach and Byron Bay), but there's not
a single swimsuit in sight. Instead, it's wall-to-wall
bags in classy flannel, felt, nylon or leather (sometimes
with gloves to match). They also sell pampering MOR
lotions, plus Neal's Yard Remedies creams.

Hervé Gambs *man-made flowers* `11 B5`
9bis rue des Blancs Manteaux, 4ème • 01 44 59 88 88
>> www.hervegambs.fr Open 11–7:30 Tue–Sat, 1:30–7:30 Sun

Hervé is *the* man when it comes to artificial flowers.
In fact, his silky blooms are so convincing that it's
hard to tell his white orchids, purple calla lilies or
trailing bamboo leaves from the real thing. As befits
their couture status, there are two collections a year
that reflect the latest horticultural trends.

Calligrane *paper chase* `17 A2`
4–6 rue du Pont Louis-Philippe, 4ème • 01 48 04 31 89
Open 11–7 Tue–Sat

Calligrane's three adjoining shops are devoted to the art of calligraphy
and paper products. One specializes only in Fabriano, an Italian paper
favoured by Goya and Michelangelo; another sells up-market briefcase
and desk essentials; the third stocks textured paper from India, Brazil,
Japan, China and Mexico – and holds occasional shows by artists
working with paper. Simply sublime gifts for writers and artists.

Yukiko *vintage passions* `11 C4`
97 rue Vieille du Temple, 4ème • 01 42 71 13 41
Open 1–7 Mon–Sat

Yukiko is mad about vintage clothes, particularly
furs. She searches all over the place, uncovering rare
pieces that she then customizes to sell in her snug
and charming Marais boutique.

Set on the quieter end of a bustling thoroughfare,
this hole in the wall is crammed with wonderful old
things, though contemporary gear by Stella Cadente
(see p91) is also stocked, as well as lesser-known
designers with a penchant for making old things like
new again. You might be lucky enough to stumble
upon an original Dior vanity case, some funky
leather bags from the 1970s, pristine 50s pumps
or clingy knee-high *Barbarella*-style boots. There's
lots of retro jewellery too, including flashy rings,
overstated bracelets and shiny enamel brooches.
It's hard to get out of the door without falling for
at least one of Yukiko's treasures.

Martin Grant *ladylike elegance* 11 B5

10 rue Charlot, 3ème • 01 42 71 39 49
>> www.martingrantparis.com Open 10–6 Mon–Fri

Australian designer Martin Grant has been making clothes ever since his grandmother taught him to sew at the age of seven. Several years on, he's still stitching, but now it's in a white and airy showroom that overlooks a 17th-century flagstone courtyard on the other side of the world. During his years in Paris – he's been here since 1992 – the low-key Grant has built up a loyal clientele, including actress Cate Blanchett, model Lauren Hutton and socialite Lee Radziwill (sister of Jacqueline Kennedy Onassis), as well as hordes of modern girls all over the world.

His clothes are ladylike but sexy, timeless and undeniably elegant. His frocks (calling them dresses just isn't right) have a faint echo of the 1950s about them: a strapless gown with wavy chiffon ruffles, a belted black wool sheath with built-in cape, a brocade cocktail dress in which a young Lauren Bacall would look drop-dead gorgeous. Coats, though, are his trademark, and Grant cuts them with sculptural precision (a skill no doubt gained by a four-year stint studying the art). Designs have included a single-breasted pony-skin coat with leather trim, a retro-look three-quarter-length tweed and a black Lurex evening trench. Even in summer, there's always a super-smart coat or three in the collection. Grant's clothes are made to hug those feminine curves and there's just something about the way he does it that makes the wearer look *très, très* chic. And that's just the ticket when in Paris.

Sentou *cool, contemporary living* `17 B1`
18 & 24 rue du Pont Louis-Philippe, 4ème
01 42 77 44 79 (No. 18), 01 42 71 00 01 (No. 24)
29 rue François Miron, 4ème • 01 42 78 50 60
>> www.sentou.fr Open 11–7 Tue–Sat (closed 2–3 Tue–Fri)

It describes itself as "the art of living" store and that pretty much sums it up. Opened in Paris in 1977 as an outlet for the work of furniture designer Robert Sentou, this Marais store (actually three separate shops) has morphed over the years into a quasi gallery that champions modern design. Today, Sentou carries a varied selection of contemporary designs, from the ethereal bamboo-and-paper lamps of Osamu Noguchi to the upright birch chairs of Alvar Aalto, with the supple vinyl containers of D-sign by O and playful picture plates by 100Drine in between.

The shop at No. 24, the original boutique, is now a temple to tablewares, including colourful hand-blown glassware by Sugahara, classy Stelton cutlery, coolly elegant silver and gold enamel-dipped china bowls, plates and cups by French design duo Tsé-Tsé, plus salt and pepper shakers, scented candles, containers, lacquered trays and spring vases (old test tubes wired together into snaking shapes). No. 18, meanwhile, is awash with the designs of former newspaper illustrator and furniture fabric designer 100Drine: vividly coloured, hand-painted plates with smiling faces and stacks of storage tins and notebooks dominate the space. In addition, there are roomy plastic shopping baskets and cute things for kids. Objects are displayed for easy, hands-on inspection and staff are helpful and happy to offer advice. The largest store, a five-minute stroll away on rue François Miron, houses the striking, modern furniture of Swedish company David Design and Aalto's classic tables and chairs, as well as lamps, furniture and textiles from the Sentou line.

Bô Plus *modish homewares*   `11 A5`
8 rue St-Merri, 4ème • 01 42 74 55 10
Open 11:30–8 Mon–Sat, 2–8:30 Sun

Parisians love the contemporary lines of this store's well-crafted wares, which run from vases to chairs via Limoges crockery, table linen and candlesticks. Much is the work of young designers, including Katsuhiro Kinoshita (lacquer storage boxes), Gilles Caffier (sleek furniture) and Catherine Grandidier (unusual lights).

Hervé Van der Straeten *chic designs*   `17 B1`
11 rue Ferdinand Duval, 4ème • 01 42 78 99 99
Open 9–6 Mon–Fri, noon–7 Sat

Once the creator of jewellery collections for Lacroix, YSL and Gaultier, Hervé Van der Straeten now designs his own furniture and jewellery. Almost exclusively produced in 24-carat gold-plated brass, the latter includes ornate necklaces and bracelets, and wafer-thin pendant earrings inspired by blades of grass.

A L'Olivier *gourmet oils*   `17 B1`
23 rue de Rivoli, 4ème • 01 48 04 86 59
➤➤ www.olivier-on-line.com Open 10–7 Mon–Sat

Opened in 1822 by a Parisian pharmacist specializing in cod-liver oil, A L'Olivier was relaunched in 1978 as a gourmet food store. The beautiful packaging of the extensive selection of olive oils, flavoured oils and organic vinegars would grace any shelf, and hampers of Provençal specialities can be made up to order.

Diptyque *haute-couture candles*   `17 A3`
34 boulevard St-Germain, 5ème • 01 43 26 45 27
➤➤ www.diptyqueparis.com Open 10–7 Mon–Sat

In business since 1961, Diptyque is the original and still the best when it comes to candles of distinction. Devotees include Kristin Scott-Thomas (who favours Shadow in the Water) and Donatella Versace (an admirer of Fig Tree). This elegant and highly fragrant store also sells scents and room sprays.

Karine Dupont *it's in the bag* 15 D3
16 rue du Cherche Midi, 6ème • 01 42 84 06 30
» www.karinedupont.com Open 11–7 Tue–Sat

Dupont makes practical, soft nylon bags in all shapes and sizes, from roomy totes to shoulder slingers. There are bags for every occasion, with names like Kampus Lady, Kasual Travel and Klub. They come in an array of modish colours and prints and many have handy sections that can be detached as required.

La Maison du Chocolat *choc therapy* 15 C3
19 rue de Sèvres, 6ème • 01 45 44 20 40
» www.lamaisonduchocolat.com
Open 10–7:30 Mon–Sat, 10–2 Sun

For those who believe that chocolate is one of the basic food groups, this place is heaven on a plate. Indulge in Robert Linx's handmade ginger-flavoured *ganache*, cocoa-covered truffles or potent Andalousie (chocolate cake, with lemon cream and truffle).

Tara Jamon *good-looking fashion* 16 E2
18 rue du Four, 6ème • 01 46 33 26 60
Open 10:30–7 Mon–Sat

Stepping into Tara Jamon's sunny corner shop is like stepping into spring. A Canadian expat with a French heart, she specializes in sophisticated, reasonably priced clothes. Think pert sundresses, slim-fit sheath dresses with knee-length coats, pleated skirts and silk cardigans in ice-cream colours with bags to match.

Sabbia Rosa *lush lingerie* 15 D2
73 rue des Sts-Pères, 6ème • 01 45 48 88 37
Open 10–7 Mon–Sat

Mme Rosa is renowned for her sumptuous, hand-made and exotic-looking camisoles, corsetry, bras and knickers, all of which are coveted by the likes of Madonna, Naomi Campbell and Cindy Crawford. Settle into the seductive sofa, survey the silk, satin and chiffon, and splash out on something custom-made.

Les 3 Marches de Catherine B `16 E2`
1 & 3 rue Guisarde, 6ème • 01 43 54 74 18
>> www.catherine-b.com Open 10:30–7:30 Tue–Sat

Catherine B is a luxury vintage-clothes sleuth who specializes in tracking down old Hermès and Chanel bags. Her bijou boutique is packed to the medieval rafters with scarves, jewellery and sought-after Kelly bags. The sister store next door sells a small selection of equally pricey and exquisite vintage clothes.

Agnès b *Parisian chic* `15 D2`
6 rue du Vieux Colombier, 6ème • 01 44 39 02 60 (women's);
10–12 rue du Vieux Colombier, 6ème • 01 45 49 02 05 (men's)
>> www.agnesb.fr Open 10–7 Mon–Sat

Agnès b is synonymous with quality fabrics, clean lines and quintessential French style. The modern yet classic designs – precisely tailored trousers, crisp shirts and must-have little black dresses – suit all ages and lifestyles and often work over a few seasons.

Free Lance *sharp shoes* `15 D2`
30 rue du Four, 6ème • 01 45 48 14 78
Open 10–7 Mon–Fri, 10–7:30 Sat

Whatever your footwear fancy – dainty, fur-covered, shiny or snakeskin – you'll find it, or its close kin, here. Free Lance, who have been in the business for more than 100 years, keep up with the shoe trends; often, they're creating them. Their strappy sandals and dominatrix heels are particularly hot.

APC *urban basics* `15 D4`
3 rue Fleurus, 6ème • 01 42 22 12 77 (women's);
4 rue Fleurus, 6ème • 01 45 49 19 15 (men's)
>> www.apc.fr Open 10:40–7 Mon–Fri, 11–7:30 Sat

The Atelier de Production et Création is something of an institution among Parisian hipsters who like their denim dark, rigid and slightly industrial. The girls' line includes A-line skirts and sweet summer dresses, while boys rule with those dark jeans and sober shirts.

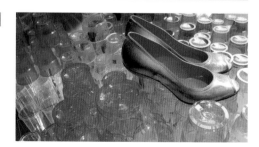

Lagerfeld Gallery *art & women's fashion* `16 E1`
40 rue de Seine, 6ème • 01 55 42 75 51
» www.karllagerfeld.com Open 11–7 Tue–Sat

This sedate and rather masculine-looking store sells Karl's own Lagerfeld Gallery line, selected items from the Fendi collection, which he also designs, and his accessories, perfumes and fabulously glossy fashion magazines. There are also regular photo exhibitions, often of Lagerfeld's own graphic compositions.

Vanessa Bruno *cross-generational clothes* `16 E3`
25 rue St-Sulpice, 6ème • 01 43 54 41 04
Open 10–7 Mon–Sat

Bruno's minimalist yet feminine garments appeal to women of all ages. They are individual, usually trend-resistant (from shapely coats and jackets to flattering trousers), and have a good quality–price ratio. A huge success since it hit the shelves in 1998 is her tote bag in sequins, leather or canvas.

Paul & Joe *for modern men* `16 E2`
40 rue du Four, 6ème • 01 45 44 97 70
» www.paulandjoe.com Open 11–7:30 Mon–Sat

The shop is named after Sophie Albou's two young sons, who are going to have to wait a while to sport the groovy slimline trousers, see-through shirts and 1930s-style jackets that their mama turns out. Confident guys go wild for the African-print tracksuits and the flamboyant pineapple-printed shirts.

Woman *erotic pursuits* `15 D2`
6 rue de Grenelle, 6ème • 01 49 54 66 21
» www.soniarykiel.fr Open 10:30–7 Mon–Sat

Nathalie, daughter of renowned designer Sonia Rykiel, caused quite a stir when she opened her "temple of pleasure" in St-Germain. The boutique's three floors offer all manner of seductive treats, from black lace lingerie and pashmina dressing gowns to designer dildos and lipstick-shaped vibrators.

Shopping

Marie Mercié *eccentric hatters* `16 E3`
23 rue St-Sulpice, 6ème • 01 43 26 45 83
Open 11–7 Mon–Sat

Beautifully finished, handmade hats are the *raison d'être* of this boutique. Celebrities including Catherine Deneuve are among the fans of Marie's stylish head-gear, which ranges from flamboyant wedding hats and cute felt cloches to skullcaps sprouting branches. Bespoke hats can be ordered (allow up to one month).

Onward *avant-garde trends* `16 E2`
147 boulevard St-Germain, 6ème • 01 55 42 77 55
Open 11–7 Mon & Sat, 10:30–7 Tue–Fri

This Left Bank institution has a reputation for show-casing experimental fashion. Clothing by maverick designers such as Bernhard Willhelm and quirky Dutch duo Viktor & Rolf are featured here as well as accessories that make bold fashion statements, such as teaspoon necklaces and jewelled handcuffs.

Jamin Puech *cheeky handbags* `16 E3`
43 rue Madame, 6ème • 01 45 48 14 85
» www.jamin-puech.com Open 11–7 Mon–Fri, noon–7 Sat

Do you crave a bag with beads, shells, embroidery, leather fringing or crocheted raffia? Designers Benoit Jamin and Isabelle Puech have that certain something to slip on to your wrist. This dramatic boutique (created by theatre designer Elisabeth Leriche) displays hundreds of their equally theatrical bags.

Loft Design by *comfortable chic* `16 E2`
56 rue de Rennes, 6ème • 01 45 44 88 99
» www.loft-design-by.com Open 11–7 Mon–Sat ✓

With its wood floors, barely there shelves and brick walls, Loft looks more like its namesake than a clothes shop. In keeping with the minimalist surroundings, designer Patrick Frèche specializes in tasteful urban basics for men and women in grey, black and white, with the occasional splash of seasonal colour.

Catherine Malandrino *distinctive fashion* `15 D2`
10 rue de Grenelle, 6ème • 01 42 22 26 95
>> www.catherinemalandrino.com Open 11–7 Mon–Sat

New York-based Malandrino has taken Manhattan by
storm with her unique mix of French glamour and
edgy sophistication. And the designer now has her
first Paris address, a futuristic glass-walled boutique
which, besides womenswear, carries an interesting
collection of accessories and shoes.

Deyrolle *animal, vegetable and mineral* `15 C1`
46 rue du Bac, 7ème • 01 42 22 30 07
>> www.princejardinier.fr Open 10–7 Mon–Sat (closed 1–2pm Mon)

In 1995, Prince Louis-Albert de Broglie traded banking for horticulture
and opened his first Paris store (Le Prince Jardinier), selling tomato
chutneys and preserves made at his Loire Valley château, plus gardening
tools and clothes, soaps and seeds. At Deyrolle – Paris's most famous
taxidermist, now also owned by the Prince – all of this is for sale, as
well as stuffed animals and mounted butterflies for your walls.

Shadé *big on style* `15 D2`
63 rue des Sts-Pères, 6ème • 01 45 49 30 37
Open 11–7:30 Tue–Sat, 1–7 Mon

Shadé is proof that size really doesn't matter.
Despite its miniscule proportions, this shop packs
quite a sartorial punch. Once inside – no easy task if
there are more than four people already browsing –
you'll be amazed at the array. Time passes quickly
when you're picking through such items as fetching,
heart-shaped silk bags with beaded appliqués and
shimmery tassels, or handmade velvet pouches
embroidered with silk flowers, many by imaginative
Brazilian designer Roberta. But this place is not just
about bags; with feathery hats, scarves, bustiers,
frou-frou skirts, Joe jeans and Converse sneakers
also on sale, women can pick up an entire outfit. Add
an umbrella with a flouncy frill, some jewellery – a
bracelet brimming with charms, a metallic heart on a
leather band or a sparkly choker – and *voilà*, you're
ready for any distraction that Paris has to offer.

>> *Say* bonjour *and* au revoir *on entering and leaving a shop; the assistants will be much friendlier*

La Grande Epicerie *culinary temptations* `15 C3`
Le Bon Marché, 38 rue de Sèvres, 7ème • 01 44 39 81 00
>> www.lebonmarche.fr Open 8:30am–9pm Mon–Sat

At Bon Marché's epicurean grocery, you can peruse 100-plus varieties of cheese, countless olive oils and vinegars, and international foodstuffs (candy-coloured Italian pasta, Zulu chilli sauce). Alternatively, snap up take-away gourmet meals and pastries. All in all, a treat for the eyes as well as the taste buds.

Iris *Italian shoe box* `15 D2`
28 rue de Grenelle, 7ème • 01 42 22 89 81
Open 10:30–7 Mon–Sat

Rue de Grenelle is a hot spot for shoe shops; there are just so many places from which to choose, but this all-white store is *the* place to visit if Italian-made shoes are what your heart desires. Venice-based Iris manufactures shoes for Marc Jacobs, Alessandro Dell'Acqua, Chloé and Véronique Branquino. *Bellissimo*!

Carine Gilson *luscious lingerie* `15 C2`
61 rue Bonaparte, 6ème • 01 43 26 46 71
>> www.carinegilson.com
Open 10:30–1:30 Tue–Fri, 10:30–7 Sat, by appt Mon

French women pay attention to the little things in life and this store has plenty of them, from lacy garters to flimsy slips and vampy black satin bras. Each collection has a theme, for example the Russian ballet or Klimt; in Gilson's hands, lingerie is an art form.

Editions de Parfums Frédéric Malle `15 C2`
37 rue de Grenelle, 7ème • 01 42 22 76 40
>> www.editionsdeparfums.com Open 11–7 Tue–Sat, 1–7 Mon

Editions de Parfums offers scents composed by nine of France's most legendary "noses". In this dimly lit labyrinth, filled with books, leather chairs and portraits of the nine perfumers, you can stop and smell the roses... and the lilacs... from vast glass "sniffing tubes" that keep the perfumes unadulterated.

Paul Smith *English class* `15 D3`
22 & 24 boulevard Raspail, 7ème • 01 42 84 15 30
≫ www.paulsmith.co.uk Open 11–7 Mon, 10–7 Tue–Sat

The Brit with a penchant for craftsmanship, tradition and humour is a favourite on this side of the Channel, too. His Paris HQ is a magnet for men who are after a sharp suit, a kimono-print shirt or a silver-and-turquoise bracelet, while women pop in for printed scarves, shoes and expertly cut jackets and dresses.

Lucien Pellat-Finet *cashmere king* `15 D1`
1 rue Montalembert, 7ème • 01 42 22 22 77
≫ www.lucienpellat-finet.com Open 10–7 Mon–Fri, 11–7 Sat

Lucien Pellat-Finet is known for his contemporary luxury knits in instantly identifiable colours and idiosyncratic patterns. His playful boutique, designed by new-generation architect Christian Biecher, perfectly matches the mood of his hooded sweaters, barely-there tank tops, bikinis and homewares.

Colors do Brasil *itsy-witsy bikinis* `15 D1`
4 rue Perronet, 7ème • 01 45 44 20 80
Open 10am–11pm Mon–Sat

This vibrant boutique sparkles with carnival colours and samba spirit, showcasing the slinkiest, sexiest bikinis in town. The swimwear is, as the name suggests, 100% made in Brazil, but it has been designed with European figures in mind – basically, a little more room up top, a little less string below!

Record Shops

While the vast emporiums of **fnac** and **Virgin** will sate any musical craving (and are open until midnight), Paris possesses other disc dealers for specialist sounds. Sixties vinyl, particularly French *chanson*, reigns at **En Avant La Zizique**, while tiny **Afric' Music** shimmies to a different beat: CDs from the Congo to Togo, with a little Caribbean thrown in. Jazz aficionados browse stacks of vinyl, secondhand CDs and old jazz magazines at **Paris Jazz Corner**, while **Wave** on rue Keller (electronica) and nearby **Techno Import** (techno and trance) are more up to date. At the other end of the musical spectrum, **Papageno** is bliss for opera buffs, with more than 4,000 vinyl albums (pre- and post-war), and rare boxed sets and CDs. For further details, *see p229*.

Shopping

Catherine Arigoni *couture collectibles* `15 D1`
14 rue Beaune, 7ème • 01 42 60 50 99
Open 2:30–7:30 Tue–Sat, by appt Mon

Former antiques dealer Arigoni is serious about vintage clothing, and couture riches abound in her wardrobe-sized shop. Try a 1960s Pierre Balmain evening dress of silk, satin and pearls, a 1930s beaded purse or 1940s black Chanel pumps in mint condition. Beware: opulent items command corresponding prices.

Jean-Baptiste Rautureau *flashy shoes* `15 D2`
24 rue de Grenelle, 7éme • 01 45 49 95 83
Open 10–7 Mon–Sat

Men's shoes are anything but tedious in the hands of Rautureau, a member of the clan that designs ever-trendy Free Lance shoes *(see p80)*. This is footwear for guys who want to make a statement – usually a loud one. Shoes come in everything from python-print and suede to red-and-white stripes and gold, but if snakeskin mules are not for you, you can also pick up some loafers with a little less attitude.

Thomas Boog *shell-shocked* `15 A1`
52 rue de Bourgogne, 7ème • 01 43 17 30 03
>> www.thomasboog.com Open 2–7 Mon, 11–7 Tue–Fri

Former shoe designer Thomas Boog is wild about shells, and it shows. He began by adorning candlesticks with them, but now he's moved on to bigger things: screens, mirror frames and chandeliers, as well as chairs made from driftwood. What's more, there's no hint of seaside kitsch in any of his creations.

The Best of the Galéries

The city's covered arcades were built in the 19th century as places for elegant ladies to promenade protected from the elements. These days, several are still attractive shopping havens. Stroll through the **Galérie Vivienne** (Map 10 F3), with its vaulted glass roof and mosaic floor, and shop for fashion at Jean-Paul Gaultier and Nathalie Garçon, or for artificial silk flowers at Emilio Robba. Nearby, the **Galérie Véro-Dodat** (Map 10 F4) houses art galleries, antiques dealers, Italian leatherware at Il Bisonte, and the purple headquarters of couture make-up queen, by Terry *(see p64)*. Farther north, the **Passage du Grand Cerf** (Map 10 H3) is a hotbed of creativity boasting everything from hat- and jewellery-makers to ceramic artists and furniture designers.

lunx *exclusive scents* `15 D1`

48–50 rue de l'Université, 7ème • 01 45 44 50 14
Open 10:30–7 Mon–Sat

lunx is a high-tech perfumery with state-of-the art
equipment. Despite the rather daunting, minimalist
design, staff are approachable and knowledgeable.
You'll soon be seduced by the store's range of creams,
gels, scented candles and ten exclusive fragrances
created by in-house "nose" Olivia Giacobetti.

Publicis Drugstore *Champs-Elysées icon* `8 F1`

133 avenue des Champs-Elysées, 8ème • 01 44 43 79 00
>> www.publicisdrugstore.com
Open 8am–2am Mon–Fri, 10am–2am Sat & Sun

Now encased in curved glass screens, this long-
established fixture on the Champs-Elysées is one of
the city's hip hangouts. Inside are restaurants, bars,
cinemas and stores, including a news kiosk (with
international press), a gift shop and a pharmacy.

Renaud Pellegrino *handbag maestro* `9 B2`

14 rue du Faubourg-St-Honoré, 8ème • 01 42 65 35 52
Open 10–7 Mon–Sat

For over 20 years, Renaud Pellegrino has been mixing
fabrics and techniques and turning out exceptional
handbags: a silk bag in the shape of a matchbox, one
dusted with Murano glass pearls, another in multi-
coloured leather and linen. Many of his creations are
inspired by the canvasses of Matisse and Braque.

Department Stores

From cutting-edge designs to must-have basics,
the city's department stores cater to all needs and
tastes. France's oldest is the swanky **Bon Marché**.
With its serious men's and women's fashion, Paris's
best lingerie selection, and photo and fashion
exhibitions, it is ideal for a bout of relaxed retail
therapy. Over on the Right Bank, **Galéries Lafayette**
has bigger crowds but offers all the top designers,
a water and champagne bar, and the chic Lafayette
Maison for homewares. The largest beauty hall of
all Parisian department stores belongs to **Printemps**:
two floors and 200 brands of make-up, fragrances
and skin care. They've also got a luxury fashion
floor and a men's store with the Nickel spa *(see
p169)*. For further details, *see p227*.

>> *In May and October, the Passage du Grand Cerf hosts the* Puces du Design *(flea market for designer goods)*

Shopping

Guerlain *classic fragrances* `8 G2`
68 avenue des Champs-Elysées, 8ème • 01 45 62 11 21
Open 11–7 Mon–Sat

This 180-year-old perfume house's glittering redesign included 350,000 pieces of gold mosaic and the addition of an immense chandelier. Have one of those famous crystal bottles filled at the "fragrance fountain", shop for limited re-editions of Guerlain classics, or have your own perfume made to measure.

Erès *make a splash* `9 C1`
2 rue Tronchet, 8ème • 01 47 42 28 82
>> www.eres.fr Open 10–7 Mon–Sat

If you cringe at the thought of donning a swimsuit, Erès is a must. This chi-chi shop is one reason why so many Frenchwomen look good on the beach: its perfectly cut bathing suits in appealing colours are flattering beyond belief, and bikini tops and bottoms are sold separately. They also do a range of underwear.

Galerie Noémie *face painting* `8 F1`
92 avenue des Champs-Elysées, 8ème • 01 45 62 78 27
>> www.galerienoemie.com Open 11–7 Mon–Thu (to 9 Fri & Sat)

Created by young painter Noémie Rocher, this make-up store puts an arty spin on cosmetics. Products are presented on artist's palettes and packaged in sweet little pots and paint tubes. Book in to have your face painted by a professional make-up artist or a bespoke shade of lip gloss specially mixed for you.

Zadig & Voltaire (de luxe) *eclectic* `8 G3`
18–20 rue François Premier, 8ème • 01 40 70 97 89
>> www.zadig-et-voltaire.com Open 10–7 Mon–Sat

Zadig & Voltaire – the French fashion and accessories line aimed at 20–45-year-olds – has boutiques all over the city, but this is their most up-market to date. In the light, airy space that is perfumed with the store's scented candles, label fans will find the design collective's own clothes mixed with choice items by Chloé, Diane von Furstenberg, Alberta Ferretti et al, plus sought-after jeans by Paper Denim. Clothes are displayed on colour-coordinated rails and the staff have a good eye for putting together outfits.

Accessories include Marc Jacobs shoes, Jamin Puech bags, Kathy Korvin jewellery and gorgeous high-heeled sandals by hot designer Jean-Michel Cazabat. The shop's philosophy of offering chic but affordable "urban luxury" also applies to the new jewellery line, mylittlejewelsdeluxe. Pieces are designed to be worn at any time of day or night.

Make Up For Ever Professional   8 H1
5 rue de la Boétie, 8ème • 01 53 05 93 30
>> www.makeupforever.fr Open 10–7 Mon–Sat

When make-up gurus Dany Sanz and Jacques Waneph created this cosmetics range in 1984 it was strictly for showbiz clients and modelling agencies. Today, the beauty emporium has widened its horizons and distributes selectively to France's main department stores. However, none can compete with this flagship boutique, which features their whole range.

A veritable Ali Baba's cave of colour, the showroom-cum-shop stocks everything from fake tattoos to their signature Pan Cake foundation. Beauty buffs will appreciate bestsellers such as Palette 5 Crèmes de Camouflage, designed to hide blemishes and scars, and Lip Plus Fixateur de Rouge à Lèvres, which helps keep lipstick in place for hours. Sanz and Waneph are also responsible for the latest arrival on Paris's cosmetics scene – the nearby Make Up For Ever Academy (8 rue de Liège, 01 53 05 93 43).

Résonances   *upscale home accessories*   9 C2
3 & 5 boulevard Malesherbes, 8ème • 01 44 51 63 70
>> www.resonances.fr Open 10–8 Mon–Sat

Walking into this bright and airy shop (one in a chain), with its aproned staff, is a bit like entering a time warp. However, while it might appear a little old-fashioned, Résonances is anything but. A cross between a bookshop, a DIY store and home-interiors shop, the store carries a wide range of traditional French wares updated for urban sophisticates.

There are accessories for every room: pint-sized cups for that first-of-the-day coffee, ceramic butter dishes and stainless-steel fruit presses for the kitchen; a multitude of soaps, lotions and towels for the bathroom; and cedar hangers and cushions for the bedroom. In addition to cookbooks, there are interior-design manuals that provide inspiration for renovations (as well as plenty of DIY gadgets to help them along), while wine buffs will appreciate a wall-mounted corkscrew that defies being misplaced.

Shopping

Roger Vivier *footwear as art* `9 B2`
29 rue du Faubourg-St-Honoré, 8ème • 01 53 43 00 00
>> www.rogervivier.com Open 10–7 Mon–Sat

Roger Vivier, the revered French shoe designer famous for his creations for Dior and YSL, died in 1998. But his legend lives on thanks to this boutique created by Italian shoe maestro Bruno Frisoni and his muse, Inès de la Fressange. Its upper floor resembles a chic Parisian apartment, where 18th-century antiques are cleverly mixed with futuristic furniture by Hervé Van der Straeten (*see p78*) and the walls are hung with art.

Rather than simply reproducing classic styles from the archives, Frisoni has updated the shoes by introducing contemporary twists. Vivier's famous curving Choc heel thus becomes the Choc-Choc, a vertiginous shoe in lime-green crocodile skin. Other revamped classics include Zorro, a shoe whose fine straps resemble the classic crusader's mask, and a more tapered version of the square-toed ballerinas Vivier created to go with YSL's famous Mondrian dress.

Stephane Kélian *fancy footwork* `9 C2`
5 rue du Faubourg-St-Honoré, 8ème • 01 44 51 64 19
>> www.stephane-kelian.fr Open 10–7 Mon–Sat

Slip your just-pedicured feet into a pair of Kélian's top-of-the-line shoes if you plan to stroll the streets in style, before hitting that upscale bar. You'll find practical (but never boring) flatties, wedges and lofty stilettos; Kélian is a rare soul who can successfully create both the classic and the fabulously fashionable.

The Golden Triangle
Trawling the three main shopping arteries of the ultra-chic *8ème* is a quintessential Right Bank experience. Start at couture heartland on avenue Montaigne with a visit to **Dior**, **Chanel** and **Christian Lacroix** and perhaps a stop-off at **Louis Vuitton**. Alternatively, shop Italian-style, taking in **Prada**, **Emmanuel Ungaro**, **Valentino**, **Dolce & Gabbana**, **Marni** and the **Gucci** mega-store. Avenue George V is home to **Givenchy**, **Balenciaga** and **Jean-Paul Gaultier** 's new Starck-designed HQ. The vibe is trendier and less intimidating on rue du Faubourg-St-Honoré: after **Chloé**, **Lanvin** and **Bottega Veneta**, head down to rue St-Honoré for **John Galliano** 's outrageous fashions and the mother of Paris concept stores, **Colette**. For further details, *see pp227–8*.

Artazart *cult canal bookshop* `11 C1`
83 quai de Valmy, 10ème • 01 40 40 24 00
>> www.artazart.com Open 10:30–7:30 Mon–Fri, 2–8 Sat & Sun

Artazart is *the* place to stock up on books (mostly French) and international magazines that deal with everything from fashion and interiors to calligraphy. The interior of the store is decorated by French graffiti artist Miss Tic. Artazart is also a great spot to pick up the latest flyers for hot club nights and local events.

Ginger Lyly *funky designs* `11 C2`
33 rue Beaurepaire, 10ème • 01 42 06 07 73
Open 11–7 Mon–Sat, 3–7 Sun

With its brightly painted frontage, Ginger Lyly draws a hip crowd on the look-out for groovy clothes and accessories. Vivid T-shirts and off-the-wall bags feature along with chintzy jewellery and raggedy hats. Walls host exhibitions by local artists and there is always some up-to-the-minute music in the air.

Antoine & Lili *colourful kitsch* `11 C1`
95 quai de Valmy, 10ème • 01 40 37 41 55
>> www.altribu.com
Open 11–8 Tue–Fri, 10–8 Sat, 11–7 Sun & Mon

The brightly painted façades of these three adjoining boutiques echo that of their contents. Young designs in vibrant colours are found in the pink house; fresh flowers, plants and homewares populate the green house; while the yellow house houses a funky café.

E2 *everything old is new again* `11 A1`
15 rue Martel, 10ème • 01 47 70 15 14
Open by appointment only

Husband-and-wife design team Michèle and Olivier Châtenet buy up classy vintage clothing (think Pucci, Hermès and Dior) and then transform it into modern must-haves. Imagine embroidered kilts, favoured by Gwyneth Paltrow and Madonna, or a whole new made-to-order outfit fashioned from a groovy old kimono.

Stella Cadente *canal style* `11 C1`
93 quai de Valmy, 10ème • 01 42 09 27 00
>> www.stella-cadente.com Open 11–7:30 daily

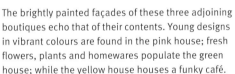

The boutique-cum-living-room of Stella Cadente (alias Ukranian-born designer Stanislassia Klein) was one of the first to appear on this street that fronts the now-trendy Canal St-Martin. Her dreamy, girly dresses, beaded cardigans and coats lined with flashy colours fit right in with the local, arty vibe.

Viveka Bergström *fantasy creations* `5 D5` ✓

23 rue de la Grange-aux-Belles, 10ème • 01 40 03 04 92
⟫ www.viveka-bergstrom.com Open noon–7 Tue–Sat

After honing her design skills at Paco Rabanne, innovative Swedish jeweller Viveka set up this cosy boutique, complete with home-from-home coffee tables and sofas. The designer, who works from a studio out back, is renowned for her pieces made from leather, precious metals and Swarovski crystals.

Coin Canal *retro heaven* `11 C1`

1 rue de Marseille, 10ème • 01 42 38 00 33
⟫ www.coincanal.com Open 11–2 & 3–7:30 Mon–Fri, 11–7:30 Sat

This corner shop is filled with lovingly selected pieces from the 1930s to the present day. Items are arranged in "rooms" and everything you see is for sale; from the Art-Deco drinks trolley to 1950s vases displayed on a 1960s wooden sideboard. Paintings by a Chinese artist, also for sale, add a contemporary touch.

Patricia Louisor *elegant bohemian* `4 F3` ✓

16 rue Houdon, 18ème • 01 42 62 10 42
⟫ www.patricialouisor.com Open noon–8 daily

One of the original boutiques that sparked the buzz about trendy Abbesses's alternative fashion scene. Louisor puts her own stylish spin on easy-to-wear garments, such as wide-legged trousers, flowing coats and jackets, and sweet *cache-coeurs* (wraparound tops) in delicate knits. Prices are very reasonable.

Lili Perpink *Japanese pick-and-mix* `4 F2`

22 rue la Vieuville, 18ème • 01 42 52 37 24
Open 11:30–1:30 & 2:30–7:30 Tue–Sat

Scarcely bigger than a walk-in wardrobe, Lili's quirky little shop is a treasure trove of vintage fashion mixed with ultra-modern Japanese creations. Lili also keeps an eye out for up-and-coming European designers, stocking elaborate hand-knits by Irish designer No and feminine prints by French designer Julie Greux.

Spree *eclectic concept store*   `4 F2`
16 rue la Vieuville, 18ème • 01 42 23 41 40
Open 11–7:30 Tue–Sat, Mon 2–7:30

When you first walk past Spree's window, it's hard to work out whether this is a retro furniture store, modern art gallery or cutting-edge fashion haven. The interior is punctuated with original Charles Eames and George Nelson chairs, and hung with Calder-like mobiles and 1960s Murano disc chandeliers, all of which can be bought. The warehouse-like space at the back of the store is devoted to fashion and boasts an excellent selection of international designers, including Comme des Garçons, Eley Kishimoto, Vanessa Bruno and Isabel Marant. Accessories scattered around the store include retro-style bags by Aurélie Mathigot, rings (designed to look as if they pierce your finger) by Pièces à Conviction and surreal silver jewellery by hip French label Lyie van Rycke. Spree is also the only place in Paris to find handmade ballerina shoes by E Porselli, otherwise available only in Italy.

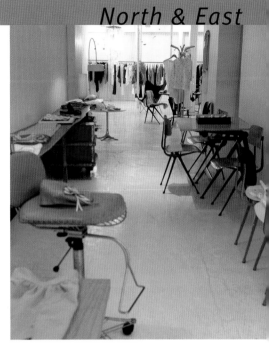

Shine *cutting-edge style*   `18 F2`
30 rue de Charonne, 11ème • 01 48 05 80 10
Open 11–7:30 Mon–Sat, 2–7 Sun

This trendy store (for women and men) stocks clothes from young designers mixed in with a sprinkling of urban sportswear and big-name labels, as well as unusual accessories. Highlights include Cacharel, See by Chloé and UK label Preen, and the delicate handknits of Macedonian designer Lidiya Georgieva.

Nuits de Satin *antique glamour*   `11 D4`
9 rue Oberkampf, 11ème • 01 43 57 65 05
➤➤ www.nuitsdesatin.com Open 12:30–7:30 Mon–Sat

An essential stop for anyone on the look-out for second-hand silk and satin lingerie. Choose from early 1900s corsets, pointy 1930s satin brassieres and sassy 50s swimsuits and suspenders. There's a good selection of groovy retro designer threads, too. No wonder this boutique is a favourite of stylists.

Shopping

Isabel Marant *ethnic chic* 18 E2
16 rue de Charonne, 11ème • 01 49 29 71 55
Open 10:30–7:30 Mon–Sat

Fashion hounds flock to this spacious Bastille boutique for Marant's youthful designs with an exotic edge. This is one designer who looks like she has some fun at her drawing board. Marant's imaginative designs favour natural fibres, often combined to create luxury items with a bohemian feel; a style that has made her one of Paris's top young designers. Clothes hang perfectly, especially fluid jersey dresses; flirty, floral tops and lots of silks and satin. When chilly winds blow, there's more substantial gear, including nubbly wool skirts cut on the bias, boiled wool coats with appliquéd or embroidered details, mohair jumpers and hippy-style bobble hats.

Recently, Marant has expanded to add accessories to her collection, in the shape of sassy bags and shoes, jewellery (delicate drop earrings and graceful silver necklaces) and perky singlets and shorts.

Alter Mundi *other worlds* 12 E5
41 rue du Chemin Vert, 11ème • 01 40 21 08 91
>> www.altermundi.com Open 11–7:30 Tue–Sat, 2–7 Sun

This boutique-cum-gallery, housed in a vast loft-like space, operates on the principles of fair trade and showcases furniture and *objets d'art* from the developing world. Highlights include sandalwood vases from Mozambique, papier-maché sculptures from Burkina Faso and Mexican silver jewellery.

La Maison de la Fausse Fourrure 17 D1
34 boulevard Beaumarchais, 11ème • 01 43 55 24 21
>> www.maisondelafaussefourrure.fr
Open 10–7 Mon–Sat (Mar–Aug: Mon–Fri)

Those who have qualms about following catwalk fur trends can ease their conscience by visiting this store. Stock up on everything from fake-fur fabric to imitation leopard-skin bags and tigerskin coats to furry lampshades and other household accessories.

Bastille Fashion Focus   18 F2

The 11th *arrondissement* tends to be associated with its nightlife buzz, but a daytime visit reveals a hive of independent fashion activity. One of the first young designers to open her *atelier-boutique* on rue Keller was **Gaëlle Barré** *(see p227)*. This young woman turns out finely tailored collections based on mixing and matching prints. Indeed, her whimsical, feminine creations often fuse polka-dots, stripes and floral patterns, all on the same garment.

Fellow rue Keller pioneer **Anne Willi** *(see p227)* works with a much more muted palette of colours, and natural fabrics such as linen and embroidered cotton. The simplicity of her style and her reversible clothes have been influenced by Japanese designers such as Yohji Yamamoto, but the charm of Willi's collections lies in the unusual details: halter-neck dresses tying with straps that dangle pebbles down the back or skirts decorated with criss-cross lacing up the side. Continuing along the street, **Des Petits Hauts** *(see p228)* is just what its name says – a boutique specializing in "little tops" of every imaginable shape and colour. Styles range from casual khaki T-shirts and basic jumpers to strappy sorbet-coloured shift tops and sophisticated black evening-wear.

On the rue de Charonne, **Florence Gaillard**'s *(see p227)* candy-pink boutique makes the perfect showcase for her floaty, feminine collections, full of flounces and girlie frills. Feathers waft fetchingly from necklines, butterflies alight delicately on shoulder straps and bags and jewellery come in assorted pastel colours that complement the clothes.

art &
architecture

The city's great historic
monuments have survived world
wars intact, and its cultural
treasures extend well beyond
its enduring landmarks – many
lesser known museums are set in
stunning mansions. But Paris
knows better than to rest on its
laurels: new architectural and
cultural projects sit next to the old,
in harmonious juxtaposition.

ART & ARCHITECTURE

Paris is blessed with an abundance of monuments, museums and galleries: even if you have lived in the city for years, it is always possible to discover something new – even just a piece of striking architecture in a side street that you notice for the first time. I love the smaller, convivial museums that focus on a single artist, but I also regularly return to the big-player art museums for their superbly conceived temporary exhibitions.

Richard Woodruff

Outdoor Attractions

History buffs shouldn't miss the **Arènes de Lutèce** *(see p104)*. Tucked away on the Left Bank, these are the city's best-preserved Roman remains. Art fans can stroll in the **Musée Rodin's** *(see p107)* sculpture garden and admire **Nemo's Murals** *(see p117)*. A boat trip on the **Canal St-Martin** *(see p112)* offers a whole new perspective on the city.

Ecclesiastical Highs

While the Gothic masterpiece of **Notre Dame** *(see p13)* is more popular, the 12th-century **Basilique St-Denis** *(see p114)* is widely considered the birthplace of this architectural genre. The classical, colonnaded **Madeleine** *(see p108)* boasts remarkable marble altars, and **St-Sulpice** *(see p105)* features some splendid Delacroix murals.

Hottest Temporary Exhibitions

The **Centre Pompidou's** *(see p13)* exhibitions are so successful they regularly travel abroad. It's also worth braving the queues for shows at the **Musée du Luxembourg** *(see p105)*. Twentieth-century artists are offered well-conceived retrospectives at the **Musée Maillol** *(see p107)*, while photographers get the limelight at the **Jeu de Paume** *(see p100)*.

choice sights

Cutting-Edge Creation

Paris boasts a vibrant art scene, most trendily exemplified by the small galleries on rue **Louise Weiss** *(see p118)* and the **Fondation Cartier** *(see p119)*. **Les Frigos** *(see p118)* is often dubbed the hub of contemporary creativity, but the **Palais de Tokyo** *(see p110)* excels in pushing artistic boundaries with its outlandish installations.

Modern Architecture

The **Bibliothèque François Mitterrand** *(see p117)* is the showpiece of the Zac Rive Gauche area, linked to the Parc de Bercy by the Simone de Beauvoir footbridge (Map 22 F2). Further upriver, the stylish **Institut du Monde Arabe** *(see p103)* and the **Musée du Quai Branly** *(see p106)* are both the work of popular contemporary architect Jean Nouvel.

One-Man Shows

Many of Paris's former artist residents now have their own museums. **Gustave Moreau** *(see p115)* even conceived his before his death, while the studio of **Constantin Branucsi** *(see p103)* has been carefully re-created. For a more grandiose experience, head to the **Musée Picasso** *(see p101)*, housed in an elegant 17th-century *hôtel particulier*.

Art & Architecture

Eglise St-Eustache *city landmark* `10 G4`
2 impasse St-Eustache, 1er • 01 42 36 31 05
>> www.st-eustache.org • Open 9:30–7 daily

The city's second-biggest church after Notre Dame *(see p13)*, St-Eustache (built 1532–1640) witnessed Louis XIV's first Communion and holds the tomb of his influential finance minister, Jean-Baptiste Colbert. Its imposing exterior is Gothic, while the interior is decidedly Renaissance.

Jeu de Paume *films and photos* `9 C3`
1 place de la Concorde, 1er • 01 47 03 12 52
>> www.jeudepaume.org
Open noon–9 Tue, noon–7 Wed–Fri, 10–7 Sat & Sun

Once an indoor court for real tennis, the Jeu de Paume is now a museum of photography and film. Shows are either retrospective or thematic, and have included a retrospective of photographer and filmmaker Cindy Sherman and British artist Craigie Horsfield. **Adm**

Bibliothèque Nationale de France Richelieu *exhibition space* `10 F3`
58 rue de Richelieu, 2ème • 01 53 79 59 59
>> www.bnf.fr Galleries open 10–5 Mon–Sat

Stripped of books since the new national library *(see p117)* opened in 1996, the original is still worth visiting for its breathtaking domed Salle Labrouse and for the frescoed galleries that host temporary exhibitions of mostly modern photography, drawings and engravings.

Musée de la Publicité *adverts as art* `10 E4`
107 rue de Rivoli, 1er • 01 44 55 57 50
>> www.museedelapub.org Open 11–6 Tue–Fri, 10–6 Sat & Sun

Temporary shows organized by theme (psychedelic posters), artist (Rene Gruau) or brand (Air France), and drawn from a fantastic array of posters, press ads and radio and TV commercials, are held within this wing of the Louvre. From the kitsch to the stylish, this collection acknowledges the power of persuasion. **Adm**

Paris Museum Pass
Providing entry to 60 of the city's biggest sights and museums, including the Musée Picasso and Musée d'Orsay, this card lets culture aficionados cut costs and queues. Valid for two, four or six consecutive days, it is available from participating museums, branches of **fnac** *(see p229)* and tourist offices. *(See www.parismuseumpass.com)*

Musée National Picasso *100% Pablo* `11 C5`

5 rue Thorigny, 3ème • 01 42 71 25 21
>> www.musee-picasso.fr
Open 9:30–5:30 Wed–Mon (summer: to 6)

On Picasso's death in 1973, the French state waived the hefty inheritance taxes due in return for prime pickings from the artist's home and studio. Subsequent donations make this one of the most complete collections of Picasso's works, and one so popular that there are often long queues to get in.

The museum's exhibits – remarkable for their sheer diversity – are a chronological record of the artist's life, from his simple but accomplished teenage sketches, through paintings of the famed Blue and Rose periods, to massive sculptures of Cubist heads. Must-sees include a series of little-known paper constructions; *Bull's Head* a witty bronze combining a bicycle saddle and handlebars to resemble the animal's head); and tribal masks from Picasso's own collection which clearly inspired his work. **Adm**

Musée Carnavalet *historical collection* `17 C1`

23 rue de Sevigné, 3ème • 01 44 59 58 58
Open 10–6 Tue–Sun

With a superb setting and exhibits that include paintings, furniture and personal artefacts, the Musée Carnavalet's colossal collection offers an authoritative and highly engaging history of Paris. Occupying two buildings, the museum was founded by Baron Haussmann, who had the foresight to preserve some of the Paris he was demolishing as he reshaped the city in the mid-1800s. The 16th-century Hôtel Carnavalet, one of the Marais' oldest *hôtels particuliers*, focuses on Paris from prehistoric times up until the 1700s. Its rooms are furnished with fabulous period furniture and paintings. The neighbouring *hôtel* picks up the story from 1789 to the present day and has France's biggest collection of Revolutionary exhibits. Check out the painting of Danton with his gargantuan head; in comparison, the portrait of fellow revolutionary Robespierre shows a far less powerful and rather prim leader. **Adm**

Art & Architecture

Musée d'Art et d'Histoire du Judaïsme
celebrating the Jewish diaspora

71 rue du Temple, 3ème • 01 53 01 86 60
>> www.mahj.org Open 11–6 Mon–Fri, 10–6 Sun

In the heart of the Jewish area, the Marais, this absorbing museum traces the history and art of Judaism from the Middle Ages to the present day. Look out for Emile Zola's original *J'accuse!* article that denounced state anti-Semitism in the 19th-century Dreyfus affair. **Adm**

Tour St-Jacques *medieval remnant* `16 H1`

Standing all alone on the place du Chatelet is a striking Gothic tower, the only remains of the 16th-century St-Jacques-La Boucherie church – a stopover point for pilgrims en route to Santiago de Compostela in Spain. Its gargoyle-covered summit witnessed the experiments into atmospheric pressure of French mathematician Blaise Pascal, whose statue stands outside. Aptly, the tower now serves as a weather station.

Patrimoine Photographique *photos* `17 C2`

62 rue St-Antoine, 4ème • 01 42 74 47 75
>> www.jeudepaume.org Open noon–7 Tue–Fri, 10–7 Sat & Sun

Twinned with the Jeu de Paume at Concorde *(see p100)* and hidden away in a peaceful garden at the back of the 17th-century Hôtel de Sully, this intimate museum is the public exhibition space for the vast national photographic archives. Shows tend to revolve around historical themes or individual photographers. **Adm**

Les Galéries de Paris

In 19th-century Paris, the city's many *galeries* and *passages* served as fashionable meeting places as much as for shopping. With their attractive metal vaulting and glass roofs, they put most modern malls to shame. **Galerie Vivienne** (Map 10 F2) is the most upmarket; **Passages des Panoramas** (Map 10 F3), built in 1800, is the oldest.

Sainte-Chapelle *island chapel* `16 G1`

4 boulevard du Palais, 1er • 01 53 40 60 80
>> www.monum.fr Open 9:30–6 daily

Hidden inside the Palais de Justice, this magical two-tiered Gothic chapel was built to house what Louis IX believed to be Christ's crown of thorns. Make straight for the upper level, which is spectacularly illuminated by huge, panoramic stained-glass windows, most of which date from the 13th century. **Adm**

Musée Cognacq-Jay *art museum* `17 C1`
8 rue Elzévir, 4ème • 01 40 27 07 21
Open 10–6 Tue–Sun

Founders of La Samaritaine department store,
Ernest Cognacq and his wife Louise Jay were also
keen collectors, notably of Rococo artists. Their
predilection for the 18th century is in evidence here,
with pieces that include gorgeous period furniture
and exquisite Saxe and Sèvres ceramics. **Adm**

Atelier Brancusi *reconstructed studio* `11 A5`
Place Centre Pompidou, 4ème • 01 44 78 12 33
» www.cnac-gp.fr Open 2–6 Wed–Mon

Part of the Centre Pompidou *(see p106)*, this space
houses the reconstructed Parisian studio of influential
Romanian sculptor Constantin Brancusi (1876–1957).
Three cosy galleries display examples of his elegant,
abstract works, while another hosts temporary shows
by modern sculptors such as Richard Deacon. **Adm**

Maison Européenne de la Photographie *picture perfect* `17 B1`
5–7 rue de Fourcy, 4ème • 01 44 78 75 00
» www.mep-fr.org Open 11–8 Wed–Sun

Of all the city's show spaces dedicated to photography,
this one is possibly the best. The venue – with its
vast, high-ceilinged rooms – usually organizes
several simultaneous temporary exhibitions,
drawing on its own and other collections. **Adm**

Institut du Monde Arabe *Arab centre* `17 B3`
1 rue des Fossés St-Bernard, 5ème • 01 40 51 38 38
» www.imarabe.org Museum open 10–6 Tue–Sun

Jean Nouvel's acclaimed building mixes modern steel
and glass with traditional Arab architecture to stunning
effect. The south-facing windows operate like a
camera aperture, automatically regulating light.
Inside, a museum houses a wide range of Arabic art
and artifacts, as well as temporary exhibitions. **Adm**

Musée National du Moyen Age `16 G3`

6 place Paul-Painlevé, 5ème • 01 53 73 78 00
>> www.musee-moyenage.fr Open 9:15–5:45 Wed–Mon

Built into the ruins of Roman baths, this handsome 15th-century mansion was formerly home to the Abbots of Cluny; it now houses a vast collection of medieval sculpture, ceramics, stained glass, furniture and tapestries. The baths themselves are a prime example of Gallo-Roman architecture: the frigidarium is spectacular, with its 15-m- (50-ft-) high vaults and traces of original mosaics. Key architectural finds from around Paris are displayed here, including the "Gallery of Kings": 21 carved stone heads, depicting the Kings of Judah, which were housed in Notre Dame for 500 years, but moved here just after the French Revolution. The museum's showpiece, however, is *The Lady and the Unicorn*, a series of six radiant Flemish tapestries. Don't overlook the museum's grounds, landscaped to echo gardening fashions of the Middle Ages. **Adm**

La Sorbonne *long-established centre of learning* `16 G3`

47 rue des Ecoles, 5ème • 01 40 46 22 11
>> www.sorbonne.fr Open to the public 7–7 Mon–Fri

Founded as a theology college in the 1200s, La Sorbonne quickly gained a reputation as an intellectual stronghold. Classes were taught in Latin, giving rise to the area's name, Le Quartier Latin. The college was the hub of the student riots of 1968; if you want to get a taste of the more sedate student life of today, attend the free lectures open to the public or visit the gilded, domed 17th-century chapel.

Arènes de Lutèce *Roman recreation* `17 A5`

Entrances on 49 rue Monge & 7 rue de Navarre, 5ème • no phone
Open summer 8–9 daily; winter 8–5 daily (9–5 Sat & Sun)

A rare remnant of the city's Roman past, this late 1st-century amphitheatre was unearthed in 1869. For 200 years, it welcomed up to 17,000 spectators at gladiatorial combats, until the Barbarians invaded Lutèce (Paris). Today, the games played here are less bloody; it's a favourite with *boules* players and skateboarders.

Musèe de l'Assistance Publique `17 A3`
47 quai de la Tournelle, 5ème • 01 40 27 50 05
» www.aphp.fr Open 10–6 Tue–Sun

This quirky museum traces the history of hospitals in Paris. Their social and religious roles are brought to life by paintings, manuscripts and a reconstructed pharmacy. Early surgical instruments also feature, including some oversized dental pliers that are a reassuring reminder of just how far medicine has come. **Adm**

Eglise Royale du Val-de-Grâce `20 F1`
227bis rue St-Jacques, 5ème • 01 40 27 50 05
Open noon–5 Tue–Wed, 1–5 Sat, 1:30–5 Sun

Built as a Benedictine abbey in the 17th century, this imposing complex includes a fine Baroque chapel and a museum on the history of the French military medical service. Gruesome exhibits include casts of the faces of disfigured soldiers who were the first subjects of maxilo-facial surgery during WWI. **Adm**

Musée du Luxembourg *art exhibitions* `16 E3`
19 rue de Vaugirard, 6ème • 01 42 34 25 95
» www.museeduluxembourg.fr
Open 11–7 Tue–Thu, 11–10 Fri–Sat & Mon, 9–7 Sun

This museum's popular temporary shows are based around two themes: the Italian Renaissance (in tribute to the palace's founder, Marie de Médici) and 19th- and 20th-century art (a nod to the venue's previous incarnation as a modern-art museum). **Adm**

Eglise St-Sulpice *Left Bank church* `16 E3`
Place St-Sulpice, 6ème • 01 42 34 59 98
Open 7:30–7:30 daily

Similar in size and layout to Notre Dame, St-Sulpice demonstrates an intriguing mix of architectural styles because it took 120 years to build, starting in 1646. Its Italianate façade is topped by two famously uneven towers. Inside, there are three notable Delacroix frescoes in the Chapelle des Sts-Anges.

Art & Architecture

Musée National Eugène Delacroix 16 E2
6 rue de Furstenberg, 6ème • 01 44 41 86 50
>> www.musee-delacroix.fr Open 9:30–5 Wed–Mon

The former apartment and studio of Romantic painter
Delacroix (1798–1863) now house an intimate
museum displaying his paintings and engravings,
and tracing his life via photographs, personal
belongings and letters. Drawings include studies for
his celebrated murals inside nearby St-Sulpice. **Adm**

Musée du Quai Branly *ethnographic art* 8 E5
55 quai Branly, 7ème • 01 56 61 70 00
>> www.quaibranly.fr 10–6:30 Tue–Sun (to 9:30 Thu)

This new heavyweight museum houses some 30,000
exhibits from the State's ethnographic collections. It
is one of the world's most extensive thanks to
colonialism and the influences of 20th-century thinkers such as Claude Lévi-Strauss. Must-see exhibits
include the fantastic array of African instruments, an
exquisite collection of Indonesian bows and arrows
and a set of 17th-century North American painted
animal hides that were once the pride of the French
royal family. Outside, the grounds offer visitors breathing space among paths, pools and almost 200 trees.

Designed to resemble the elongated shadow of
the nearby Eiffel Tower, the museum's Jean Nouvel-
designed building is impressive but many regard it
as President Chirac's attempt to emulate his
predecessor, President Mitterand, and to leave his
mark on the cityscape *(see below)*. **Adm**

Les Grands Projets

Paris's reputation may be grounded in its timeless
charm, but its cityscape has nonetheless undergone
some significant changes in the last 150 years. Most
radical was Baron Haussmann's reshaping of Paris
in the late 19th century. Charged by Napoleon III
with modernizing the city, Haussmann demolished
much of it to make room for the network of long,
wide boulevards that characterize the capital today.
Many of the city's ornate apartment buildings date
from this period, and are consequently referred to
as *Hausmannien*. Over 100 years later, President
Mitterrand's own *Grand Projets* brought about an
emblematic change to Paris in the shape of showcase modern architecture such as the Louvre
pyramid *(see p12)* and the Opéra Bastille *(see p128)*.

Musée Maillol – Fondation Dina Vierny *muse's collection*

`15 D2`

59–61 rue de Grenelle, 7ème • 01 42 22 59 58
≫ www.museemaillol.com Open 10–6 Wed–Mon

At the age of 15, Dina Vierny became the chief model and creative muse of French sculptor Aristide Maillol (1861–1944). Her subsequent collection of his work – and that of his friends and contemporaries – is show-cased in this grand *hôtel particulier*. Maillol's larger-than-life marble sculptures dominate the entrance hall, while his early years are well represented in rooms dedicated to his drawings, Nabi-influenced paintings and intricate tapestries. Other 20th-century artists featured include Gauguin, a major influence on Maillol, Pierre Bonnard and Maurice Denis *(see p112)*. Works by Picasso, Degas, Cézanne and Odilon Redon are illuminated in darkened drawing rooms, while conceptual art gets a look in with Marcel Duchamp's famed "Ready-Made" art. Note that the frequent temporary exhibitions can attract long queues. **Adm**

Musée Rodin *the sculptor's former home*

`15 A1`

77 rue de Varenne, 7ème • 01 44 18 61 10
≫ www.musee-rodin.fr
Open Apr–Sep 9:30–5:45 Tue–Sun (Oct–Mar to 4:45)

Along with artists Jean Cocteau and Henri Matisse, sculptor Auguste Rodin rented rooms in this *hôtel particulier* in 1908. Smitten with the state-owned pro-perty, he donated all his work, personal archives and belongings to the government in exchange for the foundation of a museum here. Inside, the huge bronze and marble sculptures include his famed *Kiss* and the headless *Walking Man*, as well as a number of works by Rodin's student and lover Camille Claudel. There are also paintings by Monet, Renoir and van Gogh from the artist's private collection, and furniture from his house in Meudon. The museum's real charm, however, lies outside in the spacious gardens, where *The Thinker* is framed by the gold-domed Invalides. Nearby are the triumphant *Burghers of Calais* and a masterful monument to Balzac. One of Paris's real gems. **Adm**

Art & Architecture

Eglise de la Madeleine *Classical church* 9 C2
Place de la Madeleine, 8ème • 01 44 51 69 00
>> www.eglise-lamadeleine.com Open 9–7 daily

Modelled on a Greek temple, the Madeleine church took almost 100 years to build. It was variously intended to be a stock exchange, a tribute to Napoleonic glory and a railway station before it was consecrated as a church in 1842. The magnificent marble-and-gilt interior features three stunning domes.

Eglise St-Augustin *high-rise church* 3 B5
46 boulevard Malesherbes, 8ème • 01 45 22 23 12
Open 8:30–7 daily (closed noon–2 Sun)

Built in 1860–71, this was the city's first church to incorporate a metal frame, allowing its dome to rise to 50 m (164 ft). Architect Victor Baltard filled the triangular site by placing progressively larger chapels along the nave. The painted ceilings are the work of Classicist artist William Bougereau.

Musée Jacquemart-André *wealthy collectors' home* 2 H5
158 boulevard Haussmann, 8ème • 01 45 62 11 59
>> www.musee-jacquemart-andre.com Open 10–6 daily

Dutch Masters, Italian Renaissance and 18th-century French art make the private collection of Edouard André and wife Nélie Jacquemart seem like a smaller, more manageable version of the Louvre. In addition, this purpose-built *hôtel particulier*'s opulent interior and contents create a fascinating record of 19th-century Parisian bourgeois life. **Adm**

Musée Galliéra *the story of style* 8 E3
10 avenue Pierre 1er de Serbie, 16ème • 01 56 52 86 00
Open 10–6 Tue–Sun

This museum of sartorial style has a vast collection of clothing, accessories and photos with which to stage temporary exhibitions for followers of fashion. Shows range from displays of 18th-century waistcoats to the glitzy wardrobe of Marlene Dietrich. The museum is closed for two or three months a year. **Adm**

Along the Champs-Elysées `8 G2`

It's been sung about, marched on, and plays host each year to the Bastille Day parade *(see p17)*, the Tour de France climax *(see p17)* and any other occasion for national celebration. Running from place de la Concorde up to the **Arc de Triomphe** *(see p14)*, the 3-km- (2-mile-) long avenue, built by Baron Haussmann as part of his grand plan for a new Paris, still exudes a certain grandeur, even though it has suffered from an invasion of tacky, touristy shops and food outlets.

At its lower end, the expansive but traffic-heavy place de la Concorde is dominated by a 3,300-year-old granite obelisk, a gift from the Viceroy of Egypt. From here to the midway roundabout, the Champs-Elysées is bordered by gardens on both sides. The northern stretch of greenery backs on to the high-security 18th-century presidential residence, the Palais de l'Elysée, while the southern side is dominated by the colossal glass dome of the **Grand Palais** *(see p230)* and neighbouring **Petit Palais** *(see p230)*, both remnants of the 1900 Exposition Universelle. The former hosts diverse, crowd-pulling temporary shows, while the latter is home to the city's fine-arts collection and has recently undergone a massive renovation programme to improve lighting, increase exhibition space and generally restore its former glory.

At the back of the Grand Palais, the **Palais de la Découverte** *(see p231)* is a child-friendly science museum with a planetarium and an array of inter-active exhibits relating to human biology, astronomy and meteorology. The hottest spot at the upper end of the avenue is the **Publicis Drugstore** *(see p87)*, reopened in 2004 after a daringly modern makeover by architect Michele Saee. The minimalist, curvaceous steel-and-glass-spiralled frontage sets it apart from its ornate, 19th-century neighbours.

Art & Architecture

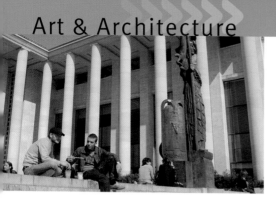

Musée d'Art Moderne de la Ville de Paris (MAMVP) *modern art*

8 E3

11 avenue du Président Wilson, 16ème • 01 53 67 40 00
Open 10–6 Tue–Sun

The city's impressive 20th-century art collection occupies part of the Palais de Tokyo, a vast building that was originally built for the 1937 Exposition Universelle. Showpieces include diptychs by Henri Matisse and Raoul Dufy's *La Fée Electricité*. **Adm**

Palais de Tokyo *contemporary art*

8 E4

13 avenue du Président Wilson, 16ème • 01 47 23 38 86
>> www.palaisdetokyo.com Open noon–midnight Tue–Sun

Complementing the adjoining MAMVP, this venue hosts cutting-edge art shows and installations. These are often site-specific, with artists creatively utilizing the vast proportions of the revamped interior. It's worth trying the basement restaurant, Tokyo Eat, for its designer good looks and food to match. **Adm**

Palais de Chaillot

7 C4

17 place du Trocadéro, 16ème
Musée de l'Homme • 01 44 05 72 72
>> www.mnhn.fr
Open 9:45–5:15 Mon & Wed–Fri, 10–6:30 Sat & Sun
Musée de la Marine • 01 53 65 69 69
>> www.musee-marine.fr Open 10–6 Wed–Mon
Cité de l'Architecture et du Patrimoine • 01 58 51 52 00

The curved twin pavilions of the Palais de Chaillot are separated by a large terrace that offers spectacular views of the Eiffel Tower. In the west wing, the Musée de la Marine features a wealth of surprisingly interesting exhibits – such as Napoleon I's flamboyant imperial barge – that trace the glories of French maritime history. Major redevelopment of the Palais has seen the scaling down of the Musée de l'Homme, while the Cité de l'Architecture et du Patrimoine occupies the entire east wing and includes historic casts of sections of heritage buildings, copies of medieval and Renaissance murals and a gallery dedicated to modern and contemporary architecture. **Adm**

Musée Marmottan-Monet *Monets galore*
2 rue Louis Boilly, 16ème • 01 44 96 50 33 • Ⓜ Ranelagh
>> www.marmottan.com Open 10–6 Tue–Sun

The Musée Marmottan-Monet boasts the world's largest collection of works by Claude Monet – all thanks to a generous donation by the artist's son. Rich pickings include an early series of Le Havre caricatures and a flurry of watercolours from travels to London, Normandy and Norway. The famous series of paintings of Rouen cathedral at different times of the day is also on show here. Don't miss the purpose-built basement, which displays a number of vibrant water-lily paintings inspired by the artist's garden at Giverny. Complementing the Monets are major works from fellow Impressionists Berthe Morisot, Manet, Degas, Renoir, Gauguin and Alfred Sisley. Most recently, the museum has added a collection of over 300 wonderfully crafted, medieval illuminated manuscripts from the English, French, Italian and Flemish schools. **Adm**

Musée Guimet *Oriental art*   `8 E3`
6 place d'Iéna, 16ème • 01 56 52 53 00
>> www.museeguimet.fr Open 10–6 Wed–Mon

The four floors of this excellent museum of Asian art contain *objets*, paintings and sculptures from most of the major Eastern cultures over five millennia. Highlights include exquisite Japanese wood-block prints, archaeological finds from Pondicherry in India, and Chinese ceramics. **Adm**

Fondation Le Corbusier *modern architecture*
Villa La Roche, 10 sq du Dr Blanche, 16ème • 01 42 88 41 53
>> www.fondationlecorbusier.asso.fr • Ⓜ Jasmin
Open 10–12:30 & 1:30–6 Mon–Fri (to 5pm Fri)

Modernist architect Le Corbusier designed this private house in 1923 for his fellow countryman, the Swiss art collector Raoul La Roche. The adjoining Villa Jeanneret was built for Le Corbusier's brother and is now home to the Foundation's offices. Originally conceived as part of a larger development, only these two houses were actually built. Pioneering his now-celebrated five points of architecture, Le Corbusier harnessed natural light and applied his Purist theory to the colour scheme. Villa La Roche itself, with its triple-height space, swooping curved gallery and blocks of colour, is the star of the show. Its rooms also feature small displays of the architect's paintings, furniture, drawings and sculpture. **Adm**

Château de St-Germain *notable château*
Place Charles de Gaulle St-Germain-en-Laye • 01 39 10 13 00
» www.musee-antiquitesnationales.fr
RER St-Germain-en-Laye
Open 9–5:15 Wed–Mon (May–Sep: 10–6 Sat & Sun)

This imposing castle is set next to the River Seine, in gardens that were designed by Le Nôtre in the 1680s. Most of the building dates from the 1500s and now houses an outstanding archaeological collection. **Adm**

Musée Départemental
Maurice Denis "Le Prieuré" *Nabi art*
2bis rue Maurice Denis, St-Germain-en-Laye • 01 39 73 77 87
» www.musee-mauricedenis.fr • RER St-Germain-en-Laye
Open 10–5.30 Tue–Sun (to 6.30 Sat & Sun)

An exceptional collection tracing the birth of early 20th-century avant-garde art, the museum here includes works by Denis and his fellow Nabi painters. Don't miss the pretty sculpture-lined garden and chapel. **Adm**

Canal St-Martin Boat Trip *Paris from the water* `17 D3`
Linking the Seine with the Canal d'Ourcq, the Canal St-Martin offers the opportunity to cruise through northern Paris. Barges (www.canauxrama.com) depart from Bastille's Port de l'Arsenal (9:45 & 2:30) and take two-and-a-half hours to travel through attractive tree-lined alleys, tunnels (look out for Keiichi Tahara's entrancing art installations), locks, and under swing bridges before arriving at Parc de la Villette. This large, modern park is also home to the Cité de la Musique *(see p129)*, Le Zenith *(see p130)* and Cité des Sciences et de l'Industrie *(see p114)*. **Adm**

Musée de l'Erotisme *erotic assemblage* `4 E3`
72 boulevard de Clichy, 18ème • 01 42 58 28 73
Open 10am–2am daily

The city's only museum that's open until 2am is, perhaps unsurprisingly, dedicated to erotic art and located in the red-light district of Pigalle. Ignore the tacky window displays; this is actually an intriguing collection where sacred *objets d'art* sit next to temporary exhibits by artists such as comic-book artist Robert Crumb. **Adm**

Montmartre *elevated attractions* `4 F2`

The hill of Montmartre has become even more tourist-struck since the worldwide success of the 2001 film *Amélie*. Most visitors previously stuck to the place du Tertre, with its hordes of caricaturists and wannabe artists, and the landmark **Sacré Cœur** church *(see p230)*, from which there are magnificent views of the city. Now, the tourist trail includes homages to *Amélie*'s local greengrocers, re-named Maison Collignon as in the film, and to her favourite bar, the **Café des Deux Moulins** *(see p221)*, the interior of which is hung with pictures of the leading lady, Audrey Tautou.

However, the real charm of Montmartre lies in its romantic, village atmosphere. Reminders of its past as a working-class, rural community (until absorbed into Paris in the late 19th century) include two windmills, the **Moulin de Radet** *(see p230)* and **Moulin de la Galette** *(see p230)*. Even some vineyards remain

here, like those on the rue des Saules (Map 4 F1), which produce around 1,000 bottles of perfectly drinkable wine each year.

From the 1880s, a bohemian boom attracted writers and artists aplenty: the Bateau-Lavoir (destroyed in the 70s) housed the studios of iconic painters Modigliani, Picasso and Braque; and the studios of Renoir and Dufy were located in what is now the **Musée de Montmartre** *(see p231)*. The museum offers an intriguing insight into the *quartier*'s artistic past and contains some original Toulouse-Lautrec posters. Nearby, the sculpture of a man apparently engulfed by the neighbouring wall is a tribute to Marcel Aymé's *Le Passe-Muraille*, a novel about a government worker who could walk through walls. Take a look at the fibre-optic lighting artwork installed in the stairs on rue du Chevalier de la Barre (Map 4 G1), which illuminates at night to form the shapes of different constellations.

Musée de la Musique *music matters*
Cité de la Musique, 221 avenue Jean Jaurès, 19ème
01 44 84 44 84 • Ⓜ Porte de Pantin
≫ www.cite-musique.fr Open noon–6 Tue–Sat, 10–6 Sun

With the benefit of infrared headsets, visitors can
sample sounds from Venetian lutes, Flemish harp-
sichords and a host of other instruments on display.
Each day on the free stage, musicians play everything
from 17th-century horns to modern African pipes. **Adm**

Cité des Sciences et de l'Industrie
Parc de la Villette, 30 avenue Corentin Cariou, 19ème
01 40 05 80 00 • Ⓜ Porte de Pantin
≫ www.cite-sciences.fr Open 10–6 Tue–Sat, 10–7 Sun

This well-planned centre presents science and
technology in their many forms via exhibits, audio-visual
installations and interactive displays. The complex also
contains the huge Géode dome cinema, a 3D film
theatre with moving seats, and a 1950s submarine. **Adm**

Stade de France *stunning arena*
rue Francis de Pressensé, St-Denis • 08 92 70 09 00
≫ www.stadefrance.fr • Ⓜ St-Denis Porte de Paris
Visits on the hour 10–5 daily (tours in English 10:30, 2:30)

The spectacular oval stadium dominating the St-Denis
skyline was built for the 1998 World Cup. Even the
cheapest of its 80,000 seats offers great visibility of
major sports events and rock concerts. Tours take
visitors into changing rooms and VIP boxes. **Adm**

Basilique St-Denis *royal mausoleum*
1 rue de la Légion d'Honneur, St-Denis • 01 48 09 83 54
Ⓜ Basilique de St-Denis
Open 10–7 Mon–Sat, noon–7 Sun (Oct–Mar to 5 daily)

An industrialized suburb it may be, but St-Denis, with
its majestic church, is generally considered the birthplace of Gothic architecture. It is also the resting place
for most of the French kings. Look out for the ostentatious tombs of François I and Claude de France. **Adm**

Musée d'Art et d'Histoire de St-Denis *local history*
22bis rue Gabriel Péri, St-Denis • 01 42 43 37 57
Ⓜ St-Denis Porte de Paris
Open 10–5:30 Mon–Fri (to 8 Thu), 2–6:30 Sat & Sun

Set in a former Carmelite convent, this museum alone merits a trip out to St-Denis. Highlights include the cramped reconstructed nuns' cells and a unique collection of posters from the 1871 Paris Commune. **Adm**

Musée Gustave Moreau *artist's home* `4 E4`
14 rue de la Rochefoucauld, 9ème • 01 48 74 38 50
≫ www.musee-moreau.fr Open 10–12:45 & 2–5:15 Wed–Mon

Troubled by the thought of anonymity, the Symbolist painter Moreau (1825–98) established an autobiographical museum in the studio and apartment he shared with his parents just before his death. Thousands of Moreau's often mystical paintings and drawings are on show, as well as memorabilia. **Adm**

Porte St-Denis & Porte St-Martin `11 A2`

These towering twin gates, just yards apart, were intended to lend the city a Roman grandeur. They are particularly striking today, in what has become a rather seedy part of north Paris. The larger Porte St-Denis was erected in 1672 and depicts battle scenes marking the triumph of Louis XIV's armies along the Rhine, while the Porte St-Martin was constructed two years later to commemorate the capture of Besançon.

Last Resting Places

Tree-lined **Cimetière de Père-Lachaise** is the largest, best-known cemetery in Paris. After the remains of dramatist Molière and poet La Fontaine were transferred here in 1817, it began attracting famed "residents" and skilled sculptors. The most visited grave is that of singer Jim Morrison; the quirkiest is the statue of 19th-century journalist Victor Noir: women rub his now-faded crotch to increase their chances of getting pregnant. The famous dead of **Cimetière de Montmartre** include the writer Zola, painter Degas and film director François Truffaut. Meanwhile, the tiny **Cimetière de Passy** has the highest density of famous names. Look out for the painter Manet, composers Debussy and Fauré, and actor Fernandel. For details, *see p229*.

≫ *The Cité des Sciences et de l'Industrie (see p114) can be reached by boat along the Canal St-Martin (see p112)*

Art & Architecture

Opéra Garnier *lavish venue* 9 D1

Place de l'Opéra, 9ème • 08 92 89 90 90

>> www.opera-de-paris.fr Open 10:30–4:30 daily (not matinées)

Architect Charles Garnier's national opera house is a glorious monument to Second Empire opulence. The façade is magnificently decorated with friezes and sculptures, while the interior is no less impressively embellished. A museum traces opera history via paintings, photographs and set models. **Adm**

Gare du Nord *monumental railway station* 5 A4

Opened in 1864 to cope with the rapidly increasing traffic on the railways, architect Jacques Ignace Hittorff's station is a grandiose example of 19th-century iron-and-glass vaulting, often overlooked by rail travellers rushing from A to B. The vast interior is fronted by an imposing, Roman-inspired stone façade lined with statues that personify the north European towns served by the station.

Seine-side Attractions

Few people know that a scaled-down **Statue of Liberty** (Map 13 B3) stands guard on an island in the Seine in the west of Paris. Donated in 1885 by the American community in Paris, it also acts as a reminder that the New York original was a gift from the French. Towards the city centre, on the river's right bank by the Place d'Alma, the golden **Liberty Flame** (Map 8 F4) is a return gift from the city of New York. Its proximity to the tunnel where Princess Diana was killed has made it her unofficial memorial. Between these two stands Gustave Eiffel's world-famous tower, which has long survived its status as a temporary exhibit for the 1889 Exposition Universelle. The **Eiffel Tower**'s *(see p12)* recently added white lights sparkle on every nocturnal hour until 2am, and cause almost as much controversy today as the tower did when it was first erected.

Opposite the sculpture-filled **Jardin des Tuileries** *(see p171)*, the colonnaded **Assemblée Nationale** *(see p230)* is the French parliament, which can be visited on a guided tour. Further east lies the domed home to the **Académie Française** (Map 16 E1), protector of the French language. Beyond here, the Seine is divided by the **Ile de la Cité** (Map 16 G2), the largest of Paris's two central islands and home to the city's iconic Gothic cathedral, **Notre Dame** *(see p230)*. On the island's other side, the turreted **Conciergerie** *(see p230)* was a 14th-century palace and, more famously, the prison of Marie Antoinette and family. Visitors here can learn about the French Revolution and view the reconstructed royal cell.

Of the 37 Seine bridges, the most spectacular is the Art Nouveau **Pont Alexandre III** (Map 9 A4), lined with gilded lamps and cherubs. The **Pont des Arts** (Map 10 F5) is popular for romantic rendezvous.

Nemo's Murals *public art* `12 2H`

Graffiti artist Nemo has been stencilling his "Shadow Man" on building façades around Paris since 1990. The silhouetted figure with its trademark suitcase pops up in poorer districts, like the 20th *arrondissement* (most spectacularly at 36 rue Henri Chevreau). Such is Nemo's notoriety that he now receives commissions, including a project around rue Mouffetard in the *5ème* to commemorate the Bièvre, Paris's underground river.

Ministère des Finances *landmark* `22 F1`

The new headquarters of the finance ministry is a dominating, three-building riverside complex that was completed in 1989. Architects Borja Huidobro and Paul Chemetov designed the spectacularly arched Colbert building – part of which overhangs the Seine to provide boat access for visiting officials – to echo the form of the nearby Métro viaduct. The whole package is best viewed from the Pont de Bercy.

Cinémathèque Française *movie mecca* `22 G2`
51 rue de Bercy, 12ème • 01 71 19 33 33
>> www.cinemathequefrancaise.com

The former home of the ill-fated American Center was designed by Frank Gehry and renovated in 2005 to accommodate a mecca for cinephiles. The complex has four cinemas, including the mighty Cinémathèque Française, temporary exhibition space and a museum that looks back on a century of film-making. **Adm**

Bibliothèque Nationale de France – François Mitterrand *modern library* `22 F3`
11 quai François Mauriac, 13ème • 01 53 79 59 59
>> www.bnf.fr Galleries open 10–7 Tue–Sat, 1–7 Sun

A hallmark of Mitterrand's presidency was his ambitious architectural *Grands Projets*. The last of these, a controversial library building, consists of four L-shaped towers, designed to look like half-open books. It hosts regular exhibitions of photographs and drawings.

Art & Architecture

Louise Weiss Galleries *art central* `21 D3`

The vibrant art scene on rue Louise Weiss has not looked back since 1997, when a project was hatched to group a number of galleries (mostly open 11–7 Tue–Sat) on this small street in the developing 13th *arrondissement*. Try Galerie Praz-Delavallade (www.praz-delavallade.com, at No. 28), with its focus on US artists, or Galerie Philip Jousse (www.jousse-entreprise.com) at No. 34, where the emphasis is on photography.

Manufacture des Gobelins *tapestries* `21A3`

42 avenue des Gobelins, 13ème • 01 44 08 52 00
Visits Tue–Thu at 2pm & 2:45pm

Founded in 1662 to supply Louis XIV with royal furnishings, the Gobelins factory still uses 17th-century techniques to produce tapestries that are now hung in state buildings and embassies. Conducted in French, guided visits take in the factory, the Beauvais tapestry and Savonnerie carpet workshops. **Adm**

Les Frigos *warehouse studios* `22 F4`

19 rue des Frigos, 13ème • 01 44 24 96 96
>> www.les-frigos.com

After years of struggle, this huge artists' community won the right to stay in the old refrigerated SNCF warehouses where it had squatted since the 1980s. Call for details of the twice-yearly official open days, usually organized in May and September. Otherwise, impromptu individual visits are usually permitted.

Cité Universitaire *campus buildings*

Boulevard Jourdan, 14ème • 01 43 13 65 96
>> www.ciup.fr • Ⓜ Cité Universitaire

These wildly eclectic residences were built from 1925, and still house foreign university students. The Asian and Armenian colleges follow their respective national architecture; the Swiss (by Le Corbusier) and Dutch (by Willem Dudok) express these notable architects' individual styles.

Catacombes *underground Paris* `20 E3`
1 place Denfert Rochereau, 14ème • 01 43 22 47 63
Open 10–5 Tue–Sun

Illicit parties are sometimes held in the miles of
tunnels beneath Paris, but the Catacombes, an
ossuary since 1785, are easier to get into. Visitors
stroll through subterranean corridors lined – often
artistically – with bones and skulls moved here from
overcrowded cemeteries of the period. **Adm**

Fondation Cartier pour l'Art `19 D2`
Contemporain *modern exhibitions*
261 boulevard Raspail, 14ème • 01 42 18 56 50
》 www.fondation.cartier.fr Open noon–8 Tue–Sun

Jean Nouvel's spectacular glass building houses
regular exhibitions of relatively well-known
contemporary artists, such as William Eggleston and
Pierrick Sorin, with an emphasis on art installations,
videos and photography. **Adm**

Fondation Henri Cartier-Bresson `19 B2`
2 impasse Lebouis, 14ème • 01 56 80 27 00
》 www.henricartierbresson.org
Open 1–6:30 Wed–Fri & Sun (to 8:30 Wed), 11–6:45 Sat

Founder of the reputed Magnum photo agency, Henri
Cartier-Bresson intended this centre to house the bulk
of his work. At present, the affiliated museum hosts
three shows a year, occasionally including Bresson's
work, but mostly that of exciting younger artists. **Adm**

Mémorial du Maréchal Leclerc `19 B1`
23 allée de la Deuxième, 15ème • 01 40 64 39 44
Open 10–5:45 Tue–Sun

Actually two museums, the exhibits here focus on two
French WWII heroes. Projected archive footage shows
the Liberation of Paris under Leclercq, his Free France
Forces and the Allies. Photographs and posters
document the situation inside occupied France from
the perspective of Resistance martyr Jean Moulin. **Adm**

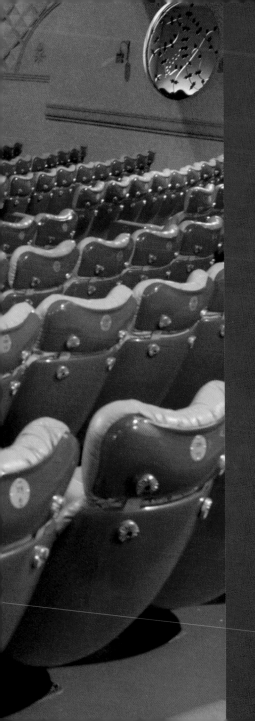

performance

From high-brow classical opera and theatre to radical circus acts and *chanson*, Paris offers a rich diversity of performance arts. Cinephiles are spoilt for choice by the city's numerous art-house cinemas, dance aficionados enjoy performances by both rising and well-established companies, and music fans can pick from leading classical orchestras and international acts.

PERFORMANCE

It's not just the sheer diversity of shows and performances that I love about Paris; it's the fact that this kaleidoscopic range is so accessible. Many theatres sell cheap last-minute tickets, the national opera house offers standing room for just 5€, independent cinemas reduce entry fees on Wednesdays, and the summer welcomes a whole wave of free entertainment. Little wonder that Parisians are so passionate about supporting their culture.

Richard Woodruff

Alternative Arts Scene

The legendary **Café de la Gare** *(see p125)* puts on excellent short plays and one-man shows and is an offbeat – yet wholeheartedly Parisian – experience. The best Anglophone equivalent is stand-up comedy at **La Java** *(see p129)*. Or try the historic **Cirque d'Hiver Bouglione** *(see p131)*, which excels in traditional circus acts with a modern spin.

Art-House Cinema

Parisians take cinema seriously, and films are usually screened in their original language with subtitles. Left-bank cinemas like **Grand Action** *(see p126)* and **Le Champollion** *(see p126)* devise excellent long-running retrospectives, while **Studio 28** *(see p129)*, which claims to be the first-ever avant-garde cinema, screens some ten films each week.

Highbrow Productions

Paris's cultural scene is far from elitist. The popular **Opéra Bastille** and **Opéra Garnier** *(see p128)* host traditional and modern productions, and all kinds of classical music lovers attend the **Théâtre du Châtelet** *(see p125)* and **Théâtre des Champs-Elysées** *(see p127)*. There's no better place to see Molière than at the **Comédie Française** *(see p125)*.

choice acts

Cutting-Edge Shows

Paris is no stranger to radical ideas and attracts trend-setting performers. The atmospheric **Bouffes du Nord** *(see p128)* offers radical programming, while the **Cartoucherie de Vincennes** *(see p131)* serves up political plays and progressive poetry readings. At the **Centre National de la Danse** *(see p130)*, expect the best in new dance talent.

Free Culture

Every summer, the **Cinéma en Plein Air** *(see p130)* is the place to be for film buffs with a penchant for the outdoors. Year round, the **Maison de la Radio France** *(see p128)* – France's national radio station – offers regular, mainly classical, concerts, while rock and pop tastes are catered for every early-evening weekday at **La Flèche d'Or** *(see p132)*.

Contemporary Music

Paris boasts relatively intimate music venues even for big-name visitors: true, **Le Zénith** *(see p130)* is large, but its ambiance is friendly. Other places with a good vibe are the **Elysée-Montmartre** *(see p129)* for indie bands, the **Café de la Danse** *(see p131)* for more eclectic tastes, or **New Morning** *(see p128)*, which attracts some of jazz's greatest exponents.

Performance

La Pagode *oriental art-house cinema* `15 A2`
57bis rue de Babylone, 7ème
01 45 55 48 48

Shipped over brick-by-brick from Japan in 1895, this striking pagoda, complete with an ornamental Japanese garden, became a cinema in the 1930s. Jean Cocteau chose it for the premiere of his *Le Testament d'Orphée* in 1959. Now classified a historical monument, it has two screens and shows recent independent films.

Forum des Images *Paris on film* `10 G4`
Forum des Halles (Porte Eustache), 1er • 01 44 76 62 00
≫ www.forumdesimages.net Research room open 1–9 daily

This centre archives films, documentaries, adverts and newsreels – anything connected with Paris. Visitors can search the database of some 6,500 films (from Lumière brothers shorts to *Superman II*) to watch on a personal screen. The cinema also screens several films a day in themed programmes. **Adm**

Le Point Virgule *small-scale comedy* `17 B1`
7 rue Ste-Croix de la Bretonnerie, 4ème • 01 42 78 67 03
≫ www.netkiri.com Performances at 8, 9:15 and 10:30pm daily

This tiny Marais *café-théâtre* organizes a prolific programme of one- and two-man comedy shows. From packed rows of slightly uncomfortable benches, spectators watch impromptu sketches, humour-spiced songs and surreal musical acts. Several shows a day are held during the popular summer Festival d'Humour.

Booking Tickets

Many venues have booking offices, but most people book tickets at branches of **fnac** and **Virgin Megastores** or online at www.ticketnet.fr. Buy half-price theatre tickets in person on the day of performance from either of **Kiosque Théâtre's** two outlets. For contact details, *see p232*. You can book cinema tickets at **Allociné** (08 92 89 28 92).

Duc des Lombards *hot jazz* `10 H5`
42 rue des Lombards, 1er • 01 42 33 22 88
≫ www.ducdeslombards.com Open Mon–Sat

Since opening in 1985, this respected jazz club has picked up several industry awards and maintained its ultra-cool reputation by attracting some of Europe's biggest names. Music ranges from free jazz to hard bop, and artists who have jammed here include trumpeter Eric Truffaz and bassist Henri Texier.

Comédie Française *classic theatre* `10 H4`
2 rue de Richelieu, 1er • 08 25 10 16 80
» www.comedie-francaise.fr Box office open 11–6:30 daily

Founded by Molière's troupe in 1680, this state theatre is famed for its classical French productions (Molière, Racine, Corneille), but an added draw is the surprisingly intimate 896-seat Italianate auditorium. Adventurous programming now sees regular forays into established modern and foreign works.

Café de la Gare *rebel humour* `11 A5`
41 rue du Temple, 4ème • 01 42 78 52 51
» www.cafe-de-la-gare.fr.st

Born out of post-1968 populism, this, the original *café-théâtre*, is still Paris's best for one-man shows, comedy and short plays. The venue brought fame to satirical comic Coluche, actor Patrick Dewaere and writer/actor Sotha, all of whose works are still performed to a mixed and enthusiastic audience.

Théâtre du Châtelet *historic venue* `16 H1`
1 place du Châtelet, 1er • 01 40 28 28 00
» www.chatelet-theatre.com Box office open 10–7 Mon–Sat

World-class ballet, opera and classical music productions are the draw at this illustrious theatre. A recent re-orientation in programming has given a more contemporary direction (music by Pierre Boulez and dance from Maurice Béjart). Excellent morning concerts (Mon, Wed, Fri) are held in the foyer (entry charged).

Le Grand Rex *cinematic grandeur* `10 H2`
1 boulevard Poissonnière, 2ème • 08 92 68 05 96
» www.legrandrex.com Tours at regular intervals

Opened in 1932, the city's largest cinema has an Art Deco façade and splendid Baroque-style decor. Audiences of up to 2,650 come here for blockbuster movies, concerts and the celebrated Christmas-time son et lumière. Entertaining behind-the-scenes tours feature Disney-esque special effects.

» *At the Comédie Française, 95 reduced-rate seats are reserved for sale one hour before each performance*

Performance

Left-Bank Cinemas *film buff's heaven* `16 G3`

Beyond the clusters of chain cinemas around Odéon and Montparnasse, the 5th and 6th *arrondissements* arguably offer the richest variety of art-house cinemas in the world. Some 20 – with a total of 39 screens between them – are located around boulevard St-Michel and form a cinephile's paradise. All films are shown in their original language (VO or *version originale*) with French subtitles where necessary, and the diversity is truly staggering. The tiny rue Champollion alone is home to three such cinemas. Film aficionados have a special affection for **Le Champollion**, a regular haunt of *Nouvelle Vague* directors Jean-Luc Godard and François Truffaut, who nurtured their encyclopedic knowledge of cinema here. The entrance is adorned with memorabilia dedicated to Jacques Tati, while the main screen has Europe's only "periscope" projector, so-called because the projection room is situated below the screen. Known for its retrospective seasons

(think Alain Resnais and Tim Burton), Le Champollion, also organizes debates in the presence of famed directors. Just down the road, the **Reflet Medicis** specializes in major classics and retrospectives, while the **Quartier Latin** (which accommodates just 70 people) prides itself on exclusive premieres.

For classic American films, try the three Action cinemas. The **Grand Action** dreams up inventive seasons that span careers, themes and genres such as Love-Hate and The 100 Best Films. The **Action Ecole** treats viewers to diverse retrospectives, while the **Action Rive Gauche** favours 1950s movies. Other popular venues include **Images d'Ailleurs** (black cinema), **Racine Odeon** (legendary all-night sessions), **Studio Galande** (weekend screenings of *The Rocky Horror Picture Show*) and **St-André-des-Arts**, where contemporary *auteurs* are just as likely to be in the audience as they are to be screened. For contact details, *see p231*.

Théâtre des Champs-Elysées

15 avenue Montaigne, 8ème • 01 49 52 50 50
>> www.theatrechampselysees.fr
Box office open 10–noon & 2–6 Mon–Fri

Described by writer Marcel Proust as "a temple to music, architecture and painting", this theatre was where the infamous premiere of Stravinsky's *Rites of Spring* (1913) ended in riots and Joséphine Baker starred in her ground-breaking *Revue Nègre* in 1925.

Today, the historic 1913 theatre, with its dome painted by Maurice Denis *(see p112)*, still hosts the *crème de la crème* of classical music. Concerts are almost unfailingly excellent: home of the Orchestre National de France and Orchestre Philharmonique de Radio-France, the venue also attracts top international orchestras (Vienna, Berlin), legendary singers (Luciano Pavarotti, Cecilia Bartoli) and renowned conductors (Pierre Boulez, Seiji Ozawa). Outstanding ballet productions have included turns by the New York City Ballet and the brilliant choreographer Maurice Béjart.

Lucernaire *one-stop entertainment* `15 D5`

53 rue Notre-Dame-des-Champs, 6ème • 01 45 44 57 34
>> www.lucernaire.fr

Converted from an old factory, this vibrant Left Bank arts centre houses two theatres, three cinemas, an art gallery, a bar and a restaurant. The eclectic theatre programming favours new talent and innovative pieces, such as one-man condensed classics, while the cinemas show recent art-house releases.

Théâtre de la Ville *hip dance* `16 H1`

2 place du Châtelet, 4ème • 01 42 74 22 77
>> www.theatredelaville-paris.com
Box office open 11–7 Mon–Sat, 11–8 Tue–Sat

This prestigious 1860s-built theatre has become the city's leading venue for contemporary dance. The 1,000-seat auditorium attracts innovative performers such as Pina Bausch and La La La Human Steps. World-music concerts and plays are also staged here.

Performance ≫≫≫

Maison de la Radio France *concerts* `13 B2`
116 avenue Président Kennedy, 16ème
01 56 40 22 22

This distinctive circular building is home to French state radio. The Salle Olivier Messiaen hosts an eclectic repertoire of classical music, usually by one of two resident orchestras. Concerts are often free, including those in the music festival Présences (Jan–Feb) and one-off gigs by big names such as Peter Gabriel.

New Morning *no-frills club* `11 A1`
7–9 rue des Petites-Ecuries, 10ème • 01 45 23 51 41
≫ www.newmorning.com

Located on a run-down street with an all-but-hidden entrance, this is possibly the city's most famous jazz venue. Beloved of serious fans and musicians alike, the club was Chet Baker's favourite and, since opening in 1981, has attracted the key exponents of jazz, blues and Latin music from Roy Ayres to Taj Mahal.

Bouffes du Nord *dilapidated charm* `5 B2`
37bis boulevard de la Chapelle, 10ème • 01 46 07 34 50
≫ www.bouffesdunord.com   Box office open 11–6 Mon–Sat

After years of neglect and with only minimal restoration, this legendary vaudeville theatre was reopened in 1974 by English director Peter Brook. The ramshackle interior provides a terrific backdrop for its often groundbreaking productions: an exciting menu of modern and reinvigorated classic plays, as well as jazz, opera and contemporary music. Performances here really benefit from the building's extraordinary acoustics.

A Night at the Opera

Crowned by Marc Chagall's gorgeous ceiling frescoes, the stunning auditorium of **Opéra Garnier** *(see p116)* is in fact used mostly for quality ballet productions and some lesser-known operas. The mainly classical repertoire is often given a modern slant in terms of design and choreography. The 2,700-capacity **Opéra Bastille** *(see p232)*, with its vast, curving glass façade, was commissioned by Mitterrand as an "opera for the people", but escalating construction costs have inflated the ticket prices (obscured views are, however, still available for just 5€). Classical opera is the mainstay here, with occasional ballet and classical-music concerts. Tickets are always in demand, so advance booking is well advised. Both venues offer daily guided tours.

For the very latest on Paris go to ≫ www.realcity.dk.com

La Java *Anglo stand-up comedy* `12 E1`

105 rue du Faubourg du Temple, 10ème • 01 42 02 20 52
» www.anythingmatters.com

Dating from the 1920s, the city's premier Latin music
club now doubles up as a venue for Anglophone
stand-up comedy. The entrance is hidden at the end
of a dingy arcade and the interior is atmospherically
ramshackle. Big-name performers (Daniel Kitson, Greg
Proops) often air new material to a mainly expat crowd.

Elysée-Montmartre *concert venue* `4 G3`

72 boulevard Rochechouart, 18ème • 08 92 69 23 92
» www.elyseemontmatre.com Box office open 9–7:30 Mon–Sat

This large Pigalle venue – now one of the city's best
for indie rock and trip-hop – stills bears vestiges of
its past life as a 19th-century music hall. Elaborate
carvings on the walls and ceiling add a certain grandeur to concerts, salsa nights and the popular twice-
monthly balls, which feature cover bands and DJs.

Studio 28 *quirky and convivial screenings* `4 E2`

10 rue Tholozé, 18ème • 01 46 06 36 07
» www.cinemastudio28.com

Opened in the 1920s, this popular independent cinema
was once frequented by film icons Luis Buñuel and
Abel Gance and, more recently, fictional local resident
Amélie. Showing current art-house releases, classics
and pre-releases, it also holds monthly debates
featuring leading directors and well-known actors.

Cité de la Musique *modern music hall*

221 avenue Jean Jaurès, 19ème • 01 44 84 44 84
» www.cite-musique.fr • Ⓜ Porte de Pantin

Designed by French architect Christian de Portzamparc,
this music-oriented complex at Parc de la Villette
includes a state-of-the-art oval auditorium that hosts
everything from classical to world music and contemporary jazz. Try to catch one of the classic silent-film
screenings that are accompanied by live music.

» *Cinema programmes change every Wednesday. Check www.allocine.fr or Pariscope for listings*

Performance

Le Zénith *giant multipurpose venue*
211 avenue Jean Jaurès, 19ème • 01 42 08 60 00
>> www.le-zenith.com/paris • Ⓜ Porte de Pantin

Purpose built by the state as a venue for popular
music, Le Zénith benefits from great acoustics and an
intimate atmosphere, despite its 6,400 capacity. The
interior of the tent-like structure can be adapted as
required, whether for French *chanson*, a big-name
rock concert, ice-skating spectacle or sport event.

Cinéma en Plein Air *picnic and a movie*
Parc de la Villette, 19ème • 01 40 03 75 75 • Ⓜ Porte de Pantin
>> www.villette.com Screenings Jul–Aug 10pm Tue–Sun

On fine summer evenings, the large lawn at Parc de la
Villette is strewn with picnickers and cinephiles enjoy-
ing the night's free film. The huge inflatable screen
shows recent blockbusters and classic foreign movies
(all in original language) based around a different
theme each year. Deck chairs are available for hire.

Centre National de la Danse *modern dance*
1 rue Victor Hugo, Pantin 93507 • 01 41 83 27 27
>> www.cnd.fr • Ⓜ Hoche RER Pantin

This 1970s concrete office building on the banks of
the Canal de l'Ourcq was refurbished in 2004 to
house the HQ of the innovative National Dance
Centre. Inside are no fewer than 11 dance studios;
three serve as cosy spaces for cutting-edge shows by
young choreographers from all over the world.

Come to the Cabaret

Cabaret is alive and kicking in the city where it first
began, but it can be an expensive night out. Shows
at the iconic **Moulin Rouge** have the expected
formula of Doriss Girls, clad in feathers, sequins and
rhinestones, dancing the cancan. At the **Lido**, it's the
Bluebell Girls who are centre stage, accompanied by
special laser effects, while at the **Paradis Latin**,
designed by Gustave Eiffel, the dancers are joined
by trapeze artists and a ventriloquist. **Crazy Horse**,
meanwhile, advertises itself as an exponent of "the
art of nudity", though it is more tasteful than the idea
of topless dance routines suggests. To escape the
domain of wealthy tourists, try the gloriously kitsch
cross-dressing at **Chez Michou** or the even camper
Chez Madame Arthur. For contact details, *see p231*.

Café de la Danse *eclectic sounds* `18 E2`
5 passage Louis-Philippe, 11ème • 01 47 00 57 59
>> www.chez.com/cafedeladanse

Despite its name, this intimate venue hosts everything from folk-rock and world music to a cappella, as well as modern dance. Overlooking the auditorium (which holds about 450 people) is a small balcony with a bar – the best vantage point from which to enjoy bands that are normally found playing bigger venues.

Cirque d'Hiver Bouglione *innovative circus acts* `11 D4`
110 rue Amelot, 11ème • 01 47 00 28 81
>> www.cirquedhiver.com Box office open 10–6 daily

Built in 1852, this spectacular, polygonal circus ring witnessed the birth of the trapeze when Jules Léotard appeared here almost 150 years ago. Each winter, the Bouglione family devise a new, enthralling show that features trapeze artists, clowns, magicians, contortionists and animal acts from around the world. And every year (Jan–Feb), the venue hosts an international festival featuring the circus stars of tomorrow.

Cartoucherie de Vincennes *radical theatre*
Route du Champ de Manœuvre, Bois de Vincennes, 12ème
01 43 74 24 08 • Ⓜ Château de Vincennes with free shuttle bus

This complex of five small theatres and three workshops was converted from a disused munitions factory in the 1970s. The site is off the beaten track and best reached by taxi, but it's worth the trek as the theatres' repertoires are prolific and stimulating.

Founded after the riots of 1968, the **Théâtre du Soleil** was the first to establish itself here and, under the direction of Arian Mnouchkine, is still turning out political epics. Philippe Adrien's energetic troupe stages a mix of the avant-garde and the classical at the **Théâtre de la Têmpète**, while Julie Brochen at the **Théâtre de l'Aquarium** programmes imaginative productions of Chekhov and Tolstoy alongside music-accompanied poetry and Japanese *butô* dance. The **Théâtre du Chaudron** favours young companies, often with women directors, while the **Théâtre de l'Epée de Bois** is known for its progressive take on contemporary works.

Performance

Bataclan *historic venue*
50 boulevard Voltaire, 11ème • 01 43 14 00 30
>> www.le-bataclan.com

12 E4

This former vaudeville theatre may have lost its original Chinese pagoda façade, but the sumptuous interior still provides an enticing setting for the varied concerts of indie, trip-hop, French *chanson* and world music. The charming auditorium has a fantastic vibe, but the acoustics can be less than perfect.

La Flèche d'Or *rock on a railway theme*
102 rue de Bagnolet, 20ème • 01 43 72 04 23
>> www.flechedor.fr • Ⓜ Alexandre Dumas, Maraîchers

Converted from an abandoned train station, the atmospheric Flèche d'Or puts on daily (mostly free) concerts of funk, hip-hop, pop and rock. Decorated with railway bric-a-brac, the large space has a bit of an underground feel and attracts an exciting mix of artists, students and late-night clubbers.

Le Regard du Cygne *experimental dance*
210 rue de Belleville, 20ème • 01 43 58 55 93
>>redcygne.free.fr • Ⓜ Télégraphe

This small and intimate dance space has been hugely influential in promoting new forms of artistic expression. The bare-bones studio is famed for its occasional Spectacles Sauvages, when artists showcase work in progress during lively ten-minute slots. Classical- and contemporary-music concerts are also held here.

La Guinguette Pirate *concerts afloat*
Quai Francois-Mauriac, 13ème • 01 43 49 68 68
>> www.guinguettepirate.com

22 F3

This three-masted Chinese junk on the Seine hosts an extremely varied programme of music for party-loving audiences of up to 200. Feel the narrow boat rock to hip-hop and indie concerts or sway gently to jazz and world music. Film screenings and improvized theatre shows also make it aboard on occasions.

Théâtre de la Cité International

21 boulevard Jourdan, 14ème • 01 43 13 50 50
RER Cité Universitaire Box office open 2–6:45 Mon–Sat
>> www.ciup.fr/culture/theatre.htm

This three-stage theatre is known for its creative and energetic shows. The Grand Théâtre puts on modern plays, dance and circus acts; the Galerie's movable seating lends itself to cutting-edge theatre; and the tiny Reserre hosts readings and small productions.

MK2 Bibliothèque *cinema complex* `22 F3`

128–62 avenue de France, 13ème • 08 92 69 84 84
>> www.mk2.com/bibliotheque/seat.html

Paris's artiest cinema chain conceived its latest outpost under the slogan "a whole life [centred] around cinema". Located next to the Bibliothèque Nationale *(see p117)*, the stylish mega-complex has 14 screens, four eateries and two shops. Two-person lovers' seats on every row are an extra draw for couples.

Spectator Sports

Most sports events are within easy reach of the city. One of the big four tennis grand-slam events, the two-week French Open, is held at **Roland Garros** at the end of May. Apply for tickets two months before the tournament; guided tours and the museum are available year round. November brings the men back for the Tennis Masters Series at the **Palais Omnisport de Paris-Bercy** (POPB), while the leading women return in March for the Open Gaz de France (at the **Stade Pierre de Coubertin**).

Although most of France's leading footballers have been lured abroad, passionate crowds still cheer on Paris St-Germain at the 50,000-capacity **Parc des Princes**. International games and Cup finals, however, are hosted at the magnificent **Stade de France**. Major athletics meetings are also held here, as well as home games of the popular Six Nations rugby tournament (tickets for which can be hard to come by). The highly successful Stade Français rugby club plays at **Stade Jean-Bouin**.

For racecourses, head to the edges of Paris's two woods. **Paris-Vincennes** favours trotting (harness racing), while **Longchamp** is reserved for flat racing, including Europe's richest race, the Prix de l'Arc de Triomphe in October. Showjumping tops the bill at POPB in March, with the Jumping International de Paris. In fact, over the year, POPB hosts everything from windsurfing and motocross to international gymnastics, basketball and ice-skating.

Tickets for most sports fixtures can be purchased at major ticket agencies *(see p124)*, as well as through department stores **La Samaritaine** and **Les Galeries Lafayette** *(see p226)*. It is wise to book in advance for most events and avoid *revendeurs* (ticket touts). For all contact details, see *p232*.

>> *The Théâtre de la Cité International is set within the Cité Universitaire* (see p118)

bars & clubs

The City of Light comes into its own after dark, when the bobos (bourgeois bohemians), beautiful people, intellectuals and other Parisian tribes set forth on their separate drinking trails. Pick your crowd, and explore the myriad bars, clubs and cafés scattered around the city – you're bound to find the cocktail and the company of your choice.

BARS & CLUBS

Paris's drinking and dancing scene really does have something for everyone. Enjoy theme bars where drinks are served in babies' bottles, top clubs where you can dance the night away, and super-swanky champagne parlours that require a black Amex card and/or a statement handbag to get in. However, don't forget the humble and ubiquitous local café. Authentic corner dives are ideal for starting things off, while cooler retro versions are perfect for big nights out.

Katherine Spenley

Fine Wine

A good glass of red (or white, or rosé) can always be found at the quirky **Le Clown Bar** *(see p155)*. A hipper option is **Wine and Bubbles** *(see p160)*, a popular venue with a pre-club crowd. **Juveniles** *(see p139)*, is a wine shop-cum-restaurant where, if you like what you sip, you can buy a bottle or two to take home.

Trad but Trendy

Pastis and Piaf are great, but the old soaks propping up the bar that are often also part of the authentic zinc-bar experience, less so. For a nostalgia trip with an up-to-date crowd, visit **Le Café Noir** *(see p141)*, **Chez Prune** *(see p153)*, **Au Petit Fer à Cheval** *(see p144)* or – the trailblazer for retro haunts – **Café Charbon** *(see p155)*.

Cocktail Chic

Where better to play cocktail connoisseur than in one of the city's palatial hotel bars. Join the fashion pack at **Le Bar du Plaza** *(see p151)*, go grown-up in the grand **Four Seasons George V** bar *(see p150)* where cocktails are served in your own personal shaker, or live like a legend at the Ritz's justifiably lauded **Hemingway Bar** *(see p139)*.

choice nightlife

Cool Clubs

You'll need to put your best (Louboutin-shod) foot forward to get into **Paris Paris** *(see p141)*, the city's current club darling, and arrive at **Le Baron** *(see p152)* before midnight to squeeze past the velvet rope. **La Suite** *(see p150)* is still flashy, but easier to get into, especially if you look the part. If not, then don't forget the much-loved **Batofar** *(see p157)*.

Out all Night

There are many places in the City of Light where the lights are left on all night. Try **Le Connetable** *(see p143)* for old-fashioned fun till dawn; **Mathi's** *(see p151)*, which is *the* place to go drinking with sophisticated (and sometimes famous) sybarites; and **The Highlander** *(see p138)*, which is popular with a young crowd who like to stay up very late.

A Place for a Pint

Sometimes only a beer will do. When that's the case in Paris, head to one of the many Frog bars for a brewed-on-site pint – my favourite is the **Frog and Princess** *(see p138)*. Nearby, **O'Neill's** *(see p138)* also has a micro-brasserie, and offers perfect pints, while **Le Pantalon** *(see p147)* serves some of the cheapest beer in town.

Bars & Clubs

Le Fumoir *chic and sleek all-rounder* `10 F5`
6 rue de L'Amiral de Coligny, 1er • 01 42 92 00 24
>> www.lefumoir.com Open to 2am daily

With its beautiful, long mahogany bar, well-stocked library and trendy terrace across from the Louvre, Le Fumoir is equally perfect for pre-dinner drinks, late-night cocktails, a little light refreshment after some art appreciation or a quiet afternoon with a pot of tea and one of the books borrowed from the groaning shelves.

Hotel Costes *sexy bar* `9 D3`
239 rue St-Honoré, 1er • 01 42 44 50 25
>> www.hotelcostes.com Open to 1am daily

The bar here is a rare creature: a hot spot that has kept its cool, despite the fact that it's been serving drinks to the style set since 1996. The plush Napoleon II bordello decor continues to provide a lush, sensual backdrop for *le beau monde*, and the intimate nooks and crannies are still likely to hide a celebrity or two.

Le Cab *posh party place* `10 F4`
2 place du Palais Royal, 1er • 01 58 62 56 25
>> www.cabaret.fr Open to 3am Mon & Tue, to 6am Wed–Sat

Very plush and upscale, Cab (formerly Cabaret) has been open for five years, but there's no such thing as growing old gracefully for a club like this. Designed by Jacques Garcia, the leather wall coverings, squishy banquettes and smooth lines have kept the beautiful people flocking here to pout, preen and party. **Adm**

Brit Pubs

While the city's bars and cafés serve all kinds of bottled beer, Parisians in search of a proper pint, anglophiles yearning for a bit of South Kensington-on-Seine and expats pining for a local all gravitate towards one of the city's pubs. Beer aficionados will love the home-brew at **O'Neils** the **Frog & Princess** and **Freedom**. Traditional pub decor and a quiet drink can be found at **The Cricketer,** or at the **Bombardier**. Irish *pubeen* fans swear by the **Corcoran** for great *craic*, or **Coolin** for Celtic cool. Whisky lovers drink at the **Auld Alliance,** while Paris's other Scottish pub, **The Highlander,** is perfect for party animals: at weekends the bar and dance floor are open late and are always packed. For further details *see pp217–220.*

138

For the very latest on Paris go to >> www.realcity.dk.com

Le Coeur Fou *lovely local*   `10 G3`
55 rue Montmartre, 2ème • no phone
Open to 2am daily

Small but beautiful, Le Coeur Fou is always packed with friendly thirtysomethings who hit this place straight from their graphic design studios/art galleries/Internet start-ups for several rounds of apéritifs. You'll find modern art on the walls, a busy bar, smiley staff and an irrepressibly sociable vibe.

Juveniles *fine wine bar*   `10F3`
47 rue de Richelieu, 1er • 01 42 97 46 49
Open to midnight Mon–Sat

Here, you'll have to pick your way past the haphazardly stacked crates of great wine – especially the New World selection – to reach the bar. The staff (who know their wine but won't patronize you if you don't) and the loyal hard-drinking hacks from nearby newspaper offices make this a top place to savour a bottle or two.

Hemingway Bar *Ritzy experience*   `9 D3`
Ritz Hotel, 15 place Vendôme, 1er • 01 43 16 33 65
>> www.ritzparis.com Open to 2am Mon–Sat, 11–5 Sun

The first thing you need to know about the Hemingway Bar is how to find it. This gem of a drinking hole is expertly concealed (no signs) within the Ritz Hotel, but the trek past the reception to the back of the building – taking a right after the overstuffed sofas and roaring fire, and continuing along the carpeted corridor – is most definitely worth it.

The Hemingway is a tiny nook of dark-wood panelling, low-lighting, black-and-white photos of Papa himself, fascinating clientele and superb cocktails. The place abounds with stories, the most famous being the tale of Hemingway "liberating" the bar at the end of WWII. Legend has it that the Old Man deemed the bar at the Ritz *the* place to enjoy the first round of "free" drinks after the Allies arrived. A high accolade indeed, given that Hemingway drank in earnest and patronized almost every bar around at the time. For further tales of

glamour, glitz and alcohol, ask head barman Colin Field, who was voted the world's best bartender for several consecutive years and is certainly Paris's most charming host. Colin's mouthwatering cocktail list is impressively extensive and includes the delicious Ritz Champagne (a wonderful mixture of apples and fizz), the Ritz 75 (a heady mix of gin, champagne and citrus fruits) and the stunning Raspberry Martini (fresh raspberries macerated in premium vodka).

This clubby den is probably the only place in Paris where you can listen to scratchy piano music played on a wind-up gramophone, watch the bartender sabre a bottle of vintage champagne, sip stunning drinks – which arrive with a flourish for the gentlemen and a flower for the ladies – and slip into a timeless reverie. The captains of industry, trust-fund babes, Lotharios and cocktail aficionados mingling at the bar aren't perturbed by the prices, and even more ordinary folk on tight budgets tend to think it's worth the splurge for a little slice of bar heaven.

>> *A pichet (carafe) of house wine is usually perfectly drinkable, and cheaper than ordering à la carte*   `139`

Kong *manga dream* `10 G5`

1 rue du Pont Neuf, 1er • 01 40 39 09 00
>> www.kong.fr Open to 2am daily

Philippe Starck's Asian-inspired project, Kong, sits atop Kenzo's flagship store and offers a riot of designer-kitsch to shoppers and bar-hoppers alike. Kong's interior is a chaotic jumble of neon lights, acid colours, Zen-grey pebble rugs, Tokyo street scenes playing on big screens, life-size images of geishas, rocking chairs, Hello Kitty and manga merchandise, and Pokemon-motif cushions. And that's all before you've headed to the top floor – as everyone does – for the views over the Seine from the bar's wrap-around windows. The upper level's toilets are also worth a look, bedecked with glitter balls and beaded curtains, and guarded by giant images of sumo children.

   This is definitely not the place to be if minimalism is your mantra. If, however, you like bright lights in your big city then the clutter and chaos of Kong is sure to tick all the boxes. The clientele is just as colourful as the backdrop: party puppies and fashionistas clamour for space at the bar, while trust-funders chill out in the rocking chairs. Cocktails are served in glasses of intense hues by surprisingly friendly aspiring models and wannabe actresses, and sipped to an eclectic soundtrack. This is played on an innovative music system that allows diners to vote for their favourite tunes from a menu of ten categories, including Sugar Pop and Glam Chic. A very reasonably priced happy hour (6–8pm daily) means that this place gets going before most of the city's other fashionable drinking destinations. It's definitely best to get there early if you want to get one of the sleek, silver Starck-designed stools in a prime spot at the bar. Another way to guarantee a seat is to book a table for dinner. But beware: as in most see-and-be-seen destinations, the food is pricey, average and really not the point.

Le Next *friendly local DJ bar*

10 H3

17 rue Tiquetonne, 2ème • 01 42 36 18 93
Open to 4am Mon–Fri, to 5am Sat

This often-rowdy joint, with its slightly schizophrenic design scheme (a nondescript bar at the front, leopard print and red velvet out back), attracts a big-drinking crowd. As its name suggests, Le Next is a perfect stop on a bar crawl, but it also cuts it as a destination drinking haunt or pre-club rendezvous.

Somo *chic and sleek*

10 G2

168 rue Montmartre, 2ème • 01 40 13 08 80
Open to 2am Mon–Thu, to 4am Fri & Sat

Somo's laid-back vibe attracts both twentysomethings and financial types from the nearby stock exchange. They come in droves for the great cocktails – try the delicious champagne-based mixes or the lethal-but-lovely mojitos. Low-slung leather chairs, chill-out music and subdued lighting complete the picture.

Le Café Noir *bobo spot*

10 G3

65 rue Montmartre, 2ème • 01 40 39 07 36
Open to 2am Mon–Sat

A retro-chic café, complete with winking neon signs, formica tables and boozy bonhomie. Le Café Noir is home from home to countless bourgeois bohemians (bobos), who come to get their creative juices flowing and discuss anything from tonight's hottest club to the trainers worn by the bloke behind the bar.

Le Rex *superstar DJs, dedicated clubbers*

10 G1

5 boulevard Poissonnière, 2ème • 01 42 36 10 96
>> www.rexclub.com Open to 6am Wed–Sat

Big on famous names and atmosphere, but low on attitude, this place is all about the music. Be prepared to queue for weekend sessions from top DJs (French and international), but other nights are ultimately no-fuss, hardcore dancing sessions led by the next big thing. Brilliant house music and truly top techno. **Adm**

Paris Paris *super-cool clubbing*

10 E4

5 avenue de l'Opéra, 1er • 01 42 60 64 45
Open to 5am daily

Word of mouth has been key to the success of Paris Paris, now the city's hottest club. It's all about friends of friends and while not an exclusive members' club, it's harder to get into (and more rewarding) than some that are. Look the part though, and once you're inside there's a glamorous house-party feel. **Adm**

>> *In clubs, buying a bottle and smiling sweetly is often the best way to get a table*

Bars & Clubs »»»»»

Harry's Bar *home of the hangover cure* `10 E2`
5 rue Daunou, 2ème • 01 42 61 71 14
»» www.harrys-bar.fr Open to 3am daily

The American accents, the saloon-bar look and US and UK college crests lining the walls might give the impression that this venerable drinking institution is little more than an ersatz slice of home for expats pining for Uncle Sam or John Bull. Not so. Harry's is a temple for all who shun temperance, regardless of their nationality. The owner's claim that the first Bloody Mary was invented in the bar comes as no surprise: given the loyalty of its regulars, the amount of time they spend propping up the bar and their commitment to all things alcoholic, inventing a brilliant hangover cure must have been a logical step. Harry's isn't for the lily-livered or the faint of heart: the measures are vast and it's a riotous place where people table-hop with gay abandon. But once you've been, you'll always come back, if only for a mean Bloody Mary the morning after the night before.

Pulp *wild club nights* `10 G1`
25 boulevard Poissonnière, 2ème • 01 40 26 01 93
»» www.pulp-paris.com Open to 6am Wed–Sat

Except for Saturday's Lesborama – one of Paris's best lesbian club nights – this spot also welcomes boys (both gay and straight). Goths, rock chicks, R&B divas and disco queens are all catered for with Pulp's varied events – the common denominator being a deep-seated desire to party. **Adm**

Café Thoumieux *sleek vodka bar* `8 H5`
4 rue de la Comète, 7ème • 01 45 51 50 40
»» www.thoumieux.com Open to 2am Mon–Sat

In the bar-deprived 7th *arrondissement*, this spot is a good bet for a quiet night spent sipping cocktails. The speciality is flavoured vodka, of which there's an impressive range behind the colourful tiled bar. The velvet banquettes and comfy stools are usually occupied by well-heeled expats and young professionals.

Andy Wahloo *trendy souk-chic* `11 A3`
69 rue des Gravilliers, 3ème • 01 42 71 20 38
Open to 2am daily

Created by the same team behind Sketch (London)
and 404 (Paris), Andy Wahloo proves that small can
be beautiful. Empty drums of paint serve as stools for
the hipsters who cram in to share a hookah, knock
back the cocktails or sip mint tea. Giant posters and
rows of pop bottles round off the atmospheric clutter.

Bliss Kfé *mainly for ladies* `17 B1`
30 rue de Roi de Sicile, 4ème • 01 42 78 49 36
≫ www.bliss.kfe.fr Open to 2am daily

This hip little spot was conceived as a meeting point
for gay men and women and their fit straight friends.
It's fairly women-centric though (especially the
downstairs cellar, where there's dancing on Friday
and Saturday nights) and pulls in a good mix of
friendly faces and femmes fatales.

Le Connetable *traditional haunt* `11 B4`
55 rue des Archives, 3ème • 01 42 77 41 40
≫ www.leconnetable.com
Open to 4am Mon–Thu, to 6am Fri & Sat

Think of all the clichés of the French *bon viveur*:
moustachioed and merry, belting out *chanson*, smiling
lasciviously, smoking furiously and getting slowly
soused over several bottles of dubious wine. Then
come and join him and his friends at Le Connetable, a
highly idiosyncratic spot that comes into its own after
midnight, when the volume level rises, the singing
kicks off, the couple in the corner start to get frisky,
and the groups at the bar freely intermingle. Don't let
the dusty silk-flower arrangements, dog-hair-covered
sofa and general rowdiness put you off – pretty young
things and aged *rouées* play up a storm on the out-of-
tune piano, notions of great philosophical importance
are hotly contested over yet another glass of red, and
fast friendships are made. One of the city's best nights
out, and one that almost always goes on until dawn.

Bars & Clubs

Amnesia *popular gay bar*   `17 B1`
42 rue Vieille du Temple, 4ème • 01 42 72 16 94
>> www.amnesia-cafe.com Open to 1:45am daily

Chilled-out by day, Amnesia turns up the tempo after
aperitif-time, when it morphs into a buzzy little bar
that is a popular pre-club venue. A Marais institution
and one of the local gay bars that welcomes straights,
this place has a well-deserved reputation as a fun
spot for drinks, discussion and delightful company.

L'Etoile Manquante *great café*   `17 B1`
34 rue Vieille du Temple, 4ème • 01 42 72 48 34
Open to 2am daily

This laid-back café is equally good for afternoon
cafés, pre-dinner drinks or late nightcaps. Modern
lighting and art perk-up the trad café decor, and
don't worry about the video installation in the toilets:
the cameras may catch you preening in the mirror,
but the images are only shown in the bathroom area.

Au Petit Fer à Cheval *venerable zinc bar*   `17 B1`
30 rue Vieille du Temple, 4ème • 01 42 72 47 47
>> www.cafeine.com Open to 2am daily

Adored by many, Au Petit Fer à Cheval sports a handsome horseshoe-shaped bar (often said to be Paris's
finest) that is invariably jammed with people sipping
good red wine. Elbow room is hard to find, though,
and it's worth settling for one of the tables for some
of the Marais's finest people-watching opportunities.

Chez Richard *relaxed chic*   `17 B1`
37 rue Vieille du Temple, 4ème • 01 42 74 31 65
Open to 2am Tue–Sat

Elegant but relaxed, Chez Richard is a great place to
go for quiet drinks or as a prelude to a big night out.
Expect exposed stone, leather banquettes, seating
for romantic tête-à-têtes, and long tables downstairs
for groups of friends or people who like to strike up
conversations with strangers.

La Belle Hortense *bookworms & barflies* `17 B1`

31 rue Vieille du Temple, 4ème • 01 48 04 71 60
≫ www.cafeine.com Open to 2am daily

A quintessentially Parisian mix of alcohol and intellectualism can be found at La Belle Hortense, an unusual combination of bookshop and bar. Serious tomes line the shelves and the clientele is encouraged to leaf through the latest Mario Vargas Llosa and indulge in a bit of lit-crit with the clever barflies perched at the zinc bar. The back room is smoke-free and quieter, with art for sale on the walls, leather banquettes, and low tables clustered together to make debating the latest hot topics that little bit easier.

The strictly French wine list, though relatively short, is well chosen and very well priced, and most of the bottles can be bought to take home. Listen, and you might hear tall tales from the regulars – who often claim to have been drinking partners with most of the 20th-century's great authors – philosophical arguments, debates about critical theory, or Sorbonne professors scoffing at their colleague's latest book. However, despite the formidable IQs present, this place is devoid of pretension, and it's not unusual for people to suddenly start dancing the tango, or engage in other less-dignified pursuits. For lofty literary minds, posters around the bar advertise plenty of events and meetings. Try the monthly Proust reading group or attend a happening book launch. (Catherine Millet's hit sexual memoir *La Vie Sexuelle de Catherine M* debuted here.) Or leaf through the piles of flyers for other cultural events taking place in venues across the city.

Bars & Clubs

Les Etages *designer grunge* `17 B1`
35 rue Vieille du Temple, 4ème • 01 42 78 72 00
Open to 2am daily

In this tall, shabby building, magnificent mojitos and a surreal dive-bar ambience awaits. Each floor of the bar – which looks more like a squat than the chic spot it is – has a different mood, though the hobo decor reigns throughout. The top floors are where the fun is, but room-swapping is the way to make new friends.

Le Cox *gay hot spot* `11 A5`
15 rue des Archives, 4ème • 01 42 72 08 00
Open to 2am daily

Almost as risqué as its name suggests, Le Cox is always full of beautifully turned-out boys. The interior – remodelled every three months to keep things looking fresh – provides a fitting backdrop. There's plenty of eye-candy and eye contact at this gay mecca, so be sure to wear your best labels and be ready to sparkle.

The Lizard Lounge *buzzing bar* `17 B1`
18 rue Bourg Tibourg, 4ème • 01 42 72 81 34
Open to 2am daily

A huge papier-mâché lizard mounted on the wall dominates this bar full of eager young professionals and hipsters getting drunk. Excellent cocktails, scrumptious Sunday brunches, occasional concerts and open-mic jam sessions in the cellar bar are the draw for a loud, friendly crowd.

Le Trésor *trendy Marais spot* `17 B1`
7 rue Trésor, 4ème • 01 42 71 35 17
Open to 1:30am daily

This perennial favourite is always packed with loyal pre-club crowds, kicking off their evening in style – whatever the day of the week. The bar is quite spacious, but it's best to arrive early as it can be difficult to get a table after 9pm. Don't miss the "rock-star" toilets with live goldfish swimming in the tanks.

Caveau des Oubliettes *weird & wacky* `16 H3`
52 rue Galande, 5ème • 01 46 34 23 09
Open to 2am Mon–Thu, to 5am Fri & Sat

Any place that lays real turf on the floor in the summer, proudly sports a huge guillotine near the bar, and organizes superb jazz jam sessions on Tuesdays in the cellar basement has got to be worth a visit. La Caveau des Oubliettes is utterly barmy, incredibly friendly and thoroughly good fun.

Le Pantalon *bargain drinks* `16 G4`
7 rue Royer Collard, 5ème • no phone
Open to 2am Mon–Sat

Due to the cheapness of the beer and wine, this bar pulls in an unlikely mix of Sorbonne students and pensioners. The bar staff are ebullient and friendly, the decor is bizarre (disco lights and palm trees in the loos) and there's always a rack of hard-boiled eggs on the counter, should you fancy a bar snack.

Le Crocodile *anti-chic cocktail bar* `16 G4`
6 rue Royer Collard, 5ème • 01 43 54 32 37
Open to 5am Mon–Sat

Yes, you do have to hammer on the closed shutters to get in, but, once there, expect a warm welcome and a phenomenal drinks list. This tiny bar offers over 200 cocktails, so don't be fazed if you are given paper and pen and a request to provide the drink's number along with its name when ordering.

Fubar *small but perfectly formed* `16 F3`
5 rue St-Sulpice, 6ème • 01 40 51 82 00
Open to 2am daily

Just steps from the main St-Germain drinking strip, but worth the stagger, the Fubar is a great spot for a few too many. The cocktails are potent and the atmosphere outstanding. The minuscule downstairs bar is often packed and rowdy, so head to the upstairs seating area if you want a quiet chat.

>> *Many bars have good-value happy hours, usually 6–8pm daily*

Le Bar du Marché *popular zinc bar* `16 F2`

75 rue de Seine, 6ème • 01 43 26 55 15
Open to 2am daily

Le Bar du Marché is one of the prime people-watching spots in St-Germain. Great views of chic Parisians bustling past and a brilliant buzz – it's lively and full of laughter inside the bar, day or night – make this a great place to while away an afternoon or make pre-dinner drinks last a very long time.

Le 10 Bar *faded charm* `16 F3`

10 rue de L'Odeon, 6ème • 01 43 26 66 83
Open to 2am daily

Bags of charm and jugs of sangria are the big draws here. Le 10 Bar is all peeling black-and-white posters, nicotine-stained walls, thick Gauloise smoke, ripped velvet banquettes, and a boisterous crowd of all ages getting noisily merry on the house special. The sangria seems innocent, but beware – it packs a mighty punch.

AZ Bar *destination drinking* `16 F2`

62 rue Mazarine, 6ème • 01 53 10 19 99
>> www.alcazar.fr Open to 2am daily

Situated above his Alcazar restaurant, Terence Conran's bar is a swanky, super-fun affair. A long bar, low banquettes, comfy chairs, candles and flattering lighting provide the perfect backdrop for the pretty PRs, young MDs and moneyed *demoiselles* who call the bar home from home. Depending on the night, the music ranges from funk to house via lounge and electro. The drinks, though, are always the same – expertly mixed, smilingly presented and a little on the expensive side. A perfect view into the "private" dining room is great for the curious, and check out the fabulous transvestite cigarette "girl", who tempts even non-smokers to buy an overpriced packet. The central pillars are just the spot to lean for those in search of stiletto-relief or trying to strike a foxy pose.

Café de la Mairie *St-Germain institution* `16 E3`
8 place St-Sulpice, 6ème • 01 43 26 67 82
Open to midnight daily

One of the 6th *arrondissement*'s "correct addresses", this chichi café is consequently popular with wealthy Parisians. Occupying a prime spot opposite St-Sulpice, the terrace is often full of ladies who lunch, gentlemen of leisure and well-heeled art students sipping champagne and watching the world go by.

L'Urgence *pre-club theme bar* `16 F3`
45 rue Monsieur Le Prince, 6ème • 01 43 26 45 69
≫ www.urgencebar.com Open 9pm–4am Tue–Sat

Hypochondriacs and medical students alike flock to this popular, if odd, venue that is decked out with medical equipment ranging from syringes and X-rays to biology text-book images of genitalia. Continuing with the theme, the bar is staffed by men in white coats who concoct drinks from a list that includes choices such as "Face Lift", "Suppository" and "Electro-Shock Therapy" – all of which, naturally, are served up in test tubes.

Don Carlos *Spanish hedonism* `16 F2`
66 rue Mazarine, 6ème • 01 43 54 53 17
Open to 5am Mon–Sat

On most nights at Don Carlos, guitarists alternately serenade beautiful girls and encourage the table-dancing crowd to indulge in rousing sing-alongs. Expect tequila shots, potent sangria, friendly staff and walls bearing photos of screen-greats who've drunk here (from Brigitte Bardot to Kevin Spacey).

WAGG *cool, classy club* `16 F2`
62 rue Mazarine, 6ème • 01 55 42 22 01
≫ www.wagg.fr Open to 5am Thu–Sat, to midnight Sun

Legend has it that this club's former incarnation, the Whisky A Go-Go, was the last stop on Jim Morrison's final big night out. The party animals who flock here today always dress to impress the terrifying *physiognomiste* (style-bouncer), so follow suit. The UK-import 70s-groove Carwash is a must on Friday nights. **Adm**

Nirvana Lounge *pricey posing* `8 H2`
3 avenue Matignon, 8ème • 01 53 89 18 91
Open to 5am daily

All curvy neon, pricey drinks and hard-to-get tables, the Nirvana Lounge is a must for poseurs and voyeurs. Claude Challe is behind the music, while Jonathan Amar dreamed up the decor, which is a mix of space-age motifs and Eastern promise and provides a perfect backdrop for the lithe and lovely crowd.

Toi *local chill-out joint* `8 H2`
27 rue Colisée, 8ème • 01 42 56 56 58
›› www.restaurant-toi.com Open to 2am daily

Pink-and-orange neon, curvaceous chairs, lava lamps and a looming Buddha set the scene at Toi – popular with the BCBG (*bon chic bon genre*) set. The taped birdsong may help soothe fevered brows after one too many Tea Tois, house specials that combine iced tea, vodka, grenadine and peach liqueur to deadly effect.

La Suite *sleek, sexy, elite* `8 F2`
40 avenue George V, 8ème • 01 53 57 49 49
Open to 2am Mon–Wed, to 6am Thu–Sat

This is the latest project from the Guettas, the people who made club Les Bains into an international code for cool. It's impressively hard to get into (be sure to look moneyed to stand a chance), but once inside, pose on a low leather stool, marvel at the pristine white decor and keep an eye out for big-name celebs.

Four Seasons George V *hotel bar* `8 F2`
31 avenue George V, 8ème • 01 49 52 70 00
›› www.fourseasons.com Open to 1am daily (to 2am Fri & Sat)

It's worth pulling out all the financial and sartorial stops to soak up the atmosphere at this swanky spot. When martinis in individual shakers are poured with a flourish at your table; when fine chocolates and cakes accompany sweet choices, and nuts in silver salvers the sour ones, the world seems a much better place.

Bar des Théâtres *unusual mix* `8 G3`
6 avenue Montaigne, 8ème • 01 47 23 34 63
Open all day to 2am daily

Popular with PRs from fashion houses, boys who work on the Bateaux Mouches, actors and audiences from the Théâtre du Champs Elysées *(see p127)* and anyone else who hangs out in Paris's Golden Triangle. A good spot for coffee or a café lunch, this is an attitude-free, rambunctious zinc bar and a rare find for the area.

Mathi's *insider address* `8 H2`
3 rue Ponthieu, 8ème • 01 53 76 01 62
Open to 2am Sun–Thu, to 5am Fri & Sat

Tucked away in a nondescript hotel, Mathi's morphs into a hedonistic haven after midnight. This petite bar fills up with super-glamorous folk flirting over the buzz of rather dire 80s music and under the eagle eye of the scary leopard-print-clad hostess. Hard to get into, but most definitely worth a try.

Le Bar du Plaza *look-at-me bar* `8 G3`
Plaza Athenée, 25 avenue Montaigne, 8ème • 01 53 67 66 65
≫ www.plaza-athenee-paris.com Open to 2am daily

Fashionistas, advertising executives and assorted beautiful people flock here to see and be seen. The interior offers high-set chairs and tables to perch at for maximum visibility, recessed seating to hide from prying eyes and flattering lighting to bring out everyone's best side. Serious cocktails at serious prices.

Le Queen *famous clubbers' favourite* `8 F1`
102 avenue des Champs Elysées, 8ème • 01 53 89 08 90
≫ www.queen.fr Open to 6am daily

A real legend, Le Queen still entices glamorous gays and hip heteros past the notoriously difficult-to access velvet rope. Disco divas love Monday's Disco Inferno, and fans of superstar DJs are bowled over by the sets of those who play here. Exhibitionists take note: women should dress scantily, men should dress tight. **Adm**

Bars & Clubs

Le Baron *uptown boys and girls*   8 F3
6 avenue Marceau, 8ème • 01 47 20 04 01
Open daily to 5am

Set up in 2005 by star graffiti artist André, Le Baron set out to lure the city's hipsters who were looking for a good time rather than just a good look. It worked. Whilst the pretty still flock here, the witty come too, to throw themselves around a tiny dance floor to nostalgic pop and a smattering of air-guitar rock. **Adm**

La Gare *posh, plush cocktail spot*
19 chaussée de la Muette, 16ème • 01 42 15 15 31
Ⓜ La Muette Open to 1:30am daily

Housed in a former train station, this is the epicentre of the smart and moneyed 16th-*arrondissement* set. The bar is a large circular room full of red velvet, gilt and glitz; the restaurant has food that is better and more reasonably priced than in similar joints. A good choice for an all-inclusive night out in this part of Paris.

Project 101 *alternative underground club*   4 E4
44 rue de la Rochefoucauld, 9ème • 01 49 95 95 85
≫ www.project-101.com Open until late Fri–Sun

An alternative to expensive, exclusive, soulless *soirées*, Project 101 is a collective of artists and DJs that hosts intimate, friendly gatherings for like-minded people. Video projections, an honesty bar (pay 10€, then help yourself), knock-out sets by up-and-coming DJs and a totally different top time. **Adm**

De la Ville Café *prime destination*   10 H2
34 boulevard de Bonne Nouvelle, 10ème • 01 48 24 48 09
Open to 2:30am daily

Once a brothel, De la Ville underwent several incarnations before emerging as a hot spot on the pre-club circuit. The rooms have different vibes from the civilized feel in the "papillon" room to the decadent atmosphere on the first floor. If you can't decide, then prop up the gorgeous zinc bar instead.

La Patache *artily distressed* `11 C1`
60 rue de Lancry, 10ème • no phone
Open to 2am daily

Just one small step away from being the wrong side of seedy, La Patache is a big hit with dishevelled creative types and their hangers-on. Pull up a rickety chair and don't be surprised if your neighbour starts sharing his haiku, bottle of rough red or theories on the meaning of life.

Chez Prune *dishevelled chic* `11 C1`
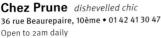
36 rue Beaurepaire, 10ème • 01 42 41 30 47
Open to 2am daily

Ever-packed Chez Prune is still the hottest spot on the Canal St-Martin. Dress vintage, drink retro (Suze is the current top tipple), ruffle your tousled hair and loudly discuss your current favourite art-house film, underground exhibition and esoteric designer – or just listen to those doing the same around you.

La Fourmi *all-day hot spot* `4 F3`
74 rue des Martyrs, 18ème • 01 42 64 70 35
Open to 2am Sun–Thu, to 4am Fri & Sat

A lively spot on the edge of Abbesses, La Fourmi is worth travelling across town for. As busy by day as by night, it's the favourite of an arts-and-media crew, who while away the hours under a huge chandelier made from wine bottles to a backdrop of loud techno music. A fantastic source of flyers for the best clubs.

Le Progres *quintessential bobo bar* `4 F2`
1 rue Yvonne le Tac, 18ème • 01 42 64 07 37
Open to 2am daily

It's all about atmosphere at Le Progres – little more than a small space stuffed with a few trestle tables, an electric heater and some uncomfortable chairs. Oh, and an über-cool art-house crowd. Having said that, it's a very friendly bar where people flit from table to table flirting and chatting over a *demi* or three.

Bars & Clubs

Le Sancerre *boisterous, fun bar* `4 E2`
35 rue des Abbesses, 18ème • 01 42 58 08 20
Open to 2am Sun–Thu, to 4am Fri & Sat

The pick of Montmartre's bistros, full of charm and character. Lovers, clubbers, transvestites and visitors all squeeze in for a rowdy time, nodding along to one of the frequent Sunday-night jazz concerts or shouting over loud techno, all the while getting through carafe after carafe of whatever is on special that day.

China Club *seductive cocktail joint* `18 E3`
50 rue Charenton, 12ème • 01 43 43 82 02
>> www.chinaclub.cc Open to 2am daily

A very sexy take on a colonial-era gentleman's club, with giant ceiling fans, deep Chesterfields, excellent cocktails (the martinis are superb) and a low buzz of civilized conversation pervading the ground floor. Upstairs, the *fumoir* offers a more romantic setting, while in the jazz cellar there's live music on weekends.

Rúla Búla *Celtic cool* `18 E2`
53 rue du Faubourg St-Antoine, 11ème • 01 49 29 92 10
>> www.rulabulabar.com Open to 2am daily

A welcome Irish addition to the Bastille, Rúla Búla (meaning "rumpus" in Gaelic) is a slick spot that pulls in a party crowd of young professionals. With its sleek granite bar, stone floor and acres of mirrors, this place may have Irish roots but it's certainly a shamrock and shillelagh-free zone.

Le Trucmush *down-to-earth bar* `18 E2`
5 passage Thiéré, 11ème • 01 48 07 11 91
Open to 2am Tue–Sat, to midnight Sun

On a quiet back street, happily hidden from the rabble of non-discriminating Bastille bar-hoppers, this tiny marvel of a bar is worth seeking out. Young and friendly, if quietly absurd (with bathtubs as seats and bidets as tables), it's the perfect place to put the world to rights over a couple of gargantuan *mojitos*.

Pop In *something for everyone*
11 D4

105 rue Amelot, 11ème • 01 48 05 56 11
Open to 2am Tue–Sun

A rather odd mix of grungy local, student haunt and fashionista central, the Pop In is, truly, all things to all people. The weeknight indie concerts give way to DJs and dancing at weekends, with music that ranges from electroclash to sugar pop. Christian Dior once threw a huge party here – it's more chic than it looks.

Le Clown Bar *themed wine bar*
11 D4

114 rue Amelot, 11ème • 01 43 55 87 35
Open to 1am daily

All manner of clown-related clutter and big-top bits and bobs can be found here. If you find Pierrot & Co unsettling, calm your nerves with several glasses of excellent wine, picked from an interesting and varied list. Don't be afraid to ask for guidance – the staff are happy to discuss the various vintages in depth.

Les Couleurs *dishevelled drinking*
12 F3

117 rue St-Maur, 11ème • 01 43 57 95 61
>> www.cafe-lescouleurs.com Open to 5am Mon–Sat

Les Couleurs represents all that's good about bric-a-brac chic. With an odds-and-ends interior and an arty clientele, this place is a good choice for a buzzy, bohemian night. Concerts and exhibitions fill the bar's cultural diary, and wine, beer and very reasonably priced cocktails make up the drinks menu.

Café Charbon *living legend*
12 F3

109 rue Oberkampf, 11ème • 01 43 57 55 13
Open to 2am Sun–Thu, to 4am Fri & Sat

The original Oberkampf HQ, Charbon is still going strong. The huge mirrors, beautiful antique lighting and Belle Epoque feel keep a loyal crowd coming back for more. Get there early for the chance of a table or space at the bar, or go very late to enter the backroom club (with eclectic music roster), Le Nouveau Casino.

Bars & Clubs

Le Zero Zero *dippy-hippy bar* `11 D5`
89 rue Amelot, 11ème • 01 49 23 51 00
Open to 2am daily

A tiny but intriguing bar that is always busy with an intensely loyal boho-chic clientele. Everyone drinks hard and chats happily: you might arrive on your own, but by the bottom of the first glass, you'll have a posse of new best friends. Don't miss the minuscule alcove out back: the fairy lights are sure to work some magic.

Wax *ace club-bar* `18 E1`
15 rue Daval, 11ème • 01 40 21 16 16
Open to 2am Tue–Thu, to 5am Fri & Sat

All psychedelic swirls, bright colours, hard house and strong cocktails, Wax sounds migraine-inducing, but it is in fact a top spot for a night out. It works equally well as a pre-club joint to get you in the groove or as a one-stop shop where you can hit the bar first and the dance floor later.

Favela Chic *Brazilian party* `11 D2`
18 rue du Faubourg du Temple, 11ème • 01 40 21 38 14
>> www.favelachic.com Open to 2am Tue–Thu, to 4am Fri & Sat

Don't turn up late: the queues here might be a drag, but missing a dancing spot on one of the refectory tables that are leapt upon at the first chance is close to tragedy. Fuelled by cracking *caipirinhas* and crowd-pleasing music (from funk to reggae and R&B), this place is hot, exhibitionistic and really good fun.

Chai 33 *hip and happening* `22 H3`
33 cour St-Emilion, 12ème • 01 53 44 01 01
>> www.chai33.com Open to 2am daily

Bercy's only really decent drinking spot, Chai 33 is a vast converted wine warehouse run by the people behind Parisian legends Barfly and the Buddha Bar. Expect an industrial look, low lights, hard-core dance music, deck chairs to kick back in and rather special wine-based cocktails.

Barrio Latino *Latin quarter* `18 E2`
46 rue du Faubourg St-Antoine, 12ème • 01 55 78 84 75
Open to 2am Sun–Fri, to 3:30am Sat

A vast, slick, opulent affair, with lots of wrought iron, red velvet, expanses of coloured glass and hoards of designer-clad beautiful people, the Barrio Latino is a must for those keen to see and be seen Latino-style. Don't bother trying to reach the top floor – only those with a special elevator key can ascend to the gods.

Le Baron Rouge *zinc wine bar* `18 F3`
1 rue Théophile Roussel, 12ème • 01 43 43 14 32
Open to 10pm Mon–Sat, 10am–3pm Sun

Just around the corner from the marché d'Aligre, this is a jolly, traditional *bistrot à vins* that is always full of contented oenophiles slurping and swilling – but never spitting – their way through the impressive wine list. Ask the bar staff for recommendations – their blackboard full of goodies changes regularly and includes a large choice of wine by the glass. On Sundays, oysters are available in season; atmosphere in abundance is on tap all year round.

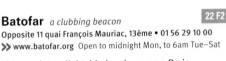

Limelight *exclusive clubbing destination* `22 F4`
162 avenue de France, 13ème • 01 56 61 44 04
» www.mk2.com Open 6pm–3am Wed–Thu, 6pm–5am Fri, 3pm–5am Sat, 3pm–3am Sun

Located inside the futuristic MK2 Bibliothèque cinema complex, the Limelight is a super-cool club with lofty ceilings, minimalist style and a terrace that can take 300 people. The management opens for one-off parties year-round and more regularly during summer. **Adm**

Batofar *a clubbing beacon* `22 F2`
Opposite 11 quai François Mauriac, 13ème • 01 56 29 10 00
» www.batofar.org Open to midnight Mon, to 6am Tue–Sat

This scarlet ex-lightship has become a Paris landmark and clubbers' institution. Big-name DJs and local unknowns, plus an unpretentious, up-for-it crowd, make it one of Paris's best nightspots. A great chill-out deck and a fantastic summertime Sunday after-party on the *quai* round off the picture. **Adm**

streetlife

Paris has sights aplenty, but the real spectacle is on the street, whether it's in the chic 7th *arrondissement* or the gritty 20th. Year round, the city's markets overflow with shoppers searching for choice seasonal produce, retro clothing and bric-a-brac bargains. And in fine weather, restaurant terraces fill with sun-seekers and people-watchers, and café life spills out onto the pavements.

Streetlife

Beaubourg and the Quartier Montorgueil `10 H4` *hipster hang-out*

With its pedestrianized streets, quirky shops, good-value restaurants and eclectic bars and clubs, the area stretching west from the Centre Pompidou to the place des Victoires is one of the city's best districts for some retail therapy and just hanging out. Before 10 or 11am, try rue Montorgueil, an atmospheric shopping street that also has a variety of cafés – try **Les Petits Carreaux** (the most traditional) or **Santi** (the trendiest). From mid-morning, the area around the Pompidou swings into action: drinks on the terrace at the **Café Beaubourg**, opposite its namesake, are a Parisian institution, and ideal before or after taking in a show.

To the west is Les Halles, a hideous underground mall that's best avoided (especially on Saturdays, when it's a magnet for bored suburban youths). Instead, rue Etienne Marcel and rue Tiquetonne (running parallel and full of cute little shops) are much more attractive propositions for shoppers. Highlights

are offbeat women's boutique **Barbara Bui** *(see p69)*; trendy second-hand store **Killiwatch** *(see p69)*; **Le Shop**, a funky warehouse full of designer concessions; and **NotsoBig**, which sells all kinds of items for cool kids. Further west, everyone who's anyone heads to the indefinably chic **L'Eclaireur** *(see p67)*, while around the place des Victoires, the scene becomes noticeably more up-market, with plenty of top designers.

The area's night-time scene is buzzing too: try trendy **Le Café** or **Etienne Marcel** or **Wine and Bubbles** *(see p217 for all)* for fabulous fizz and the best wines. Other top drinking spots are **Le Next** *(see p141)* and **Le Café Noir** *(see p141)*, while clubs include one of Paris's best jazz spots, **Le Duc des Lombards** *(see p124)*, and, on rue Bourg l'Abbeye, the once legendary **Les Bains**, whose slip in status means that mere mortals can now get through the door. For late-night nibbles, **Au Pied de Cochon** *(see p28)* and **La Tour de Montlhèry** *(see p29)* both keep serving through the early hours of the morning after the long night before.

For the very latest on Paris go to >> **www.realcity.dk.com**

Le Marais *falafal, fashion and fun* `17 B1`

Historically the city's Jewish ghetto and an area where market gardens were once cultivated, Le Marais (the marsh) is today one of Paris's most vibrant *quartiers*. Thronged by day and by night, it's a cosmopolitan mix; one where gay bars, kosher restaurants, boutiques, museums and antiques shops comfortably co-exist in beautiful buildings that have stood here for centuries.

The Marais is especially busy on Sunday afternoons, when most shops along rue des Francs Bourgeois defy the law by opening their doors. Among the most popular boutiques are **Abou d'Abi Bazar** *(see p72)*, source of affordable bobo (bohemian bourgeois) clothing; the unfailingly fashionable **Camper** for shoes; **A-poc** *(see p74)* showcasing Issey Miyake's innovative creations; and the hip home accessories store **La Chaise Longue** *(see p72)*. Heading north, on the way to the Musée National Picasso *(see p101)* is rue Elzévir, recently colonized by stylish African restaurants and shops selling clothing and arty imported objects for the home. Further north, the up-and-coming rue Charlot is home to galleries and

trendy restaurants, such as **R'Aliment** *(see p32)*. The real heart of the Marais, though, is the ancient, narrow rue des Rosiers, where falafal shops such as **L'As du Fallafal** *(see p33)* vie to out-crunch each other, and chic designer boutiques lure in wealthy trend-spotters. Around the corner, rue Vieille du Temple has a high concentration of cool cafés and restaurants, including **Les Petits Marseillais** *(see p32)*, **Au Petit Fer à Cheval** *(see p144)* and **Les Etages** *(see p146)*. This particular stretch is also a hub for the gay scene.

Down towards Bastille, the perfectly symmetrical 17th-century place des Vosges was once home to Victor Hugo and is now the playground of beautifully attired French toddlers, as well as unusually talented buskers. Locals gather here on weekends to picnic, watch the little ones frolic and generally take in the scene. Just to the south, the busy rue St-Antoine is where the locals do their food shopping in the traditional shops and supermarkets, while rue St-Paul hosts a notable collection of antiques shops and one of the city's best bakeries, **Boulangerie Malineau**, which sells an exceptional baguette.

Streetlife

St-Germain *conspicuous consumption* `16 E2`

Much of St-Germain's literary soul has been lost as scores of designer boutiques have supplanted bookshops, but the terraces of **Café de Flore** and **Les Deux Magots**, on the boulevard St-Germain, remain haunts of the area's intelligentsia and artists. But the new shops aren't all about fashion: rue Bonaparte has some serious antiques stores, while rue de Buci and neighbouring rue de Seine are both lined with gourmet food retailers. The real must for local foodies, however, is **Pierre Hermé** at No. 72 rue Bonaparte, the beauty of whose cakes rivals that of the YSL creations opposite.

In summer, there is no better place to people-watch than the terrace of **Café de la Mairie** *(see p149)*. In fact, as far as bars go, this part of town is spoilt for choice, especially along nearby rue des Canettes, aka *rue de la soif* (the street of thirst). Heading towards the river, rue St-Benoît, the jazz hub of Paris in the 1950s and 60s, still has a couple of good jazz clubs and a great Japanese noodle restaurant, **Yen** *(see p38)*.

Rue Cler *edible elegance* `14 G1`

The sedate 7th *arrondissement* seems suddenly sexy when you discover this lively street market (open 8am–1pm & 4–7pm Tue–Sat, 8am–1pm Sun) on one of the few streets in Paris that hasn't been taken over by chain shops. Extra draws are patisserie **Lenôtre** and **Davoli**, a temple to porcine delights. The **Café du Marché**, is where the locals soak up the scene all year round thanks to its heated terrace.

Champ de Mars and Trocadéro `14 E1`

For all the formality of its design, the verdant Champ de Mars – a former parade ground – is a laid-back place to watch the world go by in summer, and a prime spot from which to appreciate the engineering marvel that is the Tour Eiffel. Over the bridge, at Trocadéro, exhibition-goers mill around the beautiful Palais de Chaillot *(see p110)*, people cool down in the fountains and skateboarders show off their moves.

Les Champs-Elysées   *broad walk*   8 F1

It may seem clichéd, but "Les Champs" is still a place to head for, especially on a Sunday, when its shops – mostly flagship stores – are open (unusual for Paris). Wandering up the avenue from place de la Concorde is a popular pastime, not to be missed when the Mairie (city hall) is staging one of its regular cultural events (recent extravaganzas have included TGV trains parked on the pavement and avant-garde art exhibitions).

At night, the lights along the avenue are spectacular, and there are several stores that are open late, as well as some large multiscreen cinemas. Don't overlook the avenue's car showrooms: **Toyota** at No. 79 and **Renault** at No. 53, both of which feature in-store bars and restaurants and are trendy destinations for a unique and slightly bizarre combination of cars, cocktails and cuisine. The revamped **Publicis Drugstore** *(see p87)* contains a handful of shops and a very cool restaurant overseen by chef Alain Ducasse and at No. 65 is **Culture Bière**, Heinekin's new temple to beer.

Boulevard des Batignolles   *market*   3 B3

Below the Sacré Coeur and seedy place de Clichy, the tree-lined boulevard des Batignolles plays host every Saturday to the city's best organic market, where many of the stallholders sell their own produce (as opposed to food bought from wholesale markets). Producers hawk everything – from perfectly ripe cheeses, to giant goose eggs and vegetables galore – to the area's increasingly trendy population.

Canal St-Martin   *bohemian rhapsody*   5 C5

A hub for Parisian hipsters, this area looks and feels like nowhere else in the city. A stroll along the leafy quai de Jemmapes or quai de Valmy, on either side of the tranquil canal, is a popular weekend pursuit. There are plenty of stops to choose from, including the café **Chez Prune** *(see p153)*, the music venue **Hotel du Nord**, and trendy boutiques such as Stella Cadente *(see p91)* and **Coin Canal** *(see p92)*.

>> *Boat trips up the Canal St-Martin are a good way to soak up the local vibe (see p112)*

Streetlife

Abbesses   *having a high old time*   `4 F2`

The heart of Montmartre is one of the city's loveliest districts in which to while away some time. Expect winding cobbled streets, dilapidated old windmills, charm by the bucket-load and interesting company – the local Montmartrois include lots of bohemian types and artists. While many of the shops, such as the funky **Spree** concept store *(see p93)* and **Patricia Louisor** *(see p92)*, are worth crossing town for during the day, don't leave too soon, as it's in the evening that things really start to kick off here.

As well as outstanding restaurants – **La Famille** *(see p52)*, **La Mascotte** *(see p53)* and **Café Burq** *(see p50)* are all here – the 18th *arrondissement* has numerous atmospheric bars, such as **La Fourmi** *(see p153)* and **Le Sancerre** *(see p154)*. Other diversions come in the shape of eccentric, camp cabaret **Chez Michou** *(see p231)*, full of lip-synching, cross-dressing divas, and art-house cinema **Studio 28** *(see p129)*, with its beer garden that makes for an enchanting pre-film drink.

La Goutte d'Or   *kaleidoscope of cultures*   `5 A2`

This is perhaps the most multicultural and edgy area in central Paris. La Goutte mainly vibrates to an African beat, but other cultures are also in evidence. Head to rue de Laghouat for a taste of Algeria, rue Jean François Lépine to absorb Chinese culture and rue Gardes for young international fashion designers. For all its colour and vibrancy, this part of Paris is plagued by crime, so keep your wallet close and avoid visiting at night.

Les Puces de St-Ouen   *mother of all flea markets*

Ⓜ Port de Clignancourt
≫ www.les-puces.com Open 9:30–6 Sat–Mon

Also known as Les Puces de Clignancourt, this is the city's largest flea market where amid the piles of junk, bargains and beautiful pieces also lurk. There are 12 market areas, so if you know what you're looking for, head to the specific section: Serpette and Biron are top for antiques, while Malik has great vintage clothing.

Boulevard de Belleville   *cultural X-roads*   `12 F2`

This broad, leafy boulevard is home to one of the city's cheapest and liveliest markets (7:30–2:30 Tue & Fri) and to thriving Chinese, Jewish and Arab communities, each with its own shops and restaurants. Two of the best places to soak up the multicultural buzz are the excellent Jewish-Tunisian restaurant **Benisti** *(see p53)* and the **New Nioullaville** *(see p226)*, known for its outstanding dim sum.

For the very latest on Paris go to ≫ www.realcity.dk.com

Rue de la Butte-aux-Cailles *old Paris* `20 H5`

Attracting students from the nearby **Cité Universitaire** *(see p118)* with its cheap food and boho bars (try **Le Temps des Cerises** at No. 18 or **Chez Paul** at No. 22, a classy bistro), this street offers a slice of village life among the tower blocks of the *13ème*. Another draw is the 1920s-built outdoor pool at the **Piscine Butte-aux-Cailles** *(see below)*. But this area really comes into its own at night, when cheap drinks draw the crowds.

Les Puces de Vanves *hagglers' heaven*
Avenue Georges Lafenestre and avenue Marc Sangrier, 14ème
Ⓜ Porte de Vanves Open 7:30–6 Sat & Sun

Vanves regulars swear that this is the best place for hidden treasures. It is smaller and friendlier than the other *puces* (flea markets), with around 350 stalls selling everything from chipped china to beautiful antique furniture, as well as retro jewellery and stacks of collectible magazines and books. Haggling is expected.

Rue Oberkampf *grungy good times* `12 F3`

Despite the fact that the area around and including rue Oberkampf has been comprehensively gentrified over the past five years, it still retains a multicultural feel and an urban vibe. But these days its residents are more likely to be cash-happy creatives than struggling immigrants or salt-of-the-earth types. This part of town is essentially a night-time destination and it's packed with bars and restaurants that are all either dive-like or designer-distressed to varying degrees. The oldest are still the best: **Café Charbon** *(see p155)* and **Mecano Bar** at No. 99 continue to pull in the crowds, just as **La Cithea** at No. 112 is still a popular club choice.

Running parallel, rue Jean-Pierre Timbaud is a little more down to earth, so expect good, cheap and unpretentious food at **Astier** *(see p53)* and people drawing on the paper tablecloths (crayons provided) at **Café Cannibale** at No. 93. Linking the two, on rue St-Maur, **Les Couleurs** *(see p155)* at No. 117, is a bohemian bar that holds concerts and exhibitions.

>> *Piscine Butte-aux-Cailles, 6 place Paul Verlaine 13ème (Map 21 A5), 01 45 89 60 05*

havens

Leafy parks and gardens provide essential breathing space in Paris, both literally and metaphorically, but there are other soothing diversions. When the city's hurly-burly gets too much and only a life-enhancing massage will do, there are plenty of spas to choose from. Or there are tranquil cafés high on atmosphere and low on attitude, and chapels and churches for quiet contemplation.

Havens

Place Dauphine *historical square* `16 G1`

Built in 1607, this delightfully shady spot on the Ile de la Cité is a real slice of old Paris. Its three sides echo the pointed tip of the island and were once lined with 32 identical 17th-century houses. Today only two of the original buildings remain – they're the ones facing the statue of Henry IV atop his trusty steed. Linger over lunch in one of the local bistros, or just find a bench and take in the picturesque scene.

Square du Vert-Galant *green peace* `16 F1`

This leafy square, perched on the point of the Ile de la Cité, offers welcome respite from the hubbub of the surrounding streets. In summer, sun-seekers bypass the green benches and herbaceous borders and head for the cobblestoned quays below to work on their tans, have a waterside picnic or just enjoy the views: Seine straight ahead, Louvre to the right and the Institut de France's pretty cupola on the left.

Palais Royal *majestic oasis* `10 F3`
Place du Palais Royal, 1er
Gardens open dawn to dusk daily

The elegant arcades and quiet garden enclave of the 17th-century Palais Royal have long been popular for contemplation or a promenade, with luxury shops and restaurants as added draws. Before the Revolution, prostitutes and dissidents gathered in cafés in the arcades to plot the downfall of the old regime, and the Palais was a favoured haunt of gamblers. Today, the most illicit fun you're likely to have is devouring an extra dessert at the Restaurant du Palais Royal (*see p28*) or splashing out in one of the swish boutiques located in the building's *galeries*.

The garden is a serene oasis in the city's heart, with striking tree-lined alleyways that harbour rows of benches. Modern art fans will appreciate Pol Bury's steel-ball sculptures and Daniel Buren's once-controversial black-and-white striped columns, which echo the regularity of the architecture behind.

Nickel *male order*
48 rue des Francs Bourgeois, 3ème • 01 42 77 41 10
>> www.nickel.fr Open 9:30–7 Mon–Sat (to 9 on Thu)

11 B5

Philippe Dumont opened Nickel in 1996 so that boys wouldn't have to rub just-waxed shoulders with the girls when they were in need of a top-to-toe spruce-up. Nickel specializes in old-fashioned wet shaves, as well as treatments such as manicures and facials. There's also a range of Nickel beauty products for men.

32 Montorgueil *beauty boost*
32 rue Montorgueil, 1er • 01 55 80 71 40
>> www.john-nollet.com Open 9–7:30 Mon–Sat (to 9 Wed–Fri)

10 H3

The tiny stream running through this spa whispers "relax" – something that's instantly achievable with a solar plexus massage followed by a fruit-and-flowers exfoliation, or an acacia honey wrap and a soothing foot rub. And, for a lavish fee, hairdresser to the stars John Nollet will clip your locks into elegant submission.

St-Julien-le-Pauvre *12th-century church*
Rue St-Julien-le-Pauvre, 5ème • 01 43 54 52 16
Open 10–7:30 daily

16 H2

One of the oldest churches in Paris, St-Julien has been a place of refuge for hundreds of years. These days, it's weary tourists and workers, rather than worshippers, who find sanctuary under its barrel-vaulted ceilings and in its Gothic apses. Outside there's a calm little park with shaded benches.

L'Imprévu Café *laid-back living*
7 rue Quincampoix, 4ème • 01 42 78 23 50
Open noon–2am Mon–Sat, 1pm–2am Sun

10 H5

Pull up an old barber's chair or plump for a comfy leopard-print couch and kick back with a cocktail (or creamy coffee) after an afternoon of art appreciation in the nearby Centre Pompidou *(see p13)*. The lighting is low-key, the vibe relaxed and the mellow jazz soundtrack easy on the ears.

>> *L'Imprévu holds poetry readings on the first Tuesday of every month at 8pm*

La Grande Mosquée *exotic baths*

39 rue Geoffroy St-Hilaire, 5ème • 01 45 35 97 33
>> www.mosquee-de-paris.org Baths open 2–9 Fri,
10–9 Sat–Wed (women only: Mon, Wed, Fri & Sat; men only:
Tue & Sun); café open 9am–11pm; restaurant open lunch &
dinner daily; tours 9–noon & 2–6 Sat–Thu

Built in the 1920s, the Paris mosque – with its
immaculate white walls and intricately carved
woodwork – was inspired by the famous Alhambra in
Spain and the Boulnania Mosque in Morocco. It's an
environment where tranquillity reigns, from the grand
patio and sunken garden through to the tiled minaret
and the prayer room, all of which (except the latter)
can be visited on a guided tour. The *hammam*
(Turkish baths) and the tearoom, however, are the
main draws here. And if your idea of relaxation is
being steamed, scrubbed and massaged to within an
inch of your life, then this is definitely the place for
you. After a session in the searing sauna, followed by
a *gommage* (body scrub) and then a spirited and oily
massage, you can stretch out on a cushion in the lush
purple-and-gold rotunda and sip some sweet mint tea
as Arabic music and hushed voices float around you –
a scene straight out of Ingres's *Le Bain Turc*.

In winter, the *hammam*'s the thing, but in summer,
sipping tea in the shade of the fig tree on the blue-tiled
terrace of the Café Maure can be equally appealing.
Alternatively, drop on to one of the richly coloured
banquettes inside, under the amazing coffered ceiling,
and watch waiters dart about with trays of mint tea
and honey-drizzled cakes, or tureens of couscous
destined for the restaurant. It's another world.

City Parks and Gardens

The **Jardin du Luxembourg** (Map 16 E4) is one of the city's most beloved parks. Offering everything from fountains to *boules* pitches and chairs aplenty, it's basically a backyard for all those without one. If you want something more formal, head for the quintessential French garden, the **Jardin des Tuileries** (Map 9 D4), laid out in the 17th century by royal gardener Le Nôtre, with a sweeping central avenue bordered by geometric flower beds and topiary. **Parc Monceau** (Map 2 H4) is worlds apart with its fanciful Roman temple, Egyptian pyramid, Japanese pagoda and Dutch windmill – as well as lawns and islands of flowers. But if flowers are your pleasure, the rose garden of the **Parc de Bagatelle** *(see p220)*, with some 1,300 varieties, is heaven.

Jardins des Plantes *floral fancy* `17 B5`
Entrances on rue Buffon, rue Cuvier, rue Geoffroy St-Hilaire, place Valhubert, 5ème Open summer 7:30–8, winter 7:30–5:30

Escape dreary, wintry Paris inside steamy tropical glasshouses alive with lush cacti, ferns and orchids. In May, cherry trees add a burst of colour between the sweeping shaded avenues. And, for a dose of nature deep in the city, visit the wild *parc écologique*, which is frequented by more than 75 species of birds.

Mariage Frères *historic tearoom* `16 F1`
13 rue des Grands Augustins, 6ème • 01 40 51 82 50
» www.mariagefreres.fr Open 10:30–7:30 daily

The Mariage family have been trading tea for 150 years and this tranquil tearoom is the perfect place to discover their wares. Hardwood floors, high-backed chairs, silver tea services, white-coated waiters and 500 kinds of tea imbue this 17th-century building with a distinct aroma of the old East Indies.

Hôtel National des Invalides `15 A1`
Esplanade des Invalides, 7ème • 01 44 42 38 77
» www.invalides.org Open 10–6 daily (winter: to 5)

Built by Louis XIV to house his wounded soldiers (part of it remains a hospital today), the Hôtel des Invalides contains the grandiose tomb of Napoleon I and a massive army museum. Less well known are the restful gardens, with their perfectly trimmed triangular trees, and flowerbeds overlooking a tinkling fountain. **Adm**

Havens

Chapelle Expiatoire *fit for a king* `9 C1`
29 rue Pasquier, 8ème • 01 42 65 35 80
Open 10–1, 2–6 Thu–Sat (2–4 in winter)

Louis XVI and Marie-Antoinette (as well as other victims of the guillotine) were originally buried on this spot, which prompted Louis XVIII to build a chapel in 1815 in their memory. Rest on a bench under 100-year-old trees or peruse the huge stone tombs of the Swiss Guards who died defending the luckless Louis XVI.

Four Seasons George V *sleek spa* `8 F2`
31 avenue George V, 8ème • 01 49 52 70 00
>> www.fourseasons.com Open 6:30am–10pm daily

The spa of this five-star hotel oozes style, from the Jacuzzi and pool with trompe-l'oeil frescoes, to the relaxation lounge with linen-covered day beds, soft music and fresh fruit for the taking. Opt for a his-and-hers hot-stone massage, a tequila-based *punta mita* massage or a cosseting aromatherapy facial.

Parc des Buttes Chaumont *wild park* `6 G4`
Entrances on rue Manin and rue Boltzaris, 19ème
Open 7:30am–9pm (in summer to 11pm)

Cliffs and gushing waterfalls give this former rubbish tip and quarry an untamed alpine look. But it's all man-made, from the lake and cave complete with stalactites, to the Temple of Sybil, from which you can survey urban Paris – including the distinctive outline of the Sacré Coeur in the distance.

Cinq Mondes *world-class pampering* `9 D1`
6 square de l'Opéra Louis Jouvet, 9ème • 01 42 66 00 60
>> www.cinqmondes.com Open noon–8 Mon–Sat (to 10 Thu)

Each of Cinq Mondes' nine face and body treatments begins with a dreamy head-and-shoulder rub. Then the world tour begins: Ayurvedic massage with warm oil; a *hammam* treatment complete with black soap, vigorous scrub down and massage; or a soak in a Japanese petal-strewn *o-furo* bath, perfumed with essential oils.

For the very latest on Paris go to >> www.realcity.dk.com

La Promenade Plantée *linear park* `18 G5`

Entrances include ave Daumesnil, ave Ledru Rollin and rue Edouard-Lartet, 12ème
Open 8–6 Mon–Fri, 9–6 Sat & Sun (summer: to 9pm)

This green strip running 4.5km (3 miles) atop an old railway viaduct starts off at urbanized Bastille and ends at the verdant Bois de Vincennes, to the east of the city. Planted with roses, lavender, shrubs and herbs, the promenade appeals to joggers, strollers and the curious, as its elevated position makes it easy to gaze down at the streets below or into the apartments and offices that line the route.

Cimetière du Montparnasse *tombs* `19 C2`

3 boulevard Edgar Quinet, 14ème • 01 44 10 86 50
Open 9–5:30 daily (but times can vary)

Reflect on Paris's artistic and literary past, immortalized here. Among the graves are those of Baudelaire, Sartre and companion Simone de Beauvoir, and French crooner Serge Gainsbourg, whose grave is always covered with fans' tributes. Brancusi's superb sculpture *Kiss* commemorates the double suicide of two friends.

Parc André Citroën *themed gardens* `13 A5`

Entrances include quai André Citroën & rue St-Charles, 15ème
Open dawn–8pm Mon–Fri, 9am–8pm Sat & Sun; closing times vary according to the time of year and day of the week

Laid out on the site of the old Citroën car factory, this 21st-century French garden is a long way from the formal, keep-off-the-grass parks dotted around the city. Based on four themes – architecture, artifice, movement and nature – the park is characterized by clean lines and lots of glass, in the shape of two huge glass-house pavilions. There's a vast lawn, a black garden and a white garden, five coloured gardens designed to represent the five senses, and a moving garden (full of grasses blowing in the breeze). Water plays a central role, with canals, waterfalls and the dancing fountain – a square that shoots jets of water into the air at random heights. It's a magnet for giggling children cooling off in summer. Added attractions include leafy labyrinths for quiet contemplation and a tethered hot-air balloon for fabulous views over the city.

hotels

Hotels in Paris come in all styles and cater to all budgets. Will you plump for a charming chintz-filled pension with stunning views in Montmartre, a bohemian bedroom in the heart of the Left Bank, or a minimalist pad in one of the city's burgeoning boutique hotels? Finding a single bed in the city can be a challenge, though, so be prepared for hefty single supplements – or bring a friend.

HOTELS

Paris is famous for super-luxe hotels offering impeccable service; so if marble and gilt are your thing, you'll be in heavily mirrored heaven. Budget-friendly, often family-run, *pensions* and one- and two-star hotels are no less typical of the city's hotel scene. However, lovers of the sleek, urban look are increasingly being rewarded by hoteliers who have chosen to embrace minimalism and a more cutting-edge approach to hotel design and the hotel experience.

Katherine Spenley

Romantic Hideaways

With the right companion, any hotel in Paris is a potential love nest. However, the rooms at the **Pavillon de la Reine** *(see p178)* are especially hard to tear yourself away from; the **Hotel de Vigny** *(see p183)*, though located off the Champs Elysées, feels like a cosy rural retreat; and the themed decor at **L'Hotel** *(see p181)* is ideal for acting out your fantasies.

Artistic Style

Indulge your inner art buff with a stay at the **Hotel Square** *(see p185)* – a curvy architectural delight housing a mini gallery. Art aficionados could also check into **Le A** *(see p183)*, where canvases dot the walls and design tomes fill the bookcases. Over at the **Artus Hotel** *(see p181)*, the work of young, unknown painters and sculptors is on show.

Rooms with a View

Taking in the sights from your bed (or balcony) is possible if you check into one of the following: for typical Montmartre vistas head to the **Royal Fromentin** *(see p186)*; the **Hotel du Panthéon** *(see p181)* surveys the monument of the same name; and the **Hotel du Quai Voltaire** *(see p182)* allows guests to gaze out over the Seine.

choice stays

Designer Dreams

It's taken the capital of style a while to catch up with the trend for *haute-couture* hotels; now ventures by Christian Lacroix and Azzedine Alaïa have made up for the city's late entrance. Alaïa's **5 rue de Moussy** *(see p186)* is a diminuative haven for the very chic, and **Hotel du Petit Moulin** *(see p179)* features the flamboyant touches Lacroix's fans would expect.

Cheap Chic

A chic sleep with a distinctly high-street price tag can be found at the **Hotel Eldorado** *(see p185)*, loved by fashion folk and media hacks. The **Hotel du Septième Art** *(see p179)*, dedicated to the silver screen, is a quirky place to crash with panache, and **Hotel Mayet** *(see p182)* offers urban style at candlewick-bedspread prices.

Hip Hotels

Hotel Costes *(see p138)* has been a favourite of the achingly hip for years, but it's now got some serious competition in the shape of **Murano Urban Resort** *(see p179)*. This outlandish riot of kitsch chic appeals to inner (and real) A-listers. Run by the same team, **Kube** *(see p187)* is so cool it's even got an ice bar to prove the point.

Hotel Tonic *pleasant retreat*

12–14 rue du Roule, 1er • 01 42 33 00 71

`10 G5`

>> www.tonichotel.com

The central location and elegant rooms are the big draws here. Some of the intimate bedrooms reveal ancient stone walls (the building dates from the 17th century) and all come complete with heavy red brocade bedspreads and simple wooden headboards. Superior rooms have Jacuzzis to soothe aching bones. **Moderate**

Hotel Roubaix *homely spot*

6 rue Greneta, 3ème • 01 42 72 89 91

`10 H3`

>> www.hotel-de-roubaix.com

Traditional decor, a rickety lift and delightfully courteous, old-school owners contribute to the Roubaix's charm. The rooms are a little faded and down at heel, but extremely clean. And the wonderful welcome from the staff – who greet both first-timers and regulars alike as if they were old family friends – more than makes up for the odd creaky bed-spring. **Cheap**

Pavillon de la Reine *17th-century treat*

28 place des Vosges, 3ème • 01 40 29 19 19

`17 D1`

>> www.pavillon-de-la-reine.com

Arguably the most romantic hotel in Paris, this place will transform even the most hardbitten cynic. The prime location is just the start; add a divine courtyard, rooms with beams and giant beds, friendly staff and a gorgeous sitting room complete with an honesty bar, and you may never want to leave. **Expensive**

Booking Agencies

The official tourist office website (www.paris-touristoffice.com) is a useful site for finding and booking a hotel on the web, though you do not need to pay online. If you arrive in Paris without a hotel, try branches of the Office du Tourisme (*see p23*) at the Gare de Lyon and the Gare du Nord. A small commission is usually charged.

Hotel Tiquetonne *budget beds*

6 rue Tiquetonne, 2ème

01 42 36 94 58

`10 H4`

It might be around the corner from the unsalubrious – though colourful – rue St-Denis, but this is a great find in the city's buzzy Montorgueil *quartier*. The hotel is located on a cobbled street full of trendy shops and quirky bars, and its airy rooms are simple, functional and bigger than most in this bracket. **Cheap**

Hotel St-Merry *memorable nights* `17 A1`
78 rue de la Verrerie, 4ème
01 42 78 14 15

Here, a boho vibe and quirky Gothic feel set the scene. Formerly part of the neighbouring church and at one point a bordello, the St-Merry has cosy rooms, one of which features a flying buttress above the bed. Only the suite has a TV, so guests staying in other rooms have to amuse themselves. **Moderate**

Murano Urban Resort *OTT interiors* `11 C3`
13 boulevard du Temple, 3ème • 01 42 71 20 00
>> www.muranoresort.com

Movie stars and music magnates love this place, so it's perfect for living out A-list fantasies. From the suites with private swimming pools and terraces, to the bedside mood lighting (flick a switch for a colour change), via the sex toys in each room's mini bar, the Murano is a very special choice. **Expensive**

Hotel du Petit Moulin *designer dreams* `11 C4`
29 rue Poitou, 3ème • 01 42 74 10 10
>> www.paris-hotel-petitmoulin.com

Christian Lacroix designed the Petit Moulin, now much loved by fashionistas and design fans. Housed in a former bakery, this hotel is a real gem. Each of the 17 rooms is different, with styles ranging from rustic to pop, including features such as cornicing and wall-size fashion sketches. Dramatic and sublime. **Moderate**

Hotel du Septième Art *on a film theme* `17 C2`
20 rue St-Paul, 4ème
01 44 54 85 00

Film fans favour this hotel that pays homage to cinema, the seventh art. The bedrooms (the quietest ones face the courtyard), stairwells and bar, full of old movie posters and kitsch Hollywood memorabilia, are a little dusty. However, the art-house atmosphere and convenient location are real pluses. **Cheap**

Hotel du Bourg Tibourg *eclectic style* `17 B1`
19 rue de Bourg Tibourg, 4ème • 01 42 78 47 39
>> www.hotelbourgtibourg.com

The little-known Bourg Tibourg is popular with those looking for some lower-price chic. Design guru Jacques Garcia has created an interior that is a sexy mish-mash of periods and styles. Expect Neo-Gothic and offbeat Orientalism, stark stripes, gilt and velvet, and black marble-clad bathrooms. **Moderate**

Hotels

Hotel les Degrés de Notre Dame *perennial favourite* 16 H3
10 rue des Grands Degrés, 5ème • 01 55 42 88 88
>> www.lesdegreshotel.com

With its beams and wood panelling, helpful staff, wonderful location set back from the Seine and great value for money, this hotel is justly popular. Be sure to try dinner on the terrace or in the candle-filled dining room, and book your room well in advance. **Moderate**

Hotel Esméralda *shabby charm* 16 H2
4 rue St-Julien-le-Pauvre, 5ème
01 43 54 19 20

Set on a pretty square across the river from Notre Dame, this charming hotel is a perfect base for indulging in some Left Bank pursuits. The 17th-century building contains 19 slightly run-down – yet romantic – rooms, complete with antique furnishings and uneven floors. Book ahead (no credit cards accepted). **Cheap**

Hotel du Lys *romantic bargain* 16 G2
23 rue Serpente, 6ème
01 43 26 97 57

The Hotel du Lys is a timeless, typically French hotel, all winding staircases, scrubbed floorboards, tapestries and fading floral arrangements. The rooms are simply furnished and some tend towards the tiny, but if you're looking for a no-fuss place to hole up with your beloved, it is ideal. **Cheap**

Villa D'Estrées *chic boutique hotel* 16 G2
17 rue Git-le-Couer, 6ème • 01 55 42 71 11
>> www.paris-hotel-latin-quarter.com

Such a closely guarded secret that it's deliberately ex-directory, the Villa D'Estrées is definitely worth knowing about. With ten beautiful rooms, conceived by Yann Descamp (protégé of über-designer Jacques Garcia), the hotel is all warm tones and Empire-style furniture. Perfect for a hush-hush weekend. **Moderate**

L'Hotel *indulgent fantasies*

16 E1

13 rue des Beaux Arts, 6ème • 01 44 41 99 00
>> www.l-hotel.com

Oscar Wilde spent his last days here, famously claiming that he was dying beyond his means. There's no
need to take it quite that far, but a night here is worth
the expense. L'Hotel is a temple to opulence, with 20
rooms – individually decorated by the ubiquitous
Jaques Garcia – leading off the circular lightwell. Part
the heavy drapes at the door of the Léopard Room to
reveal a riot of purple taffeta, velvet, gilt and leopard
print. There's also a red marble bathroom with a
sunken tub. The Roi de Naples Room features a huge
bed, a fireplace and impressive chandeliers while the
St Petersburg is an imperial dream of jade, mirrors
and marble. In the basement, the perpetual-wave
pool, mosaic steam room and circular chill-out lounge
provide a heaven for hedonists. However, shy
Sybarites will be pleased to discover that this spa area
can only be reserved for private sessions. **Expensive**

Artus Hotel *chic on the cheap*

16 E2

34 rue de Buci, 6ème • 01 43 29 07 20
>> www.artushotel.com

Superbly located, the Artus has friendly, relaxed staff,
a young and hip clientele and decent prices. The arty
touch alluded to in the hotel's name? Check out the
bedroom doors, each painted by an up-and-coming
artist. If you can, splash out on the duplex room with
a truly striking, sumptuous bathroom. **Moderate**

Hotel du Panthéon *elegant living*

16 G4

19 place du Panthéon, 5ème • 01 43 54 32 95
>> www.hoteldupantheon.com

It's always wise to book ahead for the Hotel du
Panthéon; its prime location and attentive staff have
won it a legion of fans. Booking also increases the
chance of getting one of the few rooms with spectacular
Panthéon views. All rooms have château-style furnishings, including some four-poster beds. **Moderate**

Hotels

Hotel Mayet *funky design* `15 B4`
3 rue Mayet, 6ème • 01 47 83 21 35
>> www.mayet.com

A rare departure from the chintzy interiors usually found in cheaper Parisian hotels, the Mayet's rooms are a breath of fresh air, especially those on the fifth floor, which have their own balconies. Expect fuss-free furniture, primary colours and clean lines, and guests who expect a little style for their euros. **Cheap**

Hotel des St-Pères *St-Germain star* `15 D2`
65 rue des St-Pères, 6ème • 01 45 44 50 00
>> www.esprit-de-france.com

The St-Pères is a kind of up-market boarding house for the bookish. Its rooms – elegant, individually deco-rated and opening onto an interior courtyard – and bar are popular with publishers and authors from nearby publishing houses. Romantics and art-lovers will adore the painted bathroom ceiling in Room 100. **Moderate**

Hotel Lenox *updated Art Deco* `15 D1`
9 rue de l'Université, 7ème • 01 42 96 10 95
>> www.lenoxsaintgermain.com

Follow in the footsteps of James Joyce, Ezra Pound and T S Eliot by checking into the Lenox. The Art Deco bar and lobby offer a stylish backdrop for cocktails; the exterior glass lift provides an adrenaline kick for those staying on the top floors; and the comfortable rooms are a perfect cocoon from the outside world. **Moderate**

Hotel du Quai Voltaire *room with a view* `9 D5`
19 quai Voltaire, 7ème • 01 42 61 50 91
>> www.quaivoltaire.fr

Staying here is really all about location. The rooms can be a little small and the sparse furnishing tends towards the shabby, so make sure you book a top-floor, river-facing room. These are a little larger than most, have less traffic noise and, of course, the most spectacular views. **Moderate**

Hotel Malar *characterful cheapie*
29 rue Malar, 7ème • 01 45 51 38 46
» www.hotelmalar.com

8 G5

Tucked away in this chic part of town, near the Eiffel Tower the Malar is a real gem. The reception area is all wood beams and long-stemmed roses, the interior courtyard a delightful place to breakfast, and the rooms are simple yet spotlessly clean. The charming staff offer a genuinely warm welcome. **Cheap**

Le A *urban cool*
4 rue d'Artois, 8ème • 01 42 56 99 99
» www.hotel-le-a-paris.com

8 H1

The A looks like something out of *Wallpaper** magazine and is a magnet for fashion and media folk. The all-white bedrooms boast sleek stone bathrooms and original artworks: those on the sixth floor are flooded with light via skylights. Down in the lobby, recline on a chaise longue with a long drink from the bar. **Expensive**

Hotel de Vigny *insider address*
9–11 rue Balzac, 8ème • 01 42 99 80 80
» www.hoteldevigny.com

8 F1

A palatial, prestigious hotel, the de Vigny is a well-kept secret among discerning visitors. It's the only Relais et Chateaux hotel in Paris, and offers chic and elegant rooms. A roaring fire in the mahogany-panelled lounge, an Art Deco-style bar with vintage champagne on ice, and discreet staff complete the picture. **Expensive**

Les Grandes Dames

Paris's palace hotels are temples to the art of high living, and while gilt, marble, crystal, velvet and shocking room rates are universal to them all, each has its own specialities. **Le Ritz** is perhaps the most (in)famous, and its health club is one of the world's most beautiful. **Le Crillon** is the city's poshest hotel; the quiet, sun-trap courtyard is a well-kept secret for summer drinks. The **Four Seasons George V** boasts an army of staff for each guest and a trendy spa *(see p172)*. **Le Meurice** is a little hipper than its rivals, hosting glittering private parties and offering an amazing personal-shopping service, while **La Plaza Athenée** is surrounded by the city's top designer boutiques and has a fabulous bar *(see p151)*. For further details, *see p233*.

Pershing Hall *happening scene*

49 rue Pierre-Charron, 8ème • 01 58 36 58 00
>> www.pershinghall.com

8 G2

Even if you do not usually opt for up-market accommodation, Pershing Hall, the city's hippest hotel, is really
worth the splurge. An unremarkable façade with a
small sign conceals a super-sleek haven created by
design maven Andrée Putman. The lobby sets the
offbeat, modish tone, with fashion photographs, a
bizarre tree-trunk sculpture "growing" from a pool in
the centre of the room and staff who look as if they're
filling in on their day off from the catwalk. A cascade
of beaded curtains leads to the interior courtyard
restaurant where *le beau monde* drink in the amazing
vista along with their Bollinger; the entire back wall
of the courtyard is covered with a stunning vertical
garden. And in summer, the glass roof retracts so
that guests can top up their (real) St-Tropez tans.

The rooms are as minimal and chic as one would
expect from Putman, featuring white bed linen, ash
furniture, aubergine taffeta drapes and blue-stained
parquet. Interesting extras include suites with sliding
panels that allow the bathroom to become part of the
bedroom (some rooms only have showers), state-of-
the-art plasma TV/DVDs and a free mini-bar complete
with trendy mini-bottles of Pop champagne. Take
advantage of the freebies before heading to Pershing
Lounge, the upper-level bar/club where the subdued
neon lighting, see-and-be-seen balcony area and
dove-grey leather sofas all contribute to make this
spot a favourite with Paris's party people. One of the
capital's hottest places to do drinks, the Lounge has
a different DJ every night of the week, occasional
funky-jazz concerts, upscale ladies' nights complete
with speed-dating sessions and tarot-card readings,
and an ever hip-and-happy vibe. **Expensive**

Hilton Paris Arc de Triomphe `2 G4`
51 rue de Courcelles, 8ème • 01 58 36 67 00
》 www.hilton.com

Decked it out in classic 1930s style by star designer Jacques Garcia, this vast hotel harks back to an era of elegance and sophistication. Art Deco-style furnishings dot the hallways and the rooms are fitted with ebony, imitation shark-skin wall coverings, cream leather seating and luxurious bedding. **Expensive**

Hotel Sezz *industrial chic* `13 C1`
6 avenue Fremiet, 16ème • 01 56 75 26 26
》 www.hotelsezz.com

Believe the hype about this boutique hotel – it deserves the buzz. The bathrooms are partitioned off with tinted glass, and clean lines dominate the rooms where dove-grey wall coverings and dark wood lend a masculine feel. A personal butler for every guest assures an ultra-luxurious stay. **Expensive**

Hotel Square *tastefully trendy* `13 A2`
3 rue des Boulainvilliers, 16ème • 01 44 14 91 90
》 www.hotelsquare.com

Housed in a curving granite building, this is an ideal choice for lovers of all things minimal and modern. Twenty-two tasteful rooms feature sleek furnishings, impressive hi-fi systems and stacks of arty magazines. The first-floor gallery often hosts temporary exhibitions, book launches and private parties. **Expensive**

Hotel Eldorado *hip and happening* `3 C2`
18 rue des Dames, 17ème 01 45 22 35 21
》 www.eldorado.fr

The Eldorado's attractive rooms are bright and airy, and its patio is ideal for lunching and lounging. The triples and quads are great value, but be sure to book ahead, especially during fashion weeks (Mar and Oct), when this place fills with models who aren't yet super enough to stay at a palace hotel *(see p183)*. **Cheap**

Royal Fromentin *good-value good times*   4 E3
11 rue Fromentin, 9ème • 01 48 74 85 93
>> www.hotelroyalfromentin.com

It was a swinging 1930s cabaret spot, and entertaining is still part of this hotel's soul: it is often the hotel of choice for bands playing at the nearby concert halls. The lobby bar's decor recalls the good old days, while some of the agreeable rooms have amazing views which will inspire anyone to get lyrical. **Cheap**

Hotel Terrass *lovely location*   4 E2
12–14 rue Joseph de Maistre, 18ème • 01 44 92 34 14
>> www.terrass-hotel.com

The Terrass offers a peaceful night's sleep in down-to-earth Montmartre. The decor is immaculate, if a little bland, but the welcome is warm and the trendy location hard to beat. In summer, the roof-top restaurant barbecue is very romantic and quite an "in" destination with fashionable folk. **Moderate**

Hotel Langlois *atmospheric charm*   11 D4
63 rue St-Lazare, 9ème
01 48 74 78 24

Formerly the Hotel des Croises, this place's name changed after it was featured as the Hotel Langlois in the 2002 movie *The Truth about Charlie*. The pristine Art Nouveau building hides a rickety lift that takes guests to rooms stuffed with antiques and charm, some of which boast stunning views. **Cheap**

Aparthotels

If you're after a private pad, aparthotels are the way to go. The most luxurious is the **Carré d'Or** complex off the Champs-Elysées, popular with A-listers from the worlds of film, fashion and serious wealth. The most stylish is **5 rue de Moussy** heralding Azzedine Alaïa's grand entrance into the world of "hotel" design, with just three sought-after stylish suites that are sprinkled with design *objets*. At the **Hotel Résidence Henri IV** , the atmosphere is much more intimate, with its five apartments located off a beautiful square in the *5ème*. The studios run by **Hotel les Degrés de Notre Dame** also offer a Left Bank address, but a more vibrant one. Independent lets (of at least one week) can also be found via **France Apartments**. For further details, *see p232–3.*

Hotel des Arts *picture perfect* `4 E2`
5 rue Tholoze, 18ème • 01 46 06 30 52
» www.arts-hotel-paris.com

The Hotel des Arts' location – up a steep little street, opposite one of the city's best art-house cinemas and just down from an old windmill – is quintessential Montmartre. The hotel itself doesn't disappoint either, with friendly staff and comfortable, floral bedrooms, some of which have cityscape views. **Cheap**

Kube Hotel *definitely not square* `5 B2`
1 passage Ruelle, 18ème • 01 42 05 20 00
» www.kubehotel.com

Located in a dodgy part of town, the hotel – run by the team behind Murano Urban Resort *(see p179)* – is so cool nobody cares. The funky rooms have integrated sleeping/bathing pods and multi-function computers. Book ahead for Kube's "ice bar" – and be prepared to pay for the chilling experience. **Expensive**

Hotel Utrillo *Montmartre scene* `4 E2`
7 rue Aristide Bruant, 18ème • 01 42 58 13 44
» www.hotel-paris-utrillo.com

The simple, spare rooms at the Utrillo are well kept, and the sloping ceilings of the garret rooms lend a romantic feel to this bargain sleep. In contrast, the breakfast room is much more bright and distinctly cheery. Don't forget to take advantage of the in-hotel sauna (at a small extra charge). **Cheap**

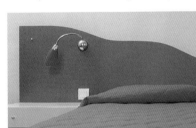

Hotel Beaumarchais *bargain chic* `11 D4`
3 rue Oberkampf, 11ème • 01 53 36 86 86
» www.hotelbeaumarchais.com

One of the first places in Paris to do reasonably priced, modern designer flair, the Beaumarchais has a loyal following. Expect bedrooms in primary colours, comfy beds and funky nick-nacks. A rue Oberkampf location means that all manner of trendy shops, bars and restaurants are just a short stroll away. **Cheap**

Novotel Tour Eiffel *luxury chain* `13 B3`
61 quai de Grenelle, 15ème • 01 40 58 20 00
» www.novotel.com

The Novotel has swathes of marble, a chic bar, two noteworthy restaurants and panoramic views. Rooms are stylish, and the small indoor pool (with retractable roof) is a terrific plus. Depending on the season, prices can be expensive, but the web often has last-minute deals year-round. **Moderate**

Paris Street Finder

Inner Paris is relatively compact and is delineated by the boulevard Périphérique. Within this ringroad, the city is divided into 20 numbered postal districts or *arrondissements*, which spiral outwards from the 1st *arrondissement* located on the Right Bank. The main map below shows the division of the

Street Finder, along with postcodes, and the smaller one shows the extent of Greater Paris. Almost every listing in this guide features a (boxed) page and grid reference to the maps in this section. The few entries that fall outside the area of these maps give transport details instead.

Key to Street Finder

- ▨ Sight/public building
- Ⓜ Metro station
- RER RER station
- 🚆 Railway station
- ⛴ River boat pier
- 🚌 Main bus stop
- 🛈 Tourist information office
- ✚ Hospital with casualty unit
- ◉ Police station
- ✛ Church
- ✡ Synagogue
- ⊗ Post office
- Ⓟ Car park
- ⁼⁼⁼ Railway line
- ▬▬ Pedestrian street
- ≡ Motorway

Scale of maps 1–22

0 metres	250
0 yards	250

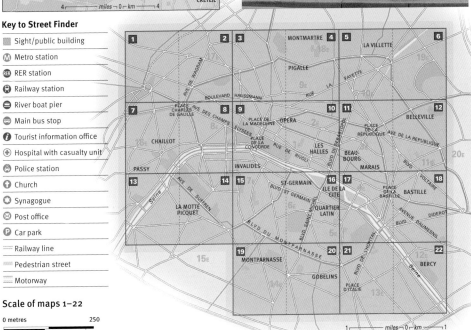

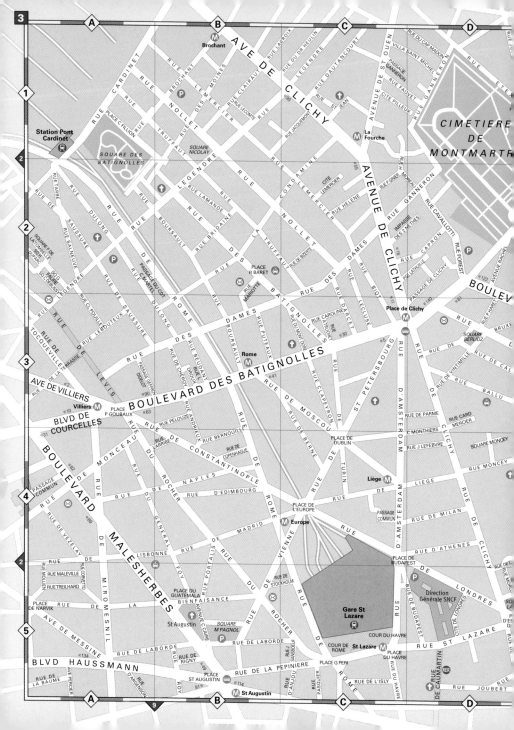

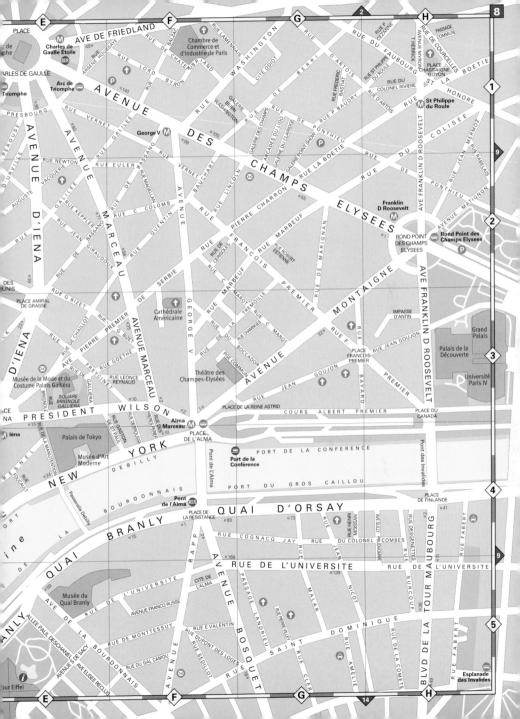

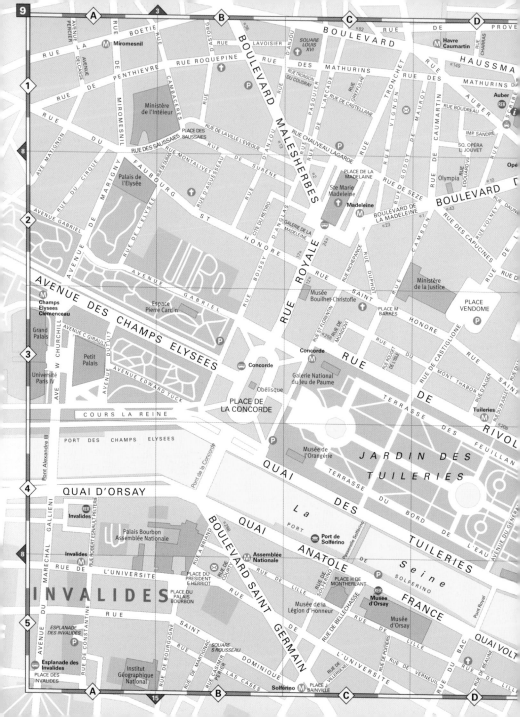

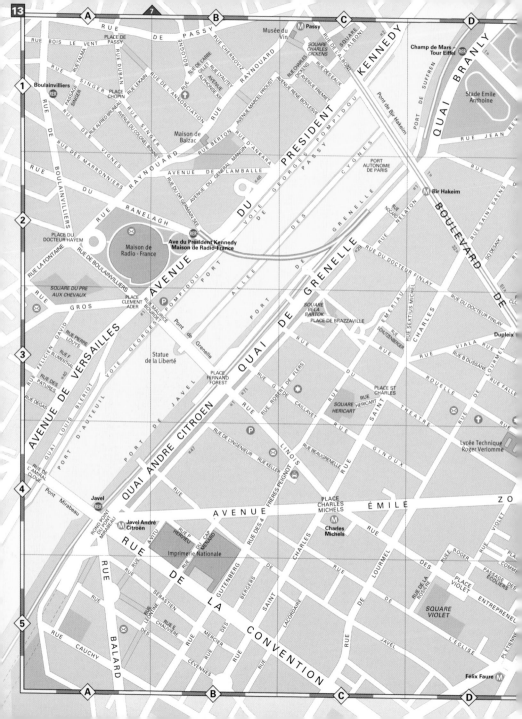

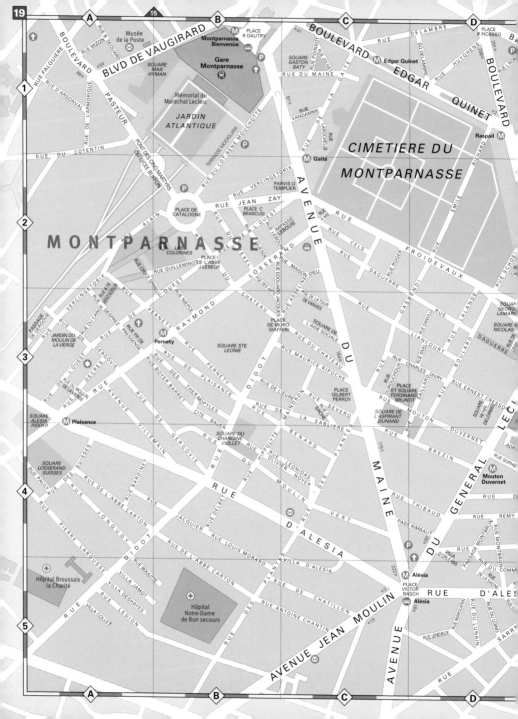

Index of Selected Streets

Index of Selected Streets

Centre

Restaurants

1st arrondissement

Angelina *(see p226)*

A Priori Thé *(see p226)*

L'Ardoise *(p28)* €€
28 rue du Mont Thabor
(Map 9 C3)
Bistro

Au Pied de Cochon *(p28)* €€€
6 rue Coquillière (Map 10 G4)
Bistro

Aux Lyonnais *(p29)* €€
32 rue St-Marc (Map 10 F2)
Bistro

Chez Vong *(p29)* €€
10 rue de la Grande Truanderie
(Map 10 H4)
Chinese

L'Espadon *(p28)* €€€
Hôtel Ritz, 15 place Vendôme
(Map 9 D2)
Haute cuisine

Higuma *(p30)* €
32bis rue Ste-Anne (Map 10 E2)
01 47 03 38 59
Japanese

Laï Laï Ken *(p30)* €
7 rue Ste-Anne (Map 10 E2)
Japanese

Le Meurice *(p29)* €€€
Hotel Meurice, 228 rue de
Rivoli (Map 9 D3)
Haute cuisine

Restaurant du Palais Royal €€
(p28)
110 galérie Valois (Map 10 F3)
Modern French

La Tour de Montlhéry *(p25)* €€
5 rue des Prouvaires
(Map 10 G4)
Bistro

2nd arrondissement

Café Moderne *(p29)* €€
40 rue Notre-Dame-des-
Victoires (Map 10 G2)
Modern French

Chez Georges *(p30)* €€
1 rue du Mail (Map 10 G3)
Bistro

Le Grand Colbert *(see p224)*

3rd arrondissement

L'Ambassade d'Auvergne €€
(p31)
22 rue du Grenier St-Lazare
(Map 11 A4)
Regional French

Anahï *(p31)* €€
49 rue Volta (Map 11 B3)
Latin American

Les Enfants Rouges *(p31)* €€
9 rue de Beauce (Map 11 C4)
Wine bar

Le Pamphlet *(p32)* €€
38 rue Debelleyme (Map 11 C4)
Bistro

Le Petit Dakar *(p30)* €
6 rue Elzévir (Map 11 C5)
African

Les Petits Marseillais *(p32)* €€
72 rue Vieille du Temple
(Map 11 B5)
Bistro

Le Potager du Marais *(p32)* €
22 rue Rambuteau (Map 11 A5)
Vegetarian

R'Aliment *(p32)* €€
57 rue Charlot (Map 11 C4)
Modern French

4th arrondissement

L'Ambroisie *(p33)* €€€
9 pl des Vosges (Map 17 C1)
Haute cuisine

L'As du Fallafal *(p33, p42)* €
34 rue des Rosiers (Map 17 B1)
Middle Eastern

Brasserie de l'Ile St-Louis
(see p224)

La Canaille *(p34)* €
4 rue Crillon (Map 17 C3)
Modern French

L'Enoteca *(p34)* €€
25 rue Charles V
(Map 17 C2)
Italian

Mon Vieil Ami *(p35)* €€
69 rue St-Louis-en-l'Ile
(Map 17 A2)
Modern French

L'Osteria *(p35)* €€
10 rue de Sévigné (Map 17 C1)
Italian

Le Vieux Bistro *(p34)* €€
14 rue du Cloître Notre Dame
(Map 16 H2)
Bistro

Robert et Louise *(p34)* €€
64 rue Vieille du Temple
(Map 11 B5)
Bistro

5th arrondissement

Anahuacalli *(p35)* €€
30 rue des Bernardins
(Map 16 H3)
Mexican

Le Balzar *(see p224)*

Le Cosi *(p36)* €€
9 rue Cujas (Map 16 G4)
Regional French

Les Délices d'Aphrodite €€
(p36)
4 rue de Candolle (Map 20 H1)
Greek

Fogon St-Julien *(p36)* €€
10 rue St-Julien-le-Pauvre
(Map 16 H2)
Spanish

Le Pré Verre *(p37)* €€
8 rue Thénard (Map 16 G3)
Bistro

Le Reminet *(p36)* €€
3 rue des Grands-Degrés
(Map 16 H3)
Bistro

Restaurant Marty *(p37)* €€
20 avenue des Gobelins
(Map 21 A2)
Brasserie

La Tour d'Argent *(p37)* €€
15–17 quai de la Tournelle
(Map 17 A3)
Haute cuisine

6th arrondissement

Abazu *(p38)* €€
3 rue André-Mazet (Map 16 F2)
Japanese

Allard *(p38)* €€
41 rue St-André-des-Arts
(Map 16 F2)
Bistro

**Le Comptoir du Relais
St-Germain** *(p38)* €€
9 carrefour de l'Odéon
(Map 16 F2)
Modern French

L'Epi Dupin *(p38)* €€
11 rue Dupin (Map 15 C3)
Bistro

La Ferrandaise *(p39)* €€
8 rue de Vaugirard (Map 16 F3)
Regional French

La Maison de la Chine
(see p226)

Le Salon d'Hélène *(p39)* €€€
4 rue d'Assas (Map 15 D3)
Regional French

Le Timbre *(p39)* €€
3 rue Ste-Beuve (Map 15 D5)
Bistro

Yen *(p38)* €€
22 rue St-Benoît (Map 16 E2)
Japanese

7th arrondissement

L'Ami Jean *(p40)* €€
27 rue Malar (Map 8 G5)
Regional French

L'Arpège *(p40)* €€€
84 rue de Varenne (Map 15 A1)
Haute cuisine

**L'Atelier de
Joël Robuchon** *(p41)* €€€
5 rue de Montalembert
(Map 15 D1)
Modern French

Au Bon Accueil *(p42)* €€
14 rue de Montessuy
(Map 8 F5)
Bistro

Bellota-Bellota *(p40)* €€
18 rue Jean-Nicot (Map 8 G5)
Spanish

Café Constant (p42)   €€
139 rue St-Dominique (Map 8 F5)
Bistro

Gaya Rive Gauche (p42)   €€
44 rue du Bac (Map 8 F5)
Modern French

Shopping

1st arrondissement

L'Artisan Parfumeur (p66)
2 rue Amiral de Coligny
(Map 10 F5)
Perfumes

by Terry (p64)
21 passage Véro-Dodat
(Map 10 F4)
Beauty

Christian Louboutin (p64)
19 rue Jean-Jacques Rousseau
(Map 10 F4)
Shoes

Colette (see p227)

L'Eclaireur (p67)
10 rue Hérold (Map 10 G3)
Fashion

Etam (see p227)

Fifi Chachnil (p64)
231 rue St-Honoré (Map 9 D3)
Lingerie

Flavie Furst (p68)
16 rue de la Soudière
(Map 10 E3)
Accessories

Helmut Lang (p65)
219 rue St-Honoré (Map 10 E4)
Fashion

John Galliano (see p227)

Lavinia (p68)
3–5 blvd de la Madeleine
(Map 9 D2)
Food & drink

Madelios (p65)
23 blvd de la Madeleine
(Map 9 C2)
Fashion

Maria Luisa (p66)
2 rue Cambon (Map 9 C3)
Fashion

Martin Margiela (p66)
23bis & 25bis rue de
Montpensier (Map 10 F3)
Fashion

Pierre Hardy (p65)
156 galérie de Valois (Map 10 F4)
Shoes

Salons du Palais Royal (p66)
25 rue de Valois (Map 10 F3)
Perfume

Ventilo (p67)
13–15 blvd de la Madeleine
(Map 9 C2)
Fashion

Yves Rocher (see p226)

2nd arrondissement

Barbara Bui (p69)
23 rue Etienne Marcel
(Map 10 H4)
Fashion

Erik & Lydie (p69)
7 passage du Grand Cerf
(Map 10 H3)
Accessories

Et Vous Stock (see p227)

Killiwatch (p69)
64 rue Tiquetonne (Map 10 G3)
Second-hand & vintage

Odette & Zoe (p67)
4 rue des Petits Champs
(Map 10 F3)
Accessories

Papageno (see p229)

3rd arrondissement

AB33 (p73)
33 rue Charlot (Map 11 C4)
Fashion

Abou d'Abi Bazar (p72)
10 rue des Francs Bourgeois
(Map 17 C1)
Fashion

La Chaise Longue (p72)
20 rue des Francs Bourgeois
(Map 17 C1)
Interiors

Food (p71)
58 rue Charlot (Map 11 C4)
Food & drink

Galerie Simone (p72)
124 rue Vieille du Temple
(Map 11 C4)
Concept store

Goumanyat & Son
Royaume (p70)
3 rue Charles François Dupuis
(Map 11 C3)
Food & drink

Martin Grant (p76)
10 rue Charlot (Map 11 B5)
Fashion

Robert Le Héros (p69)
13 rue de Saintonge (Map 11 C4)
Interiors

Shoe Bizz (p70)
48 rue Beaubourg (Map 11 A5)
Shoes

4th arrondissement

A L'Olivier (p78)
23 rue de Rivoli (Map 17 B1)
Food & drink

Antik Batik (p71)
18 rue de Turenne (Map 17 C1)
Fashion

A-poc (p74)
47 rue des Francs Bourgeois
(Map 11 B5)
Fashion

Azzedine Alaïa (p74)
7 rue de Moussy (Map 17 A1)
Fashion

Bô (p78)
8 rue St-Merri (Map 11 A5)
Interiors

Brontibay (p74)
6 rue de Sévigné (Map 17 C1)
Accessories

Calligrane (p75)
4–6 rue du Pont Louis-
Philippe (Map 17 A2)
Stationery

Comptoir des Cotonniers (p74)
33 rue des Francs Bourgeois
(Map 11 B5)
Fashion

Hervé Gambs (p75)
9bis rue des Blancs Manteaux
(Map 11 B5)
Interiors

Hervé Van der Straeten (p78)
11 rue Ferdinand Duval
(Map 17 B1)
Accessories

Nodus (p70)
22 rue Vieille du Temple
(Map 17 B1)
Fashion

Sentou (p77)
18 & 24 rue du Pont Louis-
Philippe (Map 17 B1)
29 rue François Miron
(Map 17 B1)
Interiors

Yukiko (p75)
97 rue Vieille du Temple
(Map 11 C4)
Second-hand & vintage

5th arrondissement

Diptyque (p78)
34 blvd St-Germain (Map 17 A3)
Interiors

Paris Jazz Corner (see p229)

6th arrondissement

Agnès b (p80)
6 & 12 rue du Vieux Colombier
(Map 15 D2)
Fashion

APC (p80)
3 & 4 rue Fleurus (Map 15 D4)
Fashion

Catherine Malandrino (p83)
10 rue de Grenelle
(Map 15 D2)
Fashion

Dépôt-Vente de Buci (see p227)

Free Lance (p80)
30 rue du Four (Map 15 D2)
Shoes

Jamin Puech (p82)
43 rue Madame (Map 16 E3)
Accessories

Karine Dupont (p79)
16 rue du Cherche Midi
(Map 15 D3)
Accessories

Lagerfeld Gallery (p81)
40 rue de Seine (Map 16 E1)
Fashion

Index by Area

Centre

Shopping *continued*

Loft Design by (p82)
56 rue de Rennes (Map 16 E2)
Fashion

La Maison du Chocolat (p79)
19 rue de Sèvres (Map 15 C3)
Food & drink

Marie Mercié (p82)
23 rue St-Sulpice (Map 16 E3)
Accessories

Onward (p82)
147 blvd St-Germain (Map 16 E2)
Fashion

Paul & Joe (p81)
40 rue du Four (Map 16 E2)
Fashion

Sabbia Rosa (p79)
73 rue des Sts-Pères
(Map 15 D2)
Lingerie

Shadé (p83)
63 rue des Sts-Pères
(Map 15 D2)
Fashion

**Les 3 Marches de
Catherine B** (p80)
1 & 3 rue Guisarde (Map 16 E2)
Second-hand & vintage

Tara Jamon (p79)
18 rue du Four (Map 16 E2)
Fashion

Vanessa Bruno (p81)
25 rue St-Sulpice (Map 16 E3)
Fashion

Woman (p81)
4 rue de Grenelle (Map 15 D2)
Lingerie

7th arrondissement

Le Bon Marché *(see p226)*

Carine Gilson (p84)
61 rue Bonaparte (Map 15 E1)
Lingerie

Catherine Arigoni (p86)
14 rue Beaune (Map 15 D1)
Second-hand & vintage

Colors do Brasil (p85)
4 rue Perronet (Map 15 D1)
Fashion

Deyrolle (p83)
46 rue du Bac (Map 15 C1)
Interiors

**Editions de Parfums Frédéric
Malle** (p84)
37 rue de Grenelle (Map 15 C2)
Perfumes

La Grande Epicerie (p84)
Le Bon Marché, 22 rue des
Sèvres (Map 15 C3)
Food & drink

Iris (p84)
28 rue de Grenelle (Map 15 D2)
Shoes

Iunx (p87)
48–50 rue de l'Université
(Map 15 D1)
Perfumes

Jean-Baptiste Rautureau (p86)
24 rue de Grenelle (Map 15 D2)
Shoes

Lucien Pellat-Finet (p85)
1 rue Montalembert
(Map 15 D1)
Fashion

Paul Smith (p85)
22 & 24 blvd Raspail
(Map 15 D3)
Fashion

Rue Cler (p162)
(Map 14 G1)
Markets

Thomas Boog (p86)
52 rue de Bourgogne
(Map 15 A1)
Interiors

Art & Architecture

1st arrondissement

La Conciergerie *(see p230)*

Eglise St-Eustache (p100)
2 Impasse St Eustache
(Map 10 G4)
Church

Jeu de Paume (p100)
1 pl de la Concorde (Map 9 C3)
Exhibition space

Musée du Louvre *(see p231)*

Musée de la Publicité (p100)
107 rue de Rivoli (Map 10 E4)
Museum

Sainte-Chapelle *(see p230)*

Tour St-Jacques (p102)
(Map 16 H1)
Historic building

2nd arrondissement

**Bibliothèque Nationale de
France – Richelieu** (p100)
58 rue de Richelieu (Map 10 F3)
Exhibition space

3rd arrondissement

**Musée d'Art et d'Histoire du
Judaïsme** (p102)
71 rue du Temple (Map 11 A5)
Museum

Musée Carnavalet (p101)
23 rue de Sevigné (Map 17 C1)
Museum

Musée National Picasso (p101)
5 rue Thorigny (Map 11 C5)
Museum

4th arrondissement

Atelier Brancusi (p103)
Pl Centre Pompidou (Map 11 A5)
Exhibition space

Centre Pompidou *(see p230)*

**Maison Européene de la
Photographie** (p103)
5–7 rue de Fourcy (Map 17 B1)
Exhibition space

Musée Cognacq-Jay (p103)
8 rue Elzévi (Map 17 C1)
Museum

Notre Dame *(see p230)*

Patrimoine Photographique
(p102)
62 rue St-Antoine (Map 17 C2)
Exhibition space

5th arrondissement

Arènes de Lutèce (p104)
Entrances on 49 rue Monge &
7 rue de Navarre (Map 17 A5)
Historic building

**Eglise Royale du
Val-de-Grâce** (p105)
227bis rue St-Jacques
(Map 20 F1)
Historic building

Institut du Monde Arabe (p103)
1 rue des Fossés St-Bernard
(Map 17 B3)
Exhibition space

**Musée de l'Assistance
Publique** (p105)
47 quai de la Tournelle
(Map 17 A3)
Museum

**Musée National du
Moyen Age** (p104)
6 pl Paul-Painlevé (Map 16 G3)
Museum

St-Julien-le-Pauvre (p169)
Rue St-Julien-le-Pauvre
(Map 16 H2)
Church

La Sorbonne (p104)
47 rue des Ecoles (Map 16 G3)
Historic building

6th arrondissement

Eglise St-Sulpice (p105)
Place St-Sulpice (Map 16 E3)
Church

Musée du Luxembourg (p105)
19 rue de Vaugirard (Map 16 E3)
Exhibition space

**Musée National Eugène
Delacroix** (p106)
6 rue de Furstemberg
(Map 16 E2)
Museum

7th arrondissement

Assemblée Nationale
(see p230)

Eiffel Tower *(see p230)*

**Musée Maillol – Fondation
Dina Vierny** (p107)
59–61 rue de Grenelle
(Map 15 D2)
Museum

Musée d'Orsay *(see p231)*

Musée du Quai Branly (p106)
55 quai Branly (Map 8E5)
Museum

Musée Rodin (p107)
77 rue de Varenne (Map 15 A1)
Museum

Performance
1st arrondissement

Comédie Française (p125)
1 place Colette (Map 10 E4)
Theatre

Duc des Lombards (p124)
42 rue des Lombards
(Map 10 H5)
Live music

Forum des Images (p124)
Forum des Halles (Map 10 G4)
Cinema

Théâtre du Châtelet (p125)
1 place du Châtelet (Map 16 H1)
Multi-function venue

2nd arrondissement

Le Grand Rex (p125)
1 blvd Poissonnière (Map 10 H2)
Cinema

4th arrondissement

Café de la Gare (p125)
41 rue du Temple (Map 11 A5)
Comedy

Le Point Virgule (p124)
7 rue St-Croix de la
Bretonnerie (Map 17 B1)
Comedy

Théâtre de la Ville (p127)
2 place du Châtelet
(Map 16 H1)
Multi-function venue

5th arrondissement

Action Ecole *(see p231)*

Le Champollion *(see p231)*

Grand Action *(see p231)*

Images d'Ailleurs *(see p231)*

Paradis Latin *(see p231)*

Quartier Latin *(see p231)*

Reflet Medicis *(see p231)*

Studio Galande *(see p231)*

6th arrondissement

Action Christine Odeon
(see p231)

Lucernaire (p127)
53 rue Notre-Dame-des-
Champs (Map 15 D5)
Multi-function venue

Racine Odeon *(see p231)*

St-André-des-Arts *(see p231)*

7th arrondissement

La Pagode (p124)
57bis rue de Babylone
(Map 15 A2)
Cinema

Bars & Clubs
1st arrondissement

Cab (p138)
2 pl du Palais Royal (Map 10 F4)
Club

Le Fumoir (p138)
6 rue de L'Amiral de Coligny
(Map 10 F5)
Bar

Hemingway Bar (p139)
Ritz Hotel, 15 place Vendome
(Map 9 D3)
Bar

Hotel Costes (p138)
239 rue St Honoré (Map 9 D3)
Bar

Juveniles (p139)
47 rue de Richelieu (Map 10 F3)
Bar

Kong (p140)
1 rue du Pont Neuf (Map 10 G5)
Bar

Paris Paris (p141)
5 avenue del'Opéra (Map 10 E4)
Club

Wine & Bubbles (p160)
3 rue Francaise (Map 10 H4)
01 44 76 99 84
Bar

2nd arrondissement

Le Café (p160)
62 rue Tiquetonne (Map 10 G3)
01 40 39 08 00
Bar

Le Café Noir (p141)
65 rue Montmartre (Map 10 G3)
Bar

Le Coeur Fou (p139)
55 rue Montmartre (Map 10 G3)
Bar

Etienne Marcel (p160)
34 rue Etienne Marcel
(Map 10 G3) 01 45 08 01 03
Bar

Harry's Bar (p142)
5 rue Daunou (Map 10 E2)
Bar

Le Next (p141)
17 rue Tiquetonne (Map 10 H3)
Bar

Pulp (p142)
25 blvd Poissonnière
(Map 10 G1)
Club

Le Rex (p141)
5 blvd Poissonière (Map 10 G1)
Club

Somo (p141)
168 rue Montmartre
(Map 10 G2)
Bar

3rd arrondissement

Andy Wahloo (p143)
69 rue des Gravilliers
(Map 11 A3)
Bar

Le Connetable (p143)
55 rue des Archives (Map 11 B4)
Bar

4th arrondissement

Amnesia (p144)
42 rue Vieille du Temple
(Map 17 B1)
Bar

The Auld Alliance (p138)
80 rue François Miron
(Map 17 B1)
Pub

Au Petit Fer à Cheval (p144)
30 rue Vieille du Temple
(Map 17 B1)
Bar

Bliss Kfé (p143)
30 rue de Roi de Sicile
(Map 17 B1)
Bar

La Belle Hortense (p145)
31 rue Vieille du Temple
(Map 17 B1)
Bar

Chez Richard (p144)
37 rue Vieille du Temple
(Map 17 B1)
Bar

Le Cox (p146)
15 rue des Archives (Map 11 A5)
Bar

Les Etages (p146)
35 rue Vieille du Temple
(Map 17 B1)
Bar

L'Etoile Manquante (p144)
34 rue Vieille du Temple
(Map 17 B1)
Bar

Lizard Lounge (p146)
18 rue Bourg Tibourg
(Map 17 B1)
Bar

Le Trésor (p146)
7 rue Trésor (Map 17 B1)
Bar

5th arrondissement

The Bombardier (p138)
2 pl Panthéon (Map 16 G4)
Pub

Caveau des Oubliettes (p135)
52 rue Galande (Map 16 H3)
Bar

Le Crocodile (p135)
6 rue Royer Collard
(Map 16 G4)
Bar

Le Pantalon (p135)
7 rue Royer Collard (Map 16 G4)
Bar

Index by Area

Centre

Bars & Clubs *continued*

6th arrondissement

AZ Bar (p148)
62 rue Mazarine (Map 16 F2)
Bar

Le Bar du Marché (p148)
75 rue de Seine (Map 16 F2)
Bar

Café de la Mairie (p149)
8 place St-Sulpice (Map 16 E3)
Bar

Coolin (p138)
15 rue Clément (Map 16 E2)
Pub

Corcoran (p138)
28 rue St-André des Arts
(Map 16 F2)
Pub

Don Carlos (p149)
66 rue Mazarine (Map 16 F2)
Bar

Frog & Princess (p138)
9 rue Princesse (Map 15 E2)
Pub

Fubar (p147)
5 rue St-Sulpice (Map 16 F3)
Bar

The Highlander (p138)
8 rue Nevers (Map 16 F1)
Pub

Le 10 Bar (p148)
10 rue de L'Odeon (Map 16 F3)
Bar

O'Neils (p138)
20 rue Canettes (Map 16 E2)
Pub

L'Urgence (p149)
45 rue Monsieur Le Prince
(Map 16 F3)
Bar

WAGG (p149)
62 rue Mazarine (Map 16 F2)
Club

7th arrondissement

Café Thoumieux (p142)
4 rue de la Comète (Map 8 H5)
Bar

Havens: Spas, Parks, Squares & Gardens

1st arrondissement

32 Montorgueil (p169)
32 rue Montorgueil
(Map 10 H3)

Jardin des Tuileries (p116, p171)
(Map 9 D4)

Palais Royal (p168) (Map 10 F3)

Place Dauphine (p168)
(Map 16 G1)

Square du Vert-Galant (p168)
(Map 16 F1)

3rd arrondissement

Nickel (p169)
48 rue des Francs Bourgeois
(Map 11 B5)

5th arrondissement

La Grande Mosquée (p170)
39 rue Geoffroy St-Hilaire
(Map 17 A5)

Jardins des Plantes (p171)
(Map 17 B5)

6th arrondissement

Jardin du Luxembourg
(p12, p171) (Map 16 E4)

7th arrondissement

Hôtel National des
Invalides (p171)
Esplanade des Invalides
(Map 15 A1)

Hotels

1st arrondissement

Hotel Tonic (p178)   €€
12–14 rue Roule (Map 10 G5)

Le Meurice *(see p233)*

Le Ritz *(see p233)*

2nd arrondissement

Hotel Tiquetonne (p178)   €
6 rue Tiquetonne (Map 10 H4)

3rd arrondissement

Hotel du Petit   €€€
Moulin (p179)
29 rue Poitou (Map 11 C4)

Hotel Roubaix (p178)   €
6 rue Grenetta (Map 10 H3)

Murano Urban   €€€
Resort (p179)
13 blvd du Temple (Map 11 C3)

Pavillon de la Reine (p178) €€€
28 place des Vosges
(Map 17 D1)

4th arrondissement

5 Rue de Moussy *(see p233)*

5th arrondissement

Hotel du Degrés de Notre
Dame *(see p233)*

Hotel Esméralda (p180)   €
4 rue St-Julien-le-Pauvre
(Map 16 H2)

Hotel du Panthéon (p181) €€
19 pl du Panthéon (Map 16 G4)

Hotel Résidence Henri IV
(see p233)

6th arrondissement

Artus (p181)   €€
34 rue de Buci (Map 16 E2)

L'Hotel (p181)   €€€
13 rue des Beaux Arts
(Map 16 E1)

Hotel des St-Pères (p182) €€
65 rue des St-Pères
(Map 15 D2)

Hotel du Lys (p180)   €
23 rue Serpente (Map 16 G2)

Hotel Mayet (p182)   €
3 rue Mayet (Map 15 B4)

Villa D'Estrées (p180)   €€
17 rue Git-le-Couer (Map 16 G2)

7th arrondissement

Hotel Lenox (p182)   €€
9 rue de l'Université
(Map 15 D1)

Hotel Malar (p183)   €
29 rue Malar (Map 8 G5)

Hotel du Quai Voltaire
(p182)   €€
19 quai Voltaire
(Map 9 D5)

West

Restaurants

8th arrondissement

L'Angle du   €€
Faubourg (p43)
195 rue du Faubourg
St-Honoré (Map 2 G5)
Bistro

A Toutes Vapeurs (p45)   €
7 rue de l'Isly (Map 3 C5)
Modern French

Be *(see p225)*   €€

Le Bistrot Napolitain (p43) €€
18 avenue Franklin D
Roosevelt (Map 8 H1)
Italian

Flora (p43)   €€€
36 rue de George V (Map 8 F2)
Modern French

Garnier (p43)   €€€
111 rue St-Lazare (Map 3 C5)
Brasserie

Ladurée *(see p226)*

Maison Blanche (p44)   €€
15 ave Montaigne (Map 8 G3)
Modern French

Market (p44)   €€€
15 ave Matignon (Map 9 A2)
Modern French

Savy (p45)   €€
23 rue Bayard (Map 8 G3)
Bistro

Senderens (p45)   €€€
9 pl de la Madeleine (Map 9 C2)
Haute cuisine

16th arrondissement

L'Astrance (p46)   €€€
4 rue Beethoven (Map 7 C5)
Modern French

La Butte Chaillot (p47)   €€€
110bis avenue Kléber
(Map 7 D3)
Modern French

Le Cristal Room (p44)   €€€
La Maison Baccarat, 11 place
des Etats-Unis (Map 8 E2)
Modern French

La Grande Armée (p47)   €€
3 avenue de la Grande Armée
(Map 7 E1)
Brasserie

Le Petit Rétro (p43)   €€
5 rue Mesnil (Map 7 C2)
Bistro

17th arrondissement

**Le Bistrot d'à Côte
Flaubert** (p48)   €€
10 rue Gustave-Flaubert
(Map 2 F3)
Bistro

L'Entrédejeu (p47)   €€
83 rue Laugier (Map 1 D2)
Bistro

La Braisière (p48)   €€€
54 rue Cardinet (Map 2 H2)
Modern French

Shopping

8th arrondissement

André (see p229)

Balenciaga (see p227)

Bottega Veneta (see p226)

Chanel (see p227)

Chloé (see p227)

Christian Lacroix (see p227)

Dior (see p227)

Dolce & Gabbana (see p227)

Emmanuel Ungaro (see p227)

Erès (p88)
2 rue Tronchet (Map 9 C1)
Lingerie

fnac (see p229)

Galerie Noémie (p88)
92 ave des Champs-Elysées
(Map 8 F1)
Beauty

Givenchy (see p229)

Gucci (see p226)

Guerlain (p88)
68 avenue des Champs-Elysées
(Map 8 G2)
Beauty

Jean-Paul Gaultier (see p227)

Lanvin (see p227)

Louis Vuitton (see p226)

**Make Up For Ever
Professional** (p89)
5 rue de la Boétie (Map 8 H1)
Beauty

Marni (see p228)

Prada (see p228)

Publicis Drugstore (p87)
133 ave des Champs-Elysées
(Map 8 F1)
Music & books

Renaud Pellegrino (p87)
14 rue du Faubourg-St-Honoré
(Map 9 B2)
Accessories

Résonances (p89)
3 blvd Malesherbes
(Map 9 C2)
Interiors

Roger Vivier (p90)
29 rue du Faubourg-St-Honoré
(Map 9 C2)
Shoes

Stephane Kélian (p90)
5 rue du Faubourg-St-Honoré
(Map 9 C2)
Shoes

Valentino (see p228)

Virgin Megastore (see p229)

Zadig & Voltaire (de luxe) (p88)
18–20 rue François Premier
(Map 8 G3)
Fashion

16th arrondissement

Réciproque (see p228)

Art & Architecture

8th arrondissement

Chapelle Expiatoire (p172)
29 rue Pasquier (Map 9 C1)
Church

Eglise de la Madeleine (p108)
Pl de la Madeleine (Map 9 C2)
Church

Eglise St-Augustin (p108)
46 blvd Malesherbes
(Map 3 B5)
Church

Grand Palais (see p230)

Musée Jacquemart-André
(p108)
158 blvd Haussmann (Map 2 H5)
Museum

Palais de la Découverte
(see p231)

Petit Palais (see p230)

16th arrondissement

Cimetière de Passy (p229)

Fondation Le Corbusier (p111)
Villa la Roche, 10 sq du
Dr Blanche (Ⓜ Jasmin)
Museum

**Musée d'Art Moderne de
la Ville de Paris** (MAMVP) (p110)
11 avenue du Président Wilson
(Map 8 E3)
Museum

Musée Galliéra (p108)
10 avenue Pierre 1er de Serbie
(Map 8 E3)
Museum

Musée Guimet (p111)
6 place d'Iéna (Map 8 E3)
Museum

Musée Marmottan-Monet
(p111)
2 rue Louis Boilly
(Ⓜ Ranelagh)
Museum

Palais de Chaillot (p110)
17 place du Trocadéro
(Map 7 C4)
Museum

Palais de Tokyo (p110)
13 avenue du Président Wilson
(Map 8 E3)
Exhibition space

Western Suburbs

Chateau de St-Germain (p112)
Place Charles de Gaulle
(RER St-Germain-en-Laye)
Museum

**Musée Départemental
Maurice Denis "Le Prieuré"**
(p112)
2bis rue Maurice Denis
(RER St-Germain-en-Laye)
Museum

Performance

8th arrondissement

Crazy Horse (see p231)

Lido (see p231)

Théâtre des Champs-Elysées
(p127)
15 ave Montaigne (Map 8 G3)
Multi-function venue

16th arrondissement

Hippodrome de Longchamp
(see p232)

**Maison de la Radio
France** (p128)
116 avenue Président Kennedy
(Map 13 B2)
Live music

Parc des Princes (see p232)

Stade Jean-Bouin (see p232)

Stade Pierre de Coubertin
(see p232)

Stade Roland Garros
(see p232)

Index by Area

West

Bars & Clubs

8th arrondissement

Le Bar du Plaza (p151)
Plaza Athenée, 25 avenue Montaigne (Map 8 G3)
Bar

Le Baron (p152)
10 ave Marceau (Map 8 F3)
Club

Bar des Théâtres (p151)
6 ave Montaigne (Map 8 G3)
Bar

The Cricketer (p138)
41 rue des Mathurins (Map 9 C1)
01 40 07 01 45
Pub

Four Seasons George V (p150)
31 avenue George V (Map 8 F2)
Bar

Freedom (p138)
8 rue de Berri (Map 8 G1)
01 53 75 25 50
Pub

Mathi's (p151)
3 rue Ponthieu (Map 8 H2)
Bar

Nirvana Lounge (p150)
3 avenue Matignon (Map 8 H2)
Bar

Le Queen (p151)
102 ave des Champs-Elysées (Map 8 F1)
Club

La Suite (p150)
40 ave George V (Map 8 F2)
Bar

Toi (p150)
27 rue Colisée (Map 8 H2)
Bar

16th arrondissement

La Gare (p152)
19 chausée de la Muette (Ⓜ La Muette)
Bar

Havens: Parks, Squares & Gardens

8th arrondissement

Parc Monceau (p171)
(Map 2 H4)

16th arrondissement

Parc de Bagatelle (p171)
(Ⓜ Boulogne J Jaurès)

Havens: Spas

8th arrondissement

Four Seasons Georges V (p172)
31 ave Georges V (Map 8 F2)

Hotels

8th arrondissement

Le A (p183)   €€€
4 rue d'Artois (Map 8 F1)

Le Crillon (see p233)

France Apartments (see p233)

Hilton Paris Arc de   €€€
Triomphe (p185)
51 rue de Courcelles (Map 2 G4)

Hotel de Vigny (p183)   €€€
9–11 rue Balzac (Map 8 F1)

Pershing Hall (p184)   €€€
49 rue Pierre-Charron (Map 8 G2)

La Plaza Athénée (see p233)

Residence Carré d'Or (see p233)

16th arrondissement

Hotel Sezz (p185)   €€€
6 avenue Fremiet (Map 13 C1)

Hotel Square (p185)   €€€
3 rue des Boulainvilliers (Map 13 A2)

17th arrondissement

Hotel Eldorado (p185)   €
18 rue des Dames (Map 3 C2)

North

Restaurants

9th arrondissement

Casa Olympe (p48)   €€
48 rue St-Georges (Map 4 F5)
Bistro

Cojean (see p225)

Kastoori (p48)   €
4 pl Gustave Toudouze (Map 4 F4)
Indian

Rose Bakery (p49)   €
46 rue des Martyrs (Map 4 F4)
British

Velly (p49)   €€
52 rue Lamartine (Map 4 F5)
Bistro

10th arrondissement

Brasserie Flo (see p224)

Chez Dom (p49)   €€
34 rue de Sambre et Meuse (Map 6 E5)
African

Chez Michel (p50)
10 rue de Belzunce (Map 5 A4)
Regional French

Julien (see p225)   €€

Martel (p49)   €€
3 rue Martel (Map 11 A1)
North African

Terminus Nord (p50)   €€
23 rue de Dunkerque (Map 5 A4)
Brasserie

18th arrondissement

Café Burq (p50)   €€
6 rue Burq (Map 4 E2)
Bistro

Chez Toinette (p51)   €€
20 rue Germain-Pilon (Map 4 E2)
Bistro

La Famille (p52)   €€
41 rue des Trois-Frères (Map 4 F2)
Modern French

La Mascotte (p53)   €€
52 rue des Abbesses (Map 4 E2)
Bistro

Le Poulbot Gourmet (p51)   €€
39 rue Lamarck (Map 4 F1)
Bistro

19th arrondissement

La Cave Gourmande (p51)   €€
10 rue du Général-Brunet (Ⓜ Botzaris)
Modern French

Lao Siam (p51)   €
49 rue de Belleville (Map 12 G1)
Southeast Asian

Shopping

9th arrondissement

Annexe des Créateurs (see p227)

fnac (see p229)

Galeries Lafayette (see p227)

Guerrisol (see p227)

Princesse Tam Tam (see p228)

Printemps (see p227)

Sephora (see p226)

Virgin Megastore (see p229)

10th arrondissement

Antoine & Lili (p91)
95 quai de Valmy (Map 11 C1)
Fashion

Artazart (p91)
83 quai de Valmy (Map 11 C1)
Music & book

Coin Canal (p92)
1 rue de Marseille (Map 11 C1)
Interiors

E2 (p91)
15 rue Martel (Map 11 A1)
Vintage

Ginger Lyly (p91)
33 rue Beaurepaire
(Map 11 C2)
Fashion

Stella Cadente (p91)
93 quai de Valmy (Map 11 C1)
Fashion

Viveka Bergström (p92)
23 rue de la Grange-aux-Belles
(Map 5 D5)
Accessories

18th arrondissement

En Avant La Zizique *(see p229)*

Lili Perpink (p92)
22 rue la Vieuville (Map 4 F2)
Fashion

Patricia Louisor (p92)
16 rue Houdon (Map 4 F3)
Fashion

Spree (p93)
16 rue la Vieuville (Map 4 F2)
Concept store

Northern Suburbs

Puces de St-Ouen (p164)
(Ⓜ Porte de Clignancourt)
Market

Art & Architecture

9th arrondissement

Musée Gustave Moreau (p115)
14 rue de la Rochefoucauld
(Map 4 E4)
Museum

10th arrondissement

Gare du Nord (p116)
(Map 5 A4)
Historic building

Porte St-Denis & Porte
St-Martin (p115)
(Map 11 A2)
Historic building

18th arrondissement

Café des Deux Moulins (p113)
15 rue Lepic (Map 4 E2)
01 42 54 90 50
Historic building

Cimetière de Montmartre
(see p229)

Moulin de la Galette (p113)
75 rue Lepic (Map 4 E1)
Historic building

Moulin de Radet (p113)
83 rue Lepic (Map 4 F1)
Historic building

Musée de l'Erotisme (p112)
72 blvd de Clichy (Map 4 E3)
Museum

Musée de Montmartre
(see p231)

Sacré Cœur *(see p229)*

19th arrondissement

Cité des Sciences et de
l'Industrie (p114)
Parc de la Villette, 30 ave
Corentin Cariou
(Ⓜ Porte de Pantin)
Museum

Musée de la Musique (p114)
Cité de la Musique,
221 avenue Jean Jaurès
(Ⓜ Porte de Pantin)
Museum

Northern Suburbs

Basilique St-Denis (p114)
1 rue de la Légion d'Honneur
(Ⓜ Basilique de St-Denis)
Church

Musée d'Art et d'Histoire de
St-Denis (p115)
22bis rue Gabriel Péri
(Ⓜ St-Denis Porte de Paris)
Museum

Stade de France (p204, 133)
rue Francis de Pressensé
(Ⓜ St-Denis Porte de Paris)
Modern architecture

Performance

9th arrondissement

Opéra Garnier *(see p230)*

10th arrondissement

Bouffes du Nord (p128)
37bis boulevard de la Chapelle
(Map 5 B2)
Multi-function venue

La Java (p129)
105 rue du Faubourg du Temple
(Map 11 C1)
Comedy

New Morning (p128)
7–9 rue des Petites-Ecuries
(Map 11 A1)
Live music

18th arrondissement

Bal du Moulin Rouge *(see p231)*

Chez Madame Arthur *(see p231)*

Chez Michou *(see p231)*

Elysée Montmartre (p129)
72 blvd Rochechouart
(Map 4 G3)
Live music

Studio 28 (p129)
10 rue Tholozé (Map 4 E2)
Cinema

19th arrondissement

Cinéma en Plein Air (p130)
Parc de la Villette
(Ⓜ Porte de Pontin)
Cinema

Cité de la Musique (p129)
221 avenue Jean Jaurès
(Ⓜ Porte de Pantin)
Live music

Le Zénith (p130)
211 avenue Jean Jaurès
(Ⓜ Porte de Pantin)
Multi-function venue

Northern Suburbs

Centre National de la
Danse (p130)
1 rue Victor Hugo
(Ⓜ Hoche, RER Pantin)
Dance

Stade de France (p133, p204)
rue Francis de Pressensé
(Ⓜ St-Denis Porte de Paris)
Sport

Bars & Clubs

9th arrondissement

Project 101 (p153)
44 rue de la Rochefoucauld
(Map 4 E4)
Club

10th arrondissement

Chez Prune (p153)
36 rue Beaurepaire (Map 11 C1)
Bar

De la Ville Café (p152)
34 boulevard de la Bonne
Nouvelle (Map 10 H2)
Bar/Club

La Patache (p153)
60 rue de Lancry (Map 11 C1)
Bar

18th arrondissement

La Fourmi (p152)
74 rue des Martyrs (Map 4 F3)
Bar

Le Progrès (p152)
1 rue Yvonne le Tac
(Map 4 F2)
Bar

La Sancerre (p154)
35 rue des Abbesses
(Map 4 E2)
Bar

Havens: Spas, Parks, Squares & Gardens

19th arrondissement

Parc des Buttes-Chaumont
(p172) (Map 6 G4)

Hotels

9th arrondissement

Hotel Langlois (p186)   €
63 rue St-Lazare (Map 3 D5)

Royal Fromentin (p186)   €
11 rue Fromentin (Map 4 E3)

18th arrondissement

Hotel des Arts (p187)   €
5 rue Tholoze (Map 4 E2)

>> € cheap   €€ moderate   €€€ expensive   (Price ranges: Restaurants, *see p29*, Hotels, *see p179*)   **221**

Index by Area

North

Hotels *continued*

Hotel Terrass (p186) €€
12–14 rue Joseph de Maistre
(Map 4 E2)

Hotel Utrillo (p187) €
7 rue Aristide Bruant
(Map 4 E2)

Kube Hotel (p187) €€€
1 Passage Ruelle
(Map 5 B2)

East

Restaurants

11th arrondissement

Astier (p53) €€
44 rue Jean-Pierre Timbaud
(Map 12 E3)
Bistro

Le Bistrot Paul Bert (p55) €€
18 rue Paul-Bert
(Ⓜ Faidherbe-Chaligny)
Bistro

Crêperie Bretonne €
Fleurie (p54)
67 rue de Charonne (Map 18 F2)
Regional French

Dong Huong (p54) €
14 rue Louis-Bonnet
(Map 12 F1)
Southeast Asian

L'Homme Bleu (p54) €€
55bis rue Jean-Pierre Timbaud
(Map 12 E3)
North African

Jacques Mélac (p54) €€
42 rue Léon-Frot
(Ⓜ Charonne)
Wine Bar

Le Petit Keller (p55) €€
13bis rue Keller
(Map 18 F1)
Bistro

Le Souk (p55) €€
1 rue Keller (Map 18 F2)
African

12th arrondissement

Sardegna a Tavola (p56) €€
1 rue de Cotte (Map 18 F3)
Italian

Le Square Trousseau (p56) €€
1 rue Antoine-Vollon (Map 18 F3)
Bistro

Le Train Bleu (p55) €€
Gare de Lyon, place
Louis-Armand (Map 18 E5)
Brasserie

Le Trou Gascon (p56) €€€
40 rue Taine (Ⓜ Daumesnil)
Regional French

20th arrondissement

Benisti (p53) €
108 boulevard de Belleville
(Map 12 F1)
African

Café Noir (p53) €€
15 rue St-Blaise
(Ⓜ Porte de Bagnolet)
Bistro

Shopping

11th arrondissement

Alter Mundi (p94)
41 rue du Chemin Vert
(Map 12 E5)
Fashion

Anne Willi *(see p227)*

Florence Gaillard *(see p227)*

Gaëlle Barré *(see p227)*

Isabel Marant (p94)
16 rue de Charonne (Map 18 E2)
Fashion

**La Maison de la Fausse
Fourrure** (p94)
34 blvd Beaumarchais
(Map 17 D1)
Interiors

Nuits de Satin (p93)
9 rue Oberkampf (Map 11 D4)
Second-hand & vintage

Des Petits Hauts (p95)
5 rue Keller (Map 18 F2)
01 43 38 14 39
Fashion

Shine (p93)
30 rue de Charonne (Map 18 F2)
Fashion

Techno Import *(see p229)*

Waves *(see p229)*

20th arrondissement

Boulevard de Belleville (p164)
(Map 12 F2)
Market

Art & Architecture

11th arrondissement

Canal St-Martin (p112)
(Map 17 D3)
Boat trip

12th arrondissement

Cinémathèque Française (p117)
51 rue de Bercy (Map 22 G2)
Museum

Ministère des Finances (p117)
(Map 22 F1)
Modern architecture

20th arrondissement

Cimetière de Père-Lachaise
(see p229)

Nemo's Murals (p117)
36 rue Henri Chevreau
(Map 20 H1)
Public art

Performance

11th arrondissement

Bataclan (p132)
50 blvd Voltaire (Map 12 E4)
Live music

Café de la Danse (p131)
5 passage Louis-Philippe
(Map 18 E2)
Multi-function venue

Cirque d'Hiver Bouglione
(p131)
110 rue Amelot (Map 11 D4)
Circus

12th arrondissement

Cartoucherie de Vincennes
(p131)
For individual theatres see p232
Route du Champ de
Manœuvre, Bois de Vincennes
(Ⓜ Château de Vincennes)

Hippodrome de Vincennes
(see p232)

Opéra Bastille *(see p232)*

**Palais Ominsport de
Paris-Bercy** (POPB) *(see p232)*

20th arrondissement

La Flèche d'Or (p132)
102 rue de Bagnolet
(Ⓜ Alexandre Dumas)
Live music

Le Regard du Cygne (p132)
210 rue de Belleville
(Ⓜ Télégraphe)
Dance

Bars & Clubs

11th arrondissement

Café Charbon (p155)
109 rue Oberkampf (Map 12 F3)
Bar/Club

Le Clown Bar (p155)
114 rue Amelot (Map 11 D4)
Bar

Les Couleurs (p155)
117 rue St-Maur
(Map 12 F3)
Club

Favela Chic (p156)
18 rue du Faubourg du Temple
(Map 11 D2)
Club

Pop In (p155)
105 rue Amelot (Map 11 D4)
Club

Le Trucmush (p154)
5 passage Thiéré (Map 18 E2)
Bar

Rúla Búla (p154)
53 rue du Faubourg St-Antoine
(Map 18 E2)
Bar

Wax (p156)
15 rue Daval (Map 18 E1)
Bar/Club

Le Zero Zero (p156)
89 rue Amelot (Map 11 D5)
Bar

12th arrondissement

Le Baron Rouge (p157)
1 rue Théophile Roussel
(Map 18 F3)
Bar

Barrio Latino (p157)
46 rue du Faubourg St-Antoine
(Map 18 E2)
Club

Chai 33 (p156)
33 cour St-Emilion (Map 22 H3)
Bar

China Club (p154)
50 rue Charenton (Map 18 E3)
Bar

Havens: Parks, Squares & Gardens
12th arrondissement

La Promenade Plantée (p173)
(Map 18 G5)

Hotels
11th arrondissement

Hotel Beaumarchais (p187) €
3 rue Oberkampf (Map 11 D4)

South

Restaurants

13th arrondissement

L'Avant Goût (p56) €€
26 rue Bobillot (Map 21 A4)
Bistro

Les Cailloux (p57) €€
58 rue des Cinq-Diamants
(Map 20 H5)
Italian

Tricotin (p57) €
15 avenue de Choisy
(Ⓜ Porte de Choisy)
Chinese

14th arrondissement

L'Assiette (p58) €€€
181 rue du Château (Map 19 C3)
Bistro

Au Petit Marguery (p57) €€
9 blvd de Port-Royal
(Map 20 H2)
Bistro

La Coupole (*see p224*) €€

Natacha (p57)
17bis rue Campagne-Première
(Map 19 E1)
Bistro

15th arrondissement

Chez Fung (p59) €€
32 rue de Frémicourt
(Map 14 F4)
Southeast Asian

L'Os à Moëlle & La Cave de l'Os à Moëlle (p58) €€
3 rue Vasco de Gama & 181
rue Lourmel (Ⓜ Lourmel)
Bistro

Le Père Claude (p58) €€
51 avenue de la Motte-Piquet
(Map 14 F3)
Bistro

Le Suffren (p59) €€
84 ave de Suffren (Map 14 F3)
Brasserie

Le Troquet (p59) €€
21 rue François-Bonvin
(Map 14 G5)
Bistro

Shopping
14th arrondissement

Afric' Music (*see p229*)

Cacharel (*see p227*)

Art & Architecture
13th arrondissement

Bibliothèque Nationale de France – François Mitterrand (p117)
11 quai François Mauriac
(Map 22 F3)
Exhibition space

Les Frigos (p118)
rue des Frigos (Map 22 F4)
Exhibition space

Louise Weiss, rue (p118)
(Map 21 D3)
Exhibition space

Manufacture des Gobelins (p118)
42 ave des Gobelins
(Map 21 A3)
Museum

14th arrondissement

Catacombes (p119)
1 pl Denfert Rochereau
(Map 20 E3)
Historic building

Cimetière du Montparnasse
(*see p229*)

Cité Universitaire (p118)
Boulevard Jourdan
(Ⓜ Cité Universitaire)
Modern architecture

Fondation Cartier pour l'Art Contemporain (p119)
261 boulevard Raspail
(Map 19 D2)
Exhibition space

Fondation Henri Cartier-Bresson (p119)
2 impasse Lebouis
(Map 19 B2)
Exhibition space

15th arrondissement

Mémorial du Maréchal Leclerc (p119)
23 allée de la Deuxième
(Map 19 B1)
Museum

Performance
13th arrondissement

La Guinguette Pirate (p132)
Quai Francois-Mauriac
(Map 22 F3)
Live music

MK2 Bibliothèque (p133)
128–62 ave de France
(Map 22 F3)
Cinema

14th arrondissement

Théâtre de la Cité (p133)
21 boulevard Jourdan
(RER Cité Universitaire)
Theatre

Bars & Clubs
13th arrondissement

Batofar (p157)
Opposite 11 quai François
Mauriac (Map 22 F2)
Club

Limelight (p157)
162 ave de France
(Map 22 F4)
Bar

Havens: Parks, Squares & Gardens
15th arrondissement

Parc André Citroën (p173)
(Map 13 A5)

Hotels
15th arrondissement

Novotel Tour Eiffel (p187) €€
61 quai de Grenelle
(Map 13 B3)

Index by Type

Restaurants

African

Benisti (p53) €
108 boulevard de Belleville
(Map 12 F1)
East/20th arrondissement

Chez Dom (p49) €€
34 rue de Sambre et Meuse
(Map 6 E5)
North/10th arrondissement

L'Homme Bleu (p54) €€
55bis rue Jean-Pierre Timbaud
(Map 12 E3)
East/11th arrondissement

Martel (p49) €€
3 rue Martel (Map 11 A1)
North/10th arrondissement

Le Petit Dakar (p30) €
6 rue Elzévir
(Map 11 C5)
Centre/3rd arrondissement

Le Souk (p55) €
1 rue Keller (Map 18 F2)
East/11th arrondissement

Bistros

Allard (p38) €€
41 rue St-André-des-Arts
(Map 16 F2)
Centre/6th arrondissement

L'Angle du Faubourg (p43) €€
195 rue du Faubourg
St-Honoré (Map 2 G5)
West/8th arrondissement

L'Ardoise (p28) €€
28 rue du Mont Thabor
(Map 9 C3)
Centre/1st arrondissement

L'Assiette (p58) €€€
181 rue du Chateau
(Map 19 C3)
South/14th arrondissement

Astier (p53) €€
44 rue Jean-Pierre Timbaud
(Map 12 E3)
East/11th arrondissement

Au Bon Accueil (p42) €€
14 rue de Monttessuy
(Map 8 F5)
Centre/7th arrondissement

Au Petit Marguery (p57) €€
9 boulevard de Port-Royal
(Map 20 H2)
South/14th arrondissement

Au Pied de Cochon (p28) €€
6 rue Coquillière (Map 10 G4)
Centre/1st arrondissement

Aux Lyonnais (p29) €€
32 rue St-Marc (Map 10 F2)
Centre/2nd arrondissement

L'Avant Goût (p56) €€
26 rue Bobillot (Map 21 A4)
South/13th arrondissement

Le Bistrot d'à Côté Flaubert €€
(p48)
10 rue Gustave-Flaubert
(Map 2 F3)
West/17th arrondissement

Le Bistrot Paul Bert (p55) €€
18 rue Paul-Bert
(Ⓜ Faidherbe-Chaligny)
East/11th arrondissement

Café Burq (p50) €€
6 rue Burq (Map 4 E2)
North/18th arrondissement

Café Constant (p42) €€
139 rue St-Dominique
(Map 8 F5)
Centre/7th arrondissement

Café Noir (p53) €€
15 rue St-Blaise
(Ⓜ Porte de Bagnolet)
East/20th arrondissement

Casa Olympe (p48) €€
48 rue St-Georges (Map 4 F5)
North/9th arrondissement

La Cave de l'Os à Moëlle €€
(p58)
181 rue Lourmel
(ⓂLourmel)
South/15th arrondissement

Chez Georges(p30) €€
1 rue du Mail (Map 10 G3)
Centre/2nd arrondissement

Chez Toinette (p51) €€
20 rue Germain-Pilon
(Map 4 E2)
North/18th arrondissement

L'Entrédejeu (p47) €€
83 rue Laugier (Map 1 D1)
West/17th arrondissement

L'Epi Dupin (p38) €€
11 rue Dupin
(Map 15 C3)
Centre/6th arrondissement

La Mascotte (p53) €€
52 rue des Abbesses
(Map 4 E2)
North/18th arrondissement

Natacha (p57) €€
17bis rue Campagne-Première
(Map 19 E1)
South/14th arrondissement

L'Os à Moëlle (p58) €€
3 rue Vasco de Gama
(Ⓜ Lourmel)
South/15th arrondissement

Le Pamphlet (p32) €€
38 rue Debelleyme(Map 11 C4)
Centre/3rd arrondissement

Le Père Claude (p58) €€
51 avenue de la Motte-Piquet
(Map 14 F3)
South/15th arrondissement

Le Petit Keller (p55) €€
13bis rue Keller (Map 18 F1)
East/11th arrondissement

Le Petit Retro (p47) €€
5 rue Mesnil (Map 7 C2)
West/16th arrondissement

Les Petits Marseillais (p32) €€
72 rue Vieille du Temple
(Map 11 B5)
Centre/3rd arrondissement

Le Poulbot Gourmet (p58) €€
39 rue Lamark (Map 4 F1)
North/18th arrondissement

Le Pré Verre (p37) €€
8 rue Thénard (Map 16 G3)
Centre/5th arrondissement

Le Reminet (p36) €€
3 rue des Grands-Degrés
(Map 16 H3)
Centre/5th arrondissement

Robert et Louise (p34) €€
64 rue Vieille du Temple
(Map 11 B5)
Centre/4th arrondissement

Savy (p45) €€
23 rue Bayard (Map 8 G3)
West/8th arrondissement

Le Square Trousseau (p56) €€
1 rue Antoine-Vollon
(Map 18 F3)
East/12th arrondissement

Le Timbre (p39) €€
3 rue Ste-Beuve (Map 15 D5)
Centre/6th arrondissement

La Tour de Montlhéry (p29) €€
5 rue des Prouvaires
(Map 10 G4)
Centre/1st arrondissement

Le Troquet (p59) €€
21 rue François-Bonvin
(Map 14 G5)
South/15th arrondissement

Velly (p49) €€
52 rue Lamartine (Map 4 F5)
North/9th arrondissement

Le Vieux Bistro (p34) €€
14 rue du Cloître Notre Dame
(Map 16 H2)
Centre/4th arrondissement

Brasseries

Le Balzar (p33)
49 rue des Ecoles (Map 16 G3)
01 43 54 13 67
Centre/5th arrondissement

Brasserie Flo (p33)
7 cour des Petites-Ecuries
(Map 11 A1) 01 47 70 13 59
North/10th arrondissement

Brasserie de l'Ile St-Louis (p33)
55 quai Bourbon (Map 17 A2)
01 43 54 02 59
Centre/4th arrondissement

La Coupole (p33) €€€
102 blvd de Montparnasse
(Map 15 D5)
01 43 20 14 20
South/14th arrondissement

Garnier (p43) €€€
111 rue St-Lazare (Map 3 C5)
West/8th arrondissement

La Grande Armée (p47) €€
3 avenue de la Grande Armée
(Map 7 E1)
West/16th arrondissement

Le Grand Colbert (p33)
2–4 rue Vivienne (Map 10 F3)
01 42 86 87 88
Centre/2nd arrondissement

Julien (p33) €€
16 rue du Faubourg St-Denis
(Map 11 A2)
01 47 70 12 06
North/10th arrondissement

Restaurant Marty (p37) €€
20 avenue des Gobelins
(Map 21 A2)
Centre/5th arrondissement

Le Suffren (p59) €€
84 avenue de Suffren
(Map 14 F3)
South/15th arrondissement

Terminus Nord (p50) €€
23 rue de Dunkerque
(Map 5 A4)
North/10th arrondissement

Le Train Bleu (p55) €€
Gare de Lyon, place Louis-
Armand (Map 18 E5)
East/12th arrondissement

British

Rose Bakery (p49) €€
46 rue des Martyrs (Map 4 F4)
North/9th arrondissement

Chinese

Chez Vong (p29) €€
10 rue de la Grande Truanderie
(Map 10 H4)
Centre/1st arrondissement

Tricotin (p57) €€
15 avenue de Choisy
(Ⓜ Porte de Choisy)
South/13th arrondissement

Food to Go

Be (p42)
73 boulevard de Courcelles
(Map 2 F4)
01 46 22 20 20
West/8th arrondissement

Cojean (p42)
4 rue de Sèze
(Map 9 C2)
01 40 06 08 80
North/9th arrondissement

La Grande Epicerie (p42)
(see p216)

Greek

Les Délices d'Aphrodite €€
(p36)
4 rue de Candolle
(Map 20 H1)
Centre/5th arrondissement

Haute Cuisine

L'Ambroisie (p33) €€€
9 place des Vosges
(Map 17 C1)
Centre/4th arrondissement

L'Arpège (p40) €€€
84 rue de Varenne
(Map 15 A1)
Centre/7th arrondissement

L'Espadon (p28) €€€
Hôtel Ritz, 15 place Vendôme
(Map 9 D2)
Centre/1st arrondissement

Le Meurice (p29) €€€
Hotel Meurice, 228 rue de
Rivoli (Map 9 D3)
Centre/1st arrondissement

Senderens (p45) €€€
9 place de la Madeleine
(Map 9 C2)
West/8th arrondissement

La Tour d'Argent (p37) €€€
15–17 quai de la Tournelle
(Map 17 A3)
Centre/5th arrondissement

Indian

Kastoori (p48) €
4 place Gustave Toudouze
(Map 4 F4)
North/9th arrondissement

Italian

Le Bistrot Napolitain (p43) €€
18 avenue Franklin D
Roosevelt (Map 8 H1)
West/8th arrondissement

Les Cailloux (p57) €€
58 rue des Cinq-Diamants
(Map 20 H5)
South/13th arrondissement

L'Enoteca (p34) €€
25 rue Charles V (Map 17 C2)
Centre/4th arrondissement

L'Osteria (p35) €€
10 rue de Sévigné (Map 17 C1)
Centre/4th arrondissement

Sardegna a Tavola (p56) €€
1 rue de Cotte (Map 18 F3)
East/12th arrondissement

Japanese

Abazu (p38) €€
3 rue André-Mazet
(Map 16 F2)
Centre/6th arrondissement

Higuma (p30) €
32bis rue Ste-Anne
(Map 10 E2)
01 47 03 38 59
Centre/1st arrondissement

Laï Laï Ken (p30) €
7 rue Ste-Anne (Map 10 E2)
Centre/1st arrondissement

Yen (p38) €€
22 rue St-Benoît (Map 16 E2)
Centre/6th arrondissement

Latin American

Anahï (p31) €€
49 rue Volta (Map 11 B3)
Centre/3rd arrondissement

Mexican

Anahuacalli (p35) €€
30 rue des Bernardins
(Map 16 H3)
Centre/5th arrondissement

Middle Eastern

L'As du Fallafal (p33, p42) €
34 rue des Rosiers
(Map 17 B1)
Centre/4th arrondissement

Modern French

L'Astrance (p46) €€€
4 rue Beethoven
(Map 7 C5)
West/16th arrondissement

**L'Atelier de Joël
Robuchon** (p41) €€€
5 rue de Montalembert
(Map 15 D1)
Centre/7th arrondissement

A Toutes Vapeurs (p45) €
7 rue de l'Isly (Map 3 C5)
West/8th arrondissement

La Braisière (p48) €€€
54 rue Cardinet (Map 2 H2)
West/17th arrondissement

La Butte Chaillot (p47) €€€
110bis avenue Kléber
(Map 7 D3)
West/16th arrondissement

Café Moderne (p29) €€
40 rue Notre-Dame-des-
Victoires (Map 10 G2)
Centre/2nd arrondissement

La Canaille (p34) €
4 rue Crillon (Map 17 C3)
Centre/4th arrondissement

La Cave Gourmande (p51) €
10 rue de Général-Brunet
(Ⓜ Botzaris)
North/19th arrondissement

**Le Comptoir du Relais
St-Germain** (p38) €€
9 carrefour de l'Odéon
(Map 16 F2)
Centre/6th arrondissement

Le Cristal Room (p44) €€€
La Maison Baccarat, 11 place
des Etats-Unis (Map 8 E2)
West/16th arrondissement

La Famille (p52) €€
41 rues des Trois-Frères
(Map 4 F2)
North/18th arrondissement

Flora (p43) €€
36 avenue George V
(Map 8 F2)
West/8th arrondissement

Gaya Rive Gauche (p42) €€
44 rue du Bac
(Map 8 F5)
Centre/7th arrondissement

Maison Blanche (p44) €€€
15 avenue Montaigne
(Map 8 G3)
West/8th arrondissement

Market (p44) €€€
15 avenue Matignon
(Map 9 A2)
West/8th arrondissement

Restaurants

Modern French
continued

Mon Vieil Ami (p35)   €€
69 rue St-Louis-en-l'Île
(Map 17 A2)
Centre/4th arrondissement

R'Aliment (p32)   €€
57 rue Charlot
(Map 11 C4)
Centre/3rd arrondissement

Restaurant du Palais Royal €€
(p28)
110 galérie Valois (Map 10 F3)
Centre/1st arrondissement

Regional French

L'Ambassade d'Auvergne €€
(p31)
22 rue du Grenier St-Lazare
(Map 11 A4)
Centre/3rd arrondissement

L'Ami Jean (p40)   €€
27 rue Malar (Map 8 G5)
Centre/7th arrondissement

Chez Michel (p50)   €€
10 rue de Belzunce (Map 5 A4)
North/10th arrondissement

Le Cosi (p36)   €€
9 rue Cujas (Map 16 G4)
Centre/5th arrondissement

Crêperie Bretonne Fleurie €
(p54)
67 rue de Charonne (Map 18 F2)
East/11th arrondissement

La Ferrandaise (p39)   €€
8 rue de Vaugirard
(Map 16 F3)
Centre/6th arrondissement

Le Salon d'Hélène (p39)   €€€
4 rue d'Assas
(Map 15 D3)
Centre/6th arrondissement

Le Trou Gascon (p56)   €€€
40 rue Taine
(Ⓜ Daumesnil)
East/12th arrondissement

Salons de Thé

Angelina (p59)
266 rue de Rivoli
(Map 9 C3)
Centre/1st arrondissement

A Priori Thé (p59)
35–7 galérie Vivienne
(Map 10 F3)
01 42 97 48 75
Centre/2nd arrondissement

La Grande Mosquée (p59)
(see p218)

Ladurée (p59)
16 rue Royale (Map 9 C2)
01 42 60 21 79
West/8th arrondissement

La Maison de la Chine (p59)
76 rue Bonaparte
(Map 16 E2)
01 40 51 95 00
Centre/6th arrondissement

Mariage Frères (p171)
13 rue des Grands Augustins
(Map 16 F1)
Centre/6th arrondissement

Southeast Asian

Chez Fung (p59)   €€
32 rue de Frémicourt
(Map 14 F4)
South/15th arrondissement

Dong Huong (p54)   €
14 rue Louis-Bonnet
(Map 12 F1)
East/11th arrondissement

Lao Siam (p51)   €
49 rue de Belleville
(Map 12 G1)
North/19th arrondissement

New Nioullaville (p164)   €
32 rue de l'Orillon
(Map 12 F2)
East/11th arrondissement

Spanish

Bellota-Bellota (p40)   €€
18 rue Jean-Nicot (Map 8 G5)
Centre/7th arrondissement

Fogon St-Julien (p36)   €€
10 rue St-Julien-le-Pauvre
(Map 16 H2)
Centre/5th arrondissement

Vegetarian

Le Potager du Marais (p32)   €
22 rue Rambuteau
(Map 11 A5)
Centre/3rd arrondissement

Wine Bars

Les Enfants Rouges (p31)   €€
9 rue de Beauce
(Map 11 C4)
Centre/3rd arrondissement

Jacques Mélac (p54)   €€
42 rue Léon-Frot
(Ⓜ Charonne)
East/11th arrondissement

Shopping

Accessories

Bottega Veneta (p90)
14 rue du Faubourg-St-Honoré
(Map 9 B2)
01 42 65 59 70
www.bottegaveneta.com
West/8th arrondissement

Brontibay (p74)
6 rue de Sévigné (Map 17 C1)
Centre/4th arrondissement

Erik & Lydie (p69)
7 passage du Grand Cerf
(Map 10 H3)
Centre/2nd arrondissement

Flavie Furst (p68)
16 rue de la Soudière
(Map 10 E3)
Centre/1st arrondissement

Gucci (p90)
60 ave Montaigne (Map 8 H2)
01 56 69 80 80
www.gucci.com
West/8th arrondissement

Hervé Van der Straeten (p78)
11 rue Ferdinand Duval
(Map 17 B1)
Centre/4th arrondissement

Jamin Puech (p82)
43 rue Madame (Map 16 E3)
Centre/6th arrondissement

Karine Dupont (p79)
16 rue cherche midi
(Map 15 D3)
Centre/6th arrondissement

Louis Vuitton (p90)
22 ave Montaigne (Map 8 G3)
08 10 81 00 10
www.vuitton.com
West/8th arrondissement

Marie Mercié (p82)
23 rue St-Sulpice (Map 16 E3)
Centre/6th arrondissement

Odette & Zoe (p67)
4 rue des Petits Champs
(Map 10 F3)
Centre/2nd arrondissement

Renaud Pelligrino (p90)
14 rue du Faubourg St-Honoré
(Map 9 B2)
West/8th arrondissement

Viveka Bergström (p92)
23 rue de la Grange-aux-Belles
(Map 5 D5)
North/10th arrondissement

Beauty

by Terry (p64)
21 passage Véro-Dodat
(Map 10 F4)
Centre/1st arrondissement

Galerie Noémie (p88)
92 ave des Champs-Elysées
(Map 8 F1)
West/8th arrondissement

Guerlain (p88)
68 ave des Champs-Elysées
(Map 8 G2)
West/8th arrondissement

Make Up For Ever Professional (p89)
5 rue de la Boétie (Map 8 H1)
West/8th arrondissement

Sephora (p72)
70–72 avenue des Champs-
Elysées (Map 8 G2)
01 53 93 22 50
www.sephora.fr
West/8th arrondissement

Yves Rocher (p72)
104 rue de Rivoli (Map 10 G5)
01 40 28 41 67
www.yves-rocher.fr
Centre/1st arrondissement

Concept Stores

Colette (p90)
213 rue St-Honoré (Map 9 D3)
01 55 35 33 90
www.colette.fr
Centre/1st arrondissement

Galerie Simone (p72)
124 rue Vieille du Temple
(Map 11 C4)
Centre/3rd arrondissement

Spree (p93)
16 rue la Vieuville (Map 4 F2)
North/18th arrondissement

Department Stores

Le Bon Marché (p84, p87)
24 rue des Sèvres (Map 15 C3)
01 44 39 80 00
www.lebonmarché.fr
Centre/7th arrondissement

Les Galeries Lafayette (p87)
40 blvd Haussmann (Map 9 E1)
01 42 82 34 56
www.galerieslafayette.com
North/9th arrondissement

Monoprix (p72)
50 rue de Rennes (Map 16 E2)
01 45 48 18 08
www.monoprix.fr
Centre/6th arrondissement

Printemps (p87)
64 boulevard Haussmann
01 42 82 50 00
(Map 9 D1)
www.printemps.fr
North/9th arrondissement

Fashion

AB33 (p73)
33 rue Charlot (Map 11 C4)
Centre/3rd arrondissement

Abou d'Abi Bazar (p72)
10 rue des Francs Bourgeois
(Map 17 C1)
Centre/3rd arrondissement

Agnès b (p80)
6 (women's) & 12 (men's) rue
du Vieux Colombier
(Map 15 D2)
Centre/6th arrondissement

Alter Mundi (p94)
41 rue du Chemin Vert
(Map 12 E5)
East/11th arrondissement

Anne Willi (p95)
13 rue Keller (Map 18 F2)
01 48 06 74 06
East/11th arrondissement

Annexe des Créateurs (p71)
19 rue Godot de Mauroy
(Map 9 C2)
01 42 65 46 40
North/9th arrondissement

Antik Batik (p71)
18 rue de Turenne
(Map 17 C1)
Centre/4th arrondissement

Antoine & Lili (p91)
95 quai de Valmy (Map 11 C1)
North/10th arrondissement

APC (p80)
3 & 4 rue Fleurus
(Map 15 D4)
Centre/6th arrondissement

A-poc (p74)
47 rue des Francs Bourgeois
(Map 11 B5)
Centre/4th arrondissement

Azzedine Alaïa (p74)
7 rue de Moussy (Map 17 A1)
Centre/4th arrondissement

Balenciaga (p90)
10 avenue George V (Map 8 F3)
01 47 20 21 11
www.balenciaga.com
West/8th arrondissement

Barbara Bui (p69)
23 rue Etienne Marcel
(Map 10 H4)
Centre/2nd arrondissement

Cacharel (p71)
114 rue d'Alésia (Map 19 C4)
01 45 42 53 04
www.cacharel.com
South/14th arrondissement

Catherine Malandrino (p83)
10 rue de Grenelle
(Map 15 D2)
Centre/6th arrondissement

Chanel (p90)
42 ave Montaigne (Map 8 G3)
01 47 23 74 12
www.chanel.com
West/8th arrondissement

Chloé (p90)
54–56 rue du Faubourg-
St-Honoré (Map 9 B2)
01 44 94 33 00
www.chloe.com
West/8th arrondissement

Christian Lacroix (p90)
73 rue du Faubourg-St-Honoré
(Map 9 B2)
01 42 68 79 00
www.christian-lacroix.com
West/8th arrondissement

Colors do Brasil (p85)
4 rue Perronet
(Map 15 D1)
Centre/7th arrondissement

Comptoir des Cotonniers (p74)
33 rue des Francs Bourgeois
(Map 11 B5)
Centre/4th arrondissement

Dépôt-Vente de Buci (p71)
4–6 rue Bourbon le Château
(Map 16 E2)
01 46 34 45 05
Centre/6th arrondissement

Dior (p90)
30 ave Montaigne
(Map 8 G3)
01 40 73 53 01
www.dior.com
West/8th arrondissement

Dolce & Gabbana (p90)
22 ave Montaigne (Map 8 G3)
01 42 25 68 78
www.dolcegabbana.com
West/8th arrondissement

L'Eclaireur (p67)
10 rue Hérold (Map 10 G3)
Centre/1st arrondissement

Emmanuel Ungaro (p90)
2 ave Montaigne (Map 8 F3)
01 53 57 00 22
www.emmanuelungaro.fr
West/8th arrondissement

Etam (p72)
67 rue de Rivoli (Map 17 A1)
01 44 76 73 73
www.etam.com
Centre/1st arrondissement

Et Vous Stock (p71)
17 rue de Turbigo (Map 10 H4)
01 40 13 04 12
Centre/2nd arrondissement

Florence Galliard (p95)
30bis rue de Charonne
(Map 18 F2)
East/11th arrondissement

Gaëlle Barré (p95)
17 rue Keller (Map 18 F2)
01 43 14 63 02
East/11th arrondissement

Ginger Lyly (p91)
33 rue Beaurepaire (Map 11 C2)
North/10th arrondissement

Guerrisol (p71)
17bis blvd de Rochechouart
(Map 4 H3)
01 45 26 13 12
North/9th arrondissement

Helmut Lang (p65)
219 rue St-Honoré (Map 10 E4)
Centre/1st arrondissement

Isabel Marant (p94)
16 rue de Charonne
(Map 18 F2)
East/11th arrondissement

Jean-Paul Gaultier (p90)
44 avenue George V
(Map 8 F2)
01 44 43 00 44
www.jeanpaulgaultier.com
West/8th arrondissement

John Galliano (p90)
384 rue St-Honoré
(Map 9 C3)
01 55 35 40 40
www.johngalliano.com
Centre/1st arrondissement

Kookaï (p71, p72)
82 rue Réamur (Map 11 A3)
01 45 08 93 69
www.kookai.fr
Centre/2nd arrondissement

Lagerfeld Gallery (p81)
40 rue de Seine (Map 16 E1)
Centre/6th arrondissement

Lanvin (p90)
15 rue du Faubourg-St-Honoré
(Map 19 B2)
01 44 71 31 25
www.lanvin.fr
West/8th arrondissement

Index by Type

Shopping

Fashion *continued*

Lili Perpink (p92)
22 rue Vieuville (Map 4 F2)
North/10th arrondissement

Loft Design by (p82)
56 rue de Rennes (Map 16 E2)
Centre/6th arrondissement

Lucien Pellat-Finet (p85)
1 rue Montalembert
(Map 15 D1)
Centre/7th arrondissement

Madelios (p65)
23 boulevard de la Madeleine
(Map 9 C2)
Centre/1st arrondissement

Maria Luisa (p66)
2 rue Cambon (Map 9 C3)
Centre/1st arrondissement

Marni (p90)
57 ave Montaigne (Map 8 H2)
01 56 88 08 08
www.marni.com
West/8th arrondissement

Martine Sitbon (p85)
13 rue Grenelle (Map 15 D2)
Centre/7th arrondissement

Martin Grant (p76)
10 rue de Charlot (Map 11 B5)
Centre/3rd arrondissement

Martin Margiela (p66)
23 & 25bis rue de
Montpensier (Map 10 F3)
Centre/1st arrondissement

Morgan (p72)
16 rue Turbigo (Map 10 H4)
01 44 82 02 00
www.morgan.fr
Centre/2nd arrondissement

Nodus (p70)
22 rue Vieille du Temple
(Map 17 B1)
Centre/4th arrondissement

Onward (p82)
147 boulevard St-Germain
(Map 16 E2)
Centre/6th arrondissement

Patricia Louisor (p92)
16 rue Houdon (Map 4 F3)
North/18th arrondissement

Paul & Joe (p81)
40 rue du Four (Map 16 E2)
Centre/6th arrondissement

Paul Smith (p85)
22 & 24 boulevard Raspail
(Map 15 D3)
Centre/7th arrondissement

Des Petits Hauts (p95)
5 rue Keller (Map 18 F2)
01 43 38 14 39
East/11th arrondissement

Prada (p90)
10 ave Montaigne (Map 8 G3)
01 53 23 99 40
www.prada.com
West/8th arrondissement

Réciproque (p71)
93–95, 101 & 103 rue de la
Pompe (Ⓜ Rue de la Pompe)
01 47 04 30 28
www.reciproque.fr
West/16th arrondissement

Shadé (p83)
63 rue des Sts-Pères
(Map 15 D2)
Centre/6th arrondissement

Shine (p93)
30 rue de Charonne
(Map 18 F2)
East/11th arrondissement

Stella Cadente (p91)
93 quai de Valmy
(Map 11C1)
North/10th arrondissement

Tara Jamon (p79)
18 rue du Four (Map 16 E2)
Centre/6th arrondissement

Valentino (p90)
17 ave Montaigne
(Map 8 G3)
01 47 23 64 61
www.valentino.it
West/8th arrondissement

Vanessa Bruno (p81)
25 rue St-Sulpice (Map 16 E3)
Centre/6th arrondissement

Ventilo (p67)
13–15 boulevard de la
Madeleine (Map 9 C2)
Centre/1st arrondissement

Zadig & Voltaire (de luxe)
(p88)
18–20 rue François Premier
(Map 8 G3)
West/8th arrondissement

Food & Drink

A L'Olivier (p78)
23 rue de Rivoli (Map 17 B1)
Centre/4th arrondissement

Food (p71)
58 rue Charlot (Map 11 C4)
Centre/3rd arrondissement

Goumanyat & Son Royaume
(p70)
3 rue Charles-François Dupuis
(Map 11 C3)
Centre/3rd arrondissement

La Grande Epicerie (p84)
Le Bon Marché, 22 rue des
Sèvres (Map 15 C3)
www.lebonmarché.fr
Centre/7th arrondissement

Lavinia (p68)
3–5 boulevard de la
Madeleine (Map 9 D2)
Centre/1st arrondissement

La Maison du Chocolat (p79)
19 rue de Sèvres (Map 15 C3)
Centre/6th arrondissement

Interiors

Bô (p78)
8 rue St-Merri
(Map 11 A5)
Centre/4th arrondissement

La Chaise Longue (p72)
20 rue des Francs Bourgeois
(Map 17 C1)
Centre/3rd arrondissement

Christian Tortu (p83)
6 carrefour de l'Odéon
(Map 16 F2)
Centre/6th arrondissement

Coin Canal (p92)
1 rue de Marseille
(Map 11 C1)
North/10th arrondissement

Deyrolle (p83)
46 rue du Bac (Map 15 C1)
Centre/7th arrondissement

Diptyque (p78)
34 boulevard St-Germain
(Map 17 A3)
Centre/5th arrondissement

Hervé Gambs (p75)
9bis rue des Blancs Manteaux
(Map 11 B5)
Centre/4th arrondissement

**La Maison de la Fausse
Fourrure** (p94)
34 boulevard Beaumarchais
(Map 17 D1)
East/11th arrondissement

Résonances (p89)
3 boulevard Malesherbes
(Map 9 C2)
West/8th arrondissement

Robert Le Héros (p69)
13 rue de Saintonge
(Map 11 C4)
Centre/3rd arrondissement

Sentou (p77)
18 & 24 rue du Pont Louis-
Philippe (Map 17 B1)
29 rue François Miron
(Map 17 B1)
Centre/4th arrondissement

Thomas Boog (p86)
52 rue de Bourgogne (15 A1)
Centre/7th arrondissement

Lingerie

Carine Gilson (p84)
61 rue Bonaparte (Map 16 E1)
Centre/6th arrondissement

Erès (p88)
2 rue Tronchet (Map 9 C1)
West/8th arrondissement

Fifi Chachnil (p64)
231 rue St-Honoré (Map 9 D3)
Centre/1st arrondissement

Princesse Tam Tam (p72)
79 rue St-Lazare (Map 3 D5)
01 48 78 63 31
www.princessetam-tam.com
North/9th arrondissement

Sabbia Rosa (p79)
73 rue des Sts-Pères
(Map 15 D2)
Centre/6th arrondissement

Woman (p81)
6 rue de Grenelle
(Map 15 D2)
Centre/6th arrondissement

Markets

Boulevard des Batignolles
(p162) (Map 3 B3)
North/18th arrondissement

Puces de St-Ouen (p164)
(Ⓜ Porte de Clignancourt)
North/Northern suburbs

Puces de Vanves (p165)
(Ⓜ Porte de Vanves)
South/14th arrondissement

Music & Books

Afric' Music (p85)
3 rue des Plantes (Map 19 C3)
01 45 42 43 52
South/14th arrondissement

Artazart (p91)
83 quai de Valmy (Map 11 C1)
North/10th arrondissement

En Avant la Zizique (p85)
8 rue Baudelique (Ⓜ Simplon)
01 42 62 01 02
www.la-zizique.com
North/18th arrondissement

fnac (p85, p124)
74 ave des Champs-Elysées
(Map 8 G2) 01 53 53 64 64
www.fnac.com.
West/8th arrondissement

Papageno (p85)
1 rue de Marivaux (Map 10 F1)
01 42 96 56 54
www.papageno.fr
Centre/2nd arrondissement

Paris Jazz Corner (p85)
5&7 rue de Navarre (Map 17 A5)
01 43 36 78 92
www.parisjazzcorner.com
Centre/5th arrondissement

Publicis Drugstore (p87)
133 avenue des Champs-
Elysées (Map 8 F1)
West/8th arrondissement

Techno Import (p85)
16–18 rue Taillandiers
(Map 18 F2)
01 48 05 71 56
East/11th arrondissement

Virgin Megastore (p85, p124)
52–60 ave des Champs-Elysées
(Map 8 G2)
01 49 53 50 00
www.virginmega.fr
West/8th arrondissement

Wave (p85)
36 rue Keller (Map 18 F1)
01 40 21 86 98
East/11th arrondissement

Perfumes

L'Artisan Parfumeur (p66)
2 rue Amiral de Coligny
(Map 10 F5)
Centre/1st arrondissement

**Editions de Parfums Frédéric
Malle** (p84)
37 rue de Grenelle (Map 15 C2)
Centre/7th arrondissement

Givenchy (p90)
3 avenue George V (Map 8 F3)
01 44 31 50 00
www.givenchy.com
West/8th arrondissement

Iunx (p87)
48–50 rue de l'Université
(Map 15 D1)
Centre/7th arrondissement

Salons du Palais Royal (p66)
25 rue de Valois (Map 10 F3)
Centre/1st arrondissement

Second-Hand & Vintage

Catherine Arigoni (p86)
14 rue Beaune (Map 15 D1)
Centre/7th arrondissement

E2 (p91)
15 rue Martel (Map 11 A1)
North/10th arrondissement

Killiwatch (p69)
64 rue Tiquetonne (Map 10 G3)
Centre/2nd arrondissement

Les Nuits de Satin (p93)
9 rue Oberkampf (Map 11 D4)
East/11th arrondissement

**Les 3 Marches de
Catherine B** (p80)
1 & 3 rue Guisarde (Map 16 E2)
Centre/6th arrondissement

Yukiko (p75)
97 rue Vieille du Temple
(Map 11 C4)
Centre/4th arrondissement

Shoes

André (p72)
2 rue Isly (Map 3 C5)
01 44 69 32 63
www.andre.fr
West/8th arrondissement

Christian Louboutin (p64)
19 rue Jean-Jacques Rousseau
(Map 10 F4)
Centre/1st arrondissement

Free Lance (p80)
30 rue du Four (Map 15 D2)
Centre/6th arrondissement

Iris (p84)
28 rue de Grenelle
(Map 15 D2)
Centre/7th arrondissement

Jean-Baptiste Rautureau (p86)
24 rue de Grenelle (Map 15 D2)
Centre/7th arrondissement

Pierre Hardy (p65)
156 galérie de Valois
(Map 10 F4)
Centre/1st arrondissement

Renaud Pellegrino (p87)
14 rue du Faubourg-St-Honoré
(Map 9 B2)
West/8th arrondissement

Roger Vivier (p82)
29 rue du Faubourg-St-Honoré
(Map 9 B2)
West/8th arrondissement

Shoe Bizz (p70)
48 rue Beaubourg (Map 11 A5)
Centre/3rd arrondissement

Stephane Kélian (p90)
5 rue du Faubourg-St-Honoré
(Map 9 C2)
West/8th arrondissement

Stationery

Calligrane (p75)
4–6 rue du Pont Louis-
Philippe (Map 17 A2)
Centre/4th arrondissement

Art & Architecture

Cemeteries

Cimetière du Montmartre
(p115) (Map 3 D1)
North/18th arrondissement

Cimetière du Montparnasse
(p173) (Map 19 C2)
South/14th arrondissement

Cimetière du Passy (p115)
(Map 7 C4)
West/16th arrondissement

Cimetière du Père-Lachaise
(p14, p115) (Map 12 H4)
East/20th arrondissement

Churches

Basilique St-Denis (p114)
1 rue de la Légion d'Honneur
(Ⓜ Basilique de St-Denis)
North/Northern suburbs

Chapelle Expiatoire (p172)
29 rue Pasquier (Map 9 C1)
West/8th arrondissement

Eglise de la Madeleine (p108)
Pl de la Madeleine (Map 9 C2)
West/8th arrondissement

**Eglise Royale du
Val-de-Grâce** (p105)
227bis rue St-Jacques
(Map 20 F1)
Centre/5th arrondissement

Eglise St-Augustin (p108)
46 blvd Malesherbes (Map 3 B5)
West/8th arrondissement

Eglise St-Eustache (p100)
2 impasse St-Eustache
(Map 10 G4)
Centre/1st arrondissement

Eglise St-Sulpice (p105)
Place St-Sulpice (Map 16 E3)
Centre/6th arrondissement

Index by Type

Art & Architecture

Churches
continued

Notre Dame (p13, p116)
Place du Parvis-Notre-Dame
(Map 16 H2)
01 42 34 56 10
Centre/4th arrondissement

Sacré Coeur (p15, p113)
35 rue du Chevalier de la Barre
(Map 4 G2)
01 53 41 89 00
North/18th arrondissement

Sainte-Chapelle (p15, p101)
4 blvd du Palais
(Map 16 G1)
Centre/1st arrondissement

St-Julien-le-Pauvre (p169)
Rue St-Julien-le-Pauvre
(Map 16 H2)
Centre/5th arrondissement

Exhibition Spaces

Atelier Brancusi (p103)
Place Centre Pompidou
(Map 11 A5)
Centre/4th arrondissement

Bibliothèque Nationale de France – François Mitterrand (p117)
11 quai François Mauriac
(Map 22 F3)
South/13th arrondissement

Bibliothèque Nationale de France – Richelieu (p100)
58 rue de Richelieu
(Map 10 F3)
Centre/2nd arrondissement

Fondation Cartier pour l'Art Contemporain (p119)
261 blvd Raspail (Map 19 D2)
South/14th arrondissement

Fondation Henri Cartier-Bresson (p119)
2 impasse Lebouis
(Map 19 B2)
South/14th arrondissement

Les Frigos (p118)
rue des Frigos
(Map 22 F4)
South/13th arrondissement

Grand Palais (p109)
3 avenue du Général Eisenhower (Map 9 A3)
01 44 13 17 30
West/8th arrondissement

Institut du Monde Arabe (p103)
1 rue des Fossés St-Bernard
(Map 17 B3)
Centre/5th arrondissement

Jeu de Paume (p100)
1 pl de la Concorde
(Map 9 C3)
Centre/1st arrondissement

Louise Weiss, rue (p106)
(Map 21 D3)
South/13th arrondissement

Maison Européene de la Photographie (p103)
5–7 rue de Fourcy (Map 17 B1)
Centre/4th arrondissement

Musée du Luxembourg (p105)
19 rue de Vaugirard
(Map 16 E3)
Centre/6th arrondissement

Palais du Tokyo (p110)
13 avenue du Président Wilson
(Map 8 E3)
West/16th arrondissement

Patrimoine Photographique (p102)
62 rue St-Antoine (Map 17 C2)
Centre/4th arrondissement

Petit Palais (p109)
Avenue Winston Churchill
(Map 9 A3)
01 40 05 56 78
West/8th arrondissement

Historic Buildings

Arènes de Lutèce (p104)
Entrance on 49 rue Monge & 7 rue de Navarre
(Map 17 A3)
Centre/5th arrondissement

Assemblée Nationale (p116)
126 rue de l'Université
01 40 063 60 00
(Map 9 A4)
Centre/7th arrondissement

Catacombes (p119)
1 pl Denfert Rochereau
(Map 20 E3)
South/14th arrondissement

Chateau de St-Germain (p112)
Place Charles de Gaulle
(RER St-Germain-en-Laye)
West/Western Suburbs

La Conciergerie (p116)
1 quai de l'Horloge
(Map 16 G1)
01 53 73 78 50
Centre/1st arrondissement

Eiffel Tower (p12, p116)
Champs de Mars
01 44 11 23 23
www.tour-eiffel.fr
Centre/7th arrondissement

Gare du Nord (p116)
(Map 5 A4)
North/10th arrondissement

Moulin de la Galette (p113)
75 rue Lepic
(Map 4 E1)
North/18th arrondissement

Moulin de Radet (p113)
83 rue Lepic
(Map 4 F1)
North/18th arrondissement

Opéra Garnier (p116, p128)
Place de l'Opéra
(Map 9 D1)
08 92 89 90 90
www.opera-de-paris.fr
North/9th arrondissement

La Sorbonne (p104)
47 rue des Ecoles (Map 16 G3)
Centre/5th arrondissement

Tour St-Jacques (p102)
Place du Châtelet
Centre/1st arrondissement

Modern Architecture

Cité Universitaire (p118)
Boulevard Jourdan
(M Cité Universitaire)
South/14th arrondissement

Ministère des Finances (p117)
(Map 22 F1)
East/12th arrondissement

Stade de France (p133, p204)
rue Francis de Pressensé
(M St-Denis Porte de Paris)
North/Northern suburbs

Museums

Centre Pompidou (p13, p106)
Places Georges Pompidou
(Map 11 A5)
01 44 78 12 33
www.centrepompidou.fr
Centre/4th arrondissement

Cinémathèque Française (p117)
51 rue de Bercy (Map 22 G2)
East/12th arrondissement

Cité des Sciences et de l'Industrie (p114)
Parc de la Villette, 30 ave Corentin Cariou
(M Porte de Pantin)
North/19th arrondissement

Eglise Royale du Val-de-Grâce (p105)
227bis rue St-Jacques
(Map 20 F1)
Centre/5th arrondissement

Fondation Le Corbusier (p111)
Villa la Roche, 10 square du Dr Blanche (M Jasmin)
West/16th arrondissement

Manufacture des Gobelins (p106)
42 avenue des Gobelins
(Map 21 A3)
South/13th arrondissement

Mémorial du Maréchal Leclerc (p107)
23 allée de la deuxième
(Map 19 B1)
South/15th arrondissement

Musée d'Art et d'Histoire du Judaïsme (p102)
71 rue du Temple (Map 11 A5)
Centre/3rd arrondissement

Musée d'Art et d'Histoire de St-Denis (p115)
22bis rue Gabriel Péri
(M St-Denis Porte de Paris)
North/Northern suburbs

Musée de l'Assistance Publique (p105)
47 quai de la Tournelle
(Map 17 A3)
Centre/5th arrondissement

Musée Carnavalet (p101)
23 rue de Sevigné (Map 17 C1)
Centre/3rd arrondissement

Musée Cognacq-Jay (p103)
8 rue Elzévi (Map 11 C5)
Centre/4th arrondissement

Musée Départemental Maurice Denis "Le Prieuré" (p112)
2bis rue Maurice Denis
(RER St-Germain-en-Laye)
West/Western suburbs

Musée d'Erotisme (p112)
72 blvd de Clichy (Map 4 E3)
North/18th arrondissement

Musée Galliéra (p108)
10 avenue Pierre 1er de Serbie
(Map 8 E3)
West/16th arrondissement

Musée Guimet (p111)
6 place d'Iéna (Map 8 E3)
West/16th arrondissement

Musée Gustave Moreau (p115)
14 rue de la Rochefoucauld
(Map 4 E4)
North/9th arrondissement

Musée Jacquemart-André (p115)
158 blvd Haussmann
(Map 2 H5)
West/8th arrondissement

Musée du Louvre (p12, p106)
Cour Napoléon (Map 10 E5)
01 40 20 53 17
www.louvre.fr
Centre/1st arrondissement

Musée Maillol – Fondation Dina Vierny (p107)
59–61 rue de Grenelle
(Map 15 D2)
Centre/7th arrondissement

Musée Marmottan-Monet (p111)
2 rue Louis Boilly
(Ⓜ Ranelagh)
West/16th arrondissement

Musée de Montmartre (p109)
12 rue Cortot (Map 4 F1)
01 46 06 61 11
North/18th arrondissement

Musée de la Musique (p114)
Cité de la Musique,
221 ave Jean Jaurès
(Ⓜ Porte de Pantin)
North/19th arrondissement

Musée National d'Art Moderne (MAMVP)
(p110)
11 ave du Président Wilson
(Map 8 E3)
West/16th arrondissement

Musée National Eugène Delacroix (p106)
6 rue de Furstemberg
(Map 16 E2)
Centre/6th arrondissement

Musée National du Moyen Age (p104)
6 pl Paul-Painlevé (Map 16 G3)
Centre/5th arrondissement

Musée Nationale Picasso (p101)
5 rue Thorigny (Map 11 C5)
Centre/3rd arrondissement

Musée d'Orsay (p13, p100)
1 rue de Bellechasse (Map 9 C5)
01 45 49 48 14
Centre/7th arrondissement

Musée de la Publicité (p100)
107 rue de Rivoli (Map 10 E4)
Centre/1st arrondissement

Musée du Quai Branly (p106)
55 quai Branly (Map 8 E5)
Centre/7th arrondissement

Musée Rodin (p107)
77 rue de Varenne (Map 15 A1)
Centre/7th arrondissement

Palais de Chaillot (p110)
17 pl du Trocadéro (Map 7 C4)
West/16th arrondissement

Palais de la Découverte (p109)
Avene Franklin D Roosevelt
(Map 8 H3) 01 56 43 20 21
www.palais-decouverte.fr
West/8th arrondissement

Performance

Cinema

Action Ecole (p126)
23 rue des Ecoles (Map 16 H3)
01 43 25 72 07
Centre/5th arrondissement

Action Rive Gauche (p126)
4 rue Christine (Map 16 F2)
01 43 25 85 78
Centre/6th arrondissement

Le Champollion (p126)
51 rue des Ecoles (Map 16 H3)
01 43 54 51 60
www.lechampo.com
Centre/5th arrondissement

Cinéma en Plein Air (p130)
Parc de la Villette
(Ⓜ Porte de Pontin)
North/19th arrondissement

Forum des Images (p124)
Forum des Halles (Porte
Eustache Map 10 G4
Centre/1st arrondissement

Grand Action (p126)
5 rue des Ecoles
(Map 17 A4)
01 43 54 47 62
Centre/5th arrondissement

Le Grand Rex (p125)
1 blvd Poissonnière
(Map 10 H2)
Centre/2nd arrondissement

Images d'Ailleurs (p126)
21 rue de la Clef
(Map 21 A1)
01 45 87 18 09
Centre/5th arrondissement

MK2 Bibliothèque (p133)
128–134 avenue de France
(Map 22 F3)
South/13th arrondissement

La Pagode (p124)
57 rue de Babylone
(Map 15 A2)
Centre/7th arrondissement

Quartier Latin (p126)
9 rue Champollion
(Map 16 G3)
01 43 26 84 65
Centre/5th arrondissement

Racine Odeon (p126)
6 rue de l'Ecole de Médecine
(Map16 F3)
01 46 33 43 71
Centre/6th arrondissement

Reflet Medicis (p126)
3 rue Champollion (Map 16 G3)
01 46 33 25 97
Centre/5th arrondissement

St-André-des-Arts (p126)
30 rue St André des Arts
(Map 16 F2) 01 43 26 48 18
Centre/6th arrondissement

Studio Galande (p126)
42 rue Galande (Map 16 H3)
01 43 54 72 71
www.studiogalande.fr
Centre/5th arrondissement

Studio 28 (p129)
10 rue Tholozé (Map 4 E2)
North/18th arrondissement

Circus & Cabaret

Bal du Moulin Rouge (p130)
82 blvd de Clichy (Map 4 E2)
01 53 09 82 82
www.moulinrouge.com
North/18th arrondissement

Chez Madame Arthur (p130)
75bis rue des Martyrs (Map 4 F3)
01 42 54 40 21
North/18th arrondissement

Chez Michou (p130)
80 rue des Martyrs
(Map 4 F3)
01 46 06 16 04
www.michou.com
North/18th arrondissement

Cirque d'Hiver Bouglione (p131)
110 rue Amelot (Map 11 D4)
East/11th arrondissement

Crazy Horse (p130)
12 avenue George V
(Map 8 F3)
01 47 23 97 90
www.lecrazyhorseparis.com
West/8th arrondissement

Lido (p130)
116bis avenue des Champs-
Elysées (Map 8 F1)
01 40 76 56 10
www.lido.fr
West/8th arrondissement

Paradis Latin (p130)
28 rue du Cardinal Lemoine
(Map 17 A4)
01 43 25 28 28
www.paradis-latin.com
Centre/5th arrondissement

Comedy

Café de la Gare (p125)
41 rue du Temple
(Map 11 A5)
Centre/4th arrondissement

Hotels

Aparthotels

5 rue de Moussy (p186)
5 rue de Moussy (Map 17 A1)
01 44 78 92 00
Centre/4th arrondissement

France Apartments (p186)
97 ave des Champs-Elysées
(Map 8 F1)
01 56 89 31 00
www.parisrentapart.com

Hotel du Degrès de Notre Dame (p174, p186)
10 rue des Grands Degrés
(Map 16 H3)
Centre/6th arrondissement

Hotel Résidence Henri IV (p186)
50 rue Bernadins (Map 16 H3)
01 44 41 31 81
www.residencehenri4.com
Centre/5th arrondissement

Residence Carré d'Or (p186)
46 ave George V (Map 8 F1)
01 40 70 05 05
West/8th arrondissement

Cheap

Hotel des Arts (p187)
5 rue Tholoze
(Map 4 E2)
North/18th arrondissement

Hotel Beaumarchais (p187)
3 rue Oberkampf
(Map 11 D4)
East/11th arrondissement

Hotel Eldorado (p185)
18 rue des Dames
(Map 3 C2)
West/17th arrondissement

Hotel Esméralda (p180)
4 rue St-Julien-le-Pauvre
(Map 16 H2)
Centre/5th arrondissement

Hotel Langlois (p186)
63 rue St-Lazare
(Map 3 D5)
North/9th arrondissement

Hotel du Lys (p180)
23 rue Serpente
(Map 16 G2)
Centre/6th arrondissement

Hotel Malar (p183)
29 rue Malar
(Map 8 G5)
Centre/7th arrondissement

Hotel Mayet (p182)
3 rue Mayet
(Map 15 B4)
Centre/6th arrondissement

Hotel Roubaix (p178)
6 rue Greneta
(Map 10 H3)
Centre/3rd arrondissement

Hotel Tiquetonne (p178)
6 rue Tiquetonne
(Map 10 H4)
Centre/2nd arrondissement

Hotel Utrillo (p187)
7 rue Aristide Bruant
(Map 4 E2)
North/18th arrondissement

Royal Fromentin (p186)
11 rue Fromentin
(Map 4 E3)
North/9th arrondissement

Moderate

Artus (p181)
34 rue de Buci
(Map 16 E2)
Centre/6th arrondissement

Hotel Lenox (p182)
9 rue de l'Université
(Map 15 D1)
Centre/7th arrondissement

Hotel du Panthéon (p181)
19 pl du Panthéon
(Map 16 G4)
Centre/5th arrondissement

Hotel du Petit Moulin (p179)
29 rue Poitou
(Map 11 C4)
Centre/3rd arrondissement

Hotel du Quai Voltaire (p182)
19 quai Voltaire
(Map 9 D5)
Centre/7th arrondissement

Hotel des St-Pères (p182)
65 rue des St-Pères
(Map 15 D2)
Centre/6th arrondissement

Hotel Terrass (p186)
12–14 rue Joseph de Maistre
(Map 4 E2)
North/18th arrondissement

Hotel Tonic (p178)
12–14 rue du Roule
(Map 10 G5)
Centre/1st arrondissement

Novotel Tour Eiffel (p187)
61 quai de Grenelle
(Map 13 B3)
South/15th arrondissement

Villa D'Estrées (p180)
17 rue Git-le-Coeur
(Map 16 G2)
Centre/6th arrondissement

Expensive

Le A (p183)
4 rue d'Artois
(Map 8 H1)
West/8th arrondissement

Le Crillon (p183)
10 pl de la Concorde
(Map 9 B3)
01 44 71 15 00
www.crillon.com
West/8th arrondissement

Hilton Paris Arc de Triomphe (p185)
57 rue de Courcelles
(Map 2 G4)
West/8th arrondissement

L'Hotel (p181)
13 rue des Beaux Arts
(Map 16 E1)
Centre/6th arrondissement

Hotel Sezz (p185)
6 avenue Fremiet
(Map 13 C1)
West/16th arrondissement

Hotel Square (p179)
3 rue des Boulainvilliers
(Map 13 A2)
West/16th arrondissement

Hotel de Vigny (p183)
9–11 rue Balzac
(Map 8 F1)
West/8th arrondissement

Kube Hotel (p187)
1 passage Ruelle
(Map 5 B2)
North/18th arrondissement

Le Meurice (p183)
228 rue de Rivoli
(Map 9 D3)
01 44 58 10 10
www.meuricehotel.com
Centre/1st arrondissement

Murano Urban Resort (p179)
13 boulevard du Temple
(Map 11 C3)
Centre/3rd arrondissement

Pavillon de la Reine (p178)
28 pl des Vosges
(Map 17 D1)
Centre/4th arrondissement

Pershing Hall (p184)
49 rue Pierre-Charron
(Map 8 G2)
West/8th arrondissement

La Plaza Athénée (p183)
25 ave Montaigne
(Map 8 G3)
01 53 67 66 65
www.plaza-athenee-paris.com
West/8th arrondissement

Ritz Hotel (p183)
15 pl Vendôme
(Map 9 D3)
01 43 16 30 30
www.ritzparis.com
Centre/1st arrondissement

General Index

General Index

General Index

Acknowledgments

Produced by Departure Lounge LLP
Editorial Director Naomi Peck
Art Director Lisa Kosky
Assistant Editor Debbie Woska
Designer Bernhard Wolf
Proofreaders Ella Milroy, Gary Werner and
Sylvia Tombesi-Walton
Researcher Laurie Gabay
Indexer Hilary Bird

Published by DK
Publishing Managers Jane Ewart and Scarlett O'Hara
Senior Editor Christine Stroyan
Senior Designers Paul Jackson and Marisa Renzullo
Website Editor Gouri Banerji
Cartographic Editor Casper Morris
Senior Cartographer Uma Bhattacharya
DTP Designers Jason Little and Natasha Lu
Production Coordinator Shane Higgins
Fact Checker Sadie Ryan

PHOTOGRAPHY PERMISSIONS
The publishers would like to thank all the churches, museums,
hotels, restaurants, bars, clubs, shops, galleries and other
sights for their assistance and kind permission to photograph
at their establishments.

Placement key: tc = top centre; tl = top left; tr = top right;
c = centre; ca = centre above; cb = centre below; cl = centre
left; cla = centre left above; cr = centre right; cra = centre right
above; bl = bottom left; br = bottom right.

The publishers would like to thank the following companies
and picture libraries for permission to reproduce their
photographs:

32 MONTORGUEIL: 169cl; ALAMY IMAGES: BL Images Ltd 1; LA
BISTROT D' À CÔTE FLAUBERT: 48cl; BRONTIBAY: Jérémy Fournier
74bl; LA CANAILLE: 34tr; CINÉMA EN PLEIN AIR: 123cr, 130ca;
CINQ MONDES: 172br; CNHMS Paris: 13bl, 15tl, 15cl; COLORS DO
BRASIL: 85br; L'ESPADON: 28br; L'ESTABLISSEMENT PUBLIC DU
MUSÉE ET DOMAINE NATIONAL DE VERSAILLES: 15bl; LA FLÈCHE
D'OR: 132cr; FOUR SEASONS GEORGES V: 172cl; GUERLAIN: 88cl;
HELMUT LANG: 65tl; HILTON ARC DE TRIOMPHE PARIS: 185tr;
HOTEL DU PETIT MOULIN: 177cl; HOTEL SEZZ: Manuel Zublena
185cla; BRITTA JASCHINSKI: 160bl, 160cl, 162br; KONG: Patricia
Bailer 140bl, 140br; LAVINIA: 68bl; LIMELIGHT: 157cb; MAISON
BLANCHE: 40tl; MAKE UP FOR EVER PROFESSIONAL: 89tl; M.A.N.
de Saint-Germain-en-Laye: 112tl; MURANO URBAN RESORT:
177bl, 179cra; MUSÉE DÉPARTMENTAL MAURICE DENIS "LE
PRIEURÉ": 112cl; MUSÉE DU QUAI BRANLY: Nicolas Borel 106cl;
Ianna Andréadis 106cr; Antonin Borgeaud 106cla; NICKEL:
169tr; NODUS SHIRT SHOP: 70cra; NOVOTEL TOUR EIFFEL: 187bl;
PALAIS DE TOKYO: floor, Michael Lin 110cr; PARIS TOURIST
OFFICE: Catherine Balet 63tr, 99tr, 123bl; Marc Bertrand 19tl;
Fabian Charaffi 17tr; Angélique Clément 163cr, 171bl; Amélie
Dupont 17c; StefanKraus 17tl; David LeFranc 8–9, 11tr, 12cr,
12bl, 13tr, 19tc, 162tr; Claire Pignol: 122bl; Marc Verhille 19tr;
R'ALIMENT: 28cl; RENAUD PELLEGRINO: Béatrice Drumlewiez
83cl; SENDERENS:Roberto Frankenberg 45tr; LA SUITE: 150cl;
VENTILO: 67cr; ZEFA VISUAL MEDIA: G. Rossenbach 6–7.

Full Page Picture Captions: Rollerblading along the Seine 8–9;
La Salon d'Hélène 24–5; Fifi Chachnil 60–61; Musée Gustave
Moreau 96–7; Le Grand Rex 120–21; Wax 134–5; Street scene
158–9; La Grande Mosquée 166–7; Hotel room 174–5.

Jacket Images
Front and Spine: ALAMY IMAGES: BL Images LTD.
Back: DK IMAGES: cla; Robert O'Dea ca; PARIS CONVENTION
VISITORS' BUREAU : David Lefranc cra.

Special Editions of DK Travel Guides

DK Travel Guides can be purchased in bulk quantities at
discounted prices for use in promotions or as premiums.
We are also able to offer special editions and personalized jackets, corporate imprints, and excerpts from all of
our books, tailored specifically to meet your own needs.

To find out more, please contact:
(in the United States) SpecialSales@dk.com
(in the UK) Sarah.Burgess@dk.com
(in Canada) DK Special Sales at general@tourmaline.ca
(in Australia) business.development@pearson.com.au

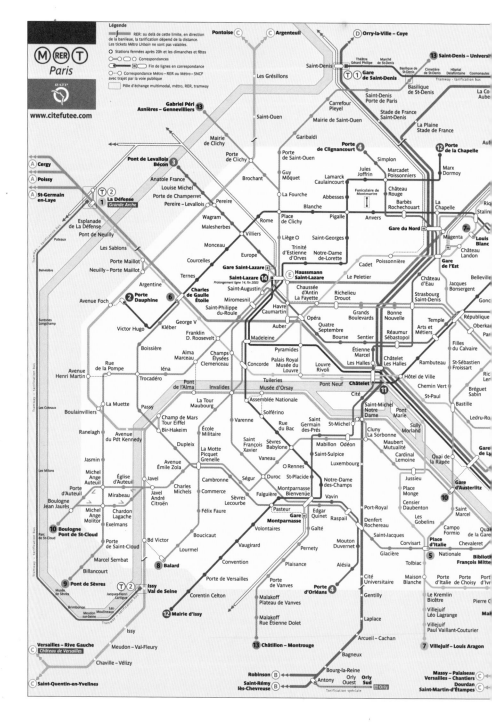